DATE DUE

Human Rights and the Search for Community

Human Rights and the Search for Community

Rhoda E. Howard

Westview Press

A Division of HarperCollinsPublishers

Parts of Chapter 6 were published previously in "Health Costs of Social Degradation and Female Self-Mutilation in North America" by Rhoda E. Howard. Kathleen E. Mahoney and Paul Mahoney, eds., *Human Rights in the Twenty-First Century: A Global Challenge.* © 1993 Kluwer Academic Publishers. Reprinted by permission of Kluwer Academic Publishers.

Published in 1995 in the United States of America by Westview Press, Inc., 5500 Central Avenue, Boulder, Colorado 80301-2877, and in the United Kingdom by Westview Press, 12 Hid's Copse Road, Cumnor Hill, Oxford OX2 9JJ

Library of Congress Cataloging-in-Publication Data
Howard, Rhoda E., 1948–
  Human rights and the search for community / Rhoda E. Howard.
    p. cm
  Includes bibliographical references and index.
  ISBN 0-8133-2578-1 (hc)—ISBN 0-8133-2579-X (pbk.)
  1. Human rights.   2. Community.   I. Title.
JC571. H69   1995
323—dc20   95-9269
                                                                              CIP

Printed and bound in the United States of America

The paper used in this publication meets the requirements of the American National Standard for Permanence of Paper for Printed Library Materials Z39.48-1984.

10 9 8 7 6 5 4 3 2 1

In Memoriam

Margarethe Käthe Hassmann Ehrenfried,
b. 1893 Leipzig, d. 1943 Sobibor

Guenther (Hassmann) Ehrenfried,
b. 1921 Berlin, d. 1941 Mauthausen

Ludwig Cohn,
b. ? Leipzig, d. 1952 Oslo, Norway

Ida Cohn,
b. 1882 Leipzig, d. 1942 Auschwitz

Lina-Gertrud Hassmann Cohn,
b. 1895 Germany, d. 1988 Oslo, Norway

Expelled from their community and denied all human rights

Contents

Acknowledgments

Many individuals and organizations have helped me in the preparation of this volume.

Several of my students assisted me in my research. From 1988 to 1994, Susan Dicklich, Lisa Kowalchuk, Ed Ezergailis, Glenn Brunetti, Dwayne Hodgson, Matthew McLean, and Patrick Reed diligently sought out sources, checked facts, read drafts, and put up with my general absentmindedness. I am deeply indebted to all of them.

From 1989 to 1991, I attended a seminar in Toronto on ethics and membership organized by Howard Adelman of York University. I am most grateful not only to him but also to my fellow participants in the seminar, especially Janet Ajzenstat, now of McMaster University; Joe Carens, Cranford Pratt, and Robert Vipond of the University of Toronto; and Peter Penz and Reg Whittaker of York University; for introducing me to material with which I had been unfamiliar and for allowing me a chance to air my views on individualism and community. I am also grateful to Iwona Irwin-Zarecka of Wilfrid Laurier University and Elaine Nardocchio of McMaster University for inviting me to present my conclusions to academic audiences in 1993.

Abdullahi Ahmed An-Na'im, now of Emory University; Ann Elizabeth Mayer of the Wharton School; and Norman Dubeski, David Hitchcock, Gary Madison, and Virginia Aksan very kindly read drafts of my work in progress. I am very thankful to all of them for their comments, as I am also to the anonymous publisher's reviewers. Parts of my argument are results of conversations with Hurst Hannum of the Fletcher School of Law and Diplomacy and James Hathaway of Osgoode Hall, York University.

Research for this volume was generously funded by the Social Sciences and Humanities Research Council of Canada, both through an individual grant to me and through a grant to the Ethics and Membership seminar group. In its final stages, research was sponsored by the Arts Research Board of McMaster University. I am very grateful to both the council and the university for their confidence in my work.

Parts of this volume have already been printed in somewhat different form elsewhere. I am grateful to Johns Hopkins University Press for permission to print a revised version of my article "Cultural Absolutism and the Search for Community" (*Human Rights Quarterly*, vol. 15, no. 2 [May 1993]: pp. 315–338). Pages 86–91 of Chapter 4 are reprinted with revisions from my "The African Debate on Human Rights: Group Versus Individual Identity," in Abdullahi Ahmed An-Na'im and Francis Deng (eds.), *Human Rights in Africa: Cross-Cultural Perspectives* (Washington, D.C.: The Brookings Institution, 1990, pp. 159–183), and I am grateful to the Brookings Institution for its permission to do so. Finally, I am grateful to Kluwer Academic Publishers of Dordrecht, the Netherlands, for permission to reprint, in revised form, parts of my "Health Costs of Social Degradation and Female Self-Mutilation in North America," in Kathleen E. Mahoney and Paul Mahoney (eds.), *Human Rights in the Twenty-First Century: A Global Challenge* (1993), pp. 503–516.

I am, as always, extremely grateful to my close friend and colleague, Jack Donnelly. He patiently read through two complete drafts of this volume, giving me his usual brutal criticism and saving me from multifarious academic sins. He was also unfailingly available with moral support and encouragement. To have an academic companion on whom one can so consistently rely is a rare privilege.

My husband, Peter McCabe, and our son, Patrick McCabe, have once again suffered through endless worries and endless dinner-table conversations about my research. I am more grateful than I can convey to them both for their patience and their sense of humor. The quality of this work, such as it is, would be much diminished had I not had access to my husband's fine intellect, and had I not had to withstand his intolerance of cant.

On this fiftieth anniversary of the end of the Holocaust, I dedicate this book to members of my paternal family persecuted by the Nazis. I dedicate it especially to my grandmother Gertrud Cohn, a German Christian twice married to Jews. Her first husband, my grandfather Bruno Hassmann, died "for the Fatherland" during World War I. In the 1930s, she refused the Nazi desire that Christians should divorce their Jewish husbands, and she escaped with Ludwig Cohn to Oslo. In Oslo, she refused an Embassy offer to admit her, but not her Jewish husband, to the United States. From 1942 to 1946, she faithfully awaited my step-grandfather, who survived Auschwitz. Like many of those who today inspire us with their dedication to human rights even in the most appalling circumstances, Gertrud Cohn was an ordinary woman who in extraordinary times never relinquished her human decency.

I alone am responsible for any errors or weaknesses in this book.

Rhoda E. Howard

1 Human Rights and the Search for Community

Human Rights as Individual Rights

This book is an argument for the principle of universal, equal, and individual human rights. Human rights are rights that one holds merely by virtue of being human. All human beings hold all human rights equally, and no one can legitimately be denied enjoyment of a human right without a fair judicial decision. Only under very limited and prescribed conditions (such as criminal conviction or the necessities of state power in warfare) may an individual be deprived of any of her human rights. The concept of human rights renders status distinctions such as race, gender, and religion politically and legally irrelevant and demands equal treatment for all, regardless of whether they fulfill expected obligations to the community.

These are statements of law and principle, not of practice. Human rights are held in law by everyone, even though they may not be enjoyed by everyone in fact. Critics of human rights reject them both for reasons of principle and because human rights are not enjoyed in practice by all people. I acknowledge deficiencies in practice but nevertheless defend the principle.

I am a sociologist and make my argument for individual human rights from a sociological perspective. The state system of the twentieth century, and the powers all political rulers hold, impel defenses of the human rights of all citizens. Everyone is under the authority of a state; there are no individuals or peoples anywhere excused from that authority. Moreover, as I will argue in this book, contemporary ideals of the right of the individual to be treated respectfully, equally with all other

1

citizens, and in a manner that guarantees her autonomy of action pervade not only Western liberal societies but increasingly most other societies. The sociological picture of late-twentieth-century society is one that demonstrates human demands for individual privacy and individual protections against the state, the society, and even the family.

Why should a sociological argument for human rights be necessary? The human rights of the individual are firmly entrenched in international law as encoded in various United Nations (UN) documents. They are also firmly ensconced as a basic principle of organized political and social life in the Western democratic world. The Cold War is over and the ideal of individual human rights is heralded throughout the former Soviet Bloc. Yet the principle of human rights is still not fully accepted.

This principle originated in Western liberal thought, as philosophers confronted both rising state power and the increasing individualization of citizens. Although economic, social, and cultural rights were added to the original liberal package of civil and political rights in the twentieth century, partly as a reaction to pressure from the Communist world, the core meaning of human rights remains liberal, with its focus on the equal and inalienable rights of the individual. States that nowadays protect human rights are perforce liberal societies, whether they exist in the West or elsewhere.[1] Liberalism as a philosophy or as a guide to law is not popular with political authoritarians, whether of right- or left-wing persuasion. Nor is it popular with those who believe that social groups of various kinds supersede the individual in importance.

There are five separate theoretical challenges in the 1990s to the UN principles of international human rights. One, which I call radical capitalism, denies the principle of economic rights. The other four are variants of communitarianism. I call these traditionalism, reactionary conservatism, left collectivism, and status radicalism.

The first challenge is the continued unwillingness of some liberals to accept the idea of economic rights. Some Western liberal thinkers reject the principle of economic rights as irrelevant and idealistic: Only civil and political rights are considered true human rights. Maurice Cranston argued, "Affirmations of [unattainable] economic and social rights ... push ... political and civil rights out of the realm of the morally compelling into the twilight world of utopian aspirations," thus diluting the principle of human rights.[2] Carnes Lord argued for the disestablishment of economic and social rights on two grounds: first, that governments can guarantee civil and political rights even when they cannot guarantee economic rights and second, that the priority of civil and political rights must be clearly established.[3]

Governments and economic actors also exhibit disquiet with the principle of economic rights. The move by states of the former Soviet

Union and Communist Eastern Europe to establish a free-market economy is taken in some quarters as a complete vindication of capitalism and as evidence that the Soviet-style stress on economic rights is at best irrelevant, and at worst dangerous, to individuals' overall freedom. The Soviet stress on economic rights was hypocritical, given its own abysmal record as a protector of such rights.[4] It was also detrimental to the cause of civil and political rights, as Soviet rhetoric in the UN and elsewhere lent support to developmental dictatorships—those authoritarian governments that claimed that they violated civil and political rights in the cause of economic development. Nevertheless, the principle of economic rights still needs to be asserted, especially in Western countries that are not social democracies and in which citizens effectively cannot make claims to economic security as a matter of human rights.

In this book I concentrate on social behavior in North America (in both the United States and Canada) to illustrate my concern with capitalist culture's rejection of economic rights.[5] The extreme version of this rejection can be termed radical capitalism, the belief that the capitalist market in and of itself is sufficient to guarantee social justice as long as private property is protected, contracts are honored, and the rules of competition are fair. The human rights concerns of radical capitalists are narrow, confined to property rights and the civil and political rights needed to carry out one's own affairs in peace. Philosophically, radical capitalists are liberal minimalists: They believe in only a very narrow set of the human rights that a liberal political regime should protect.

A behavioral manifestation of radical capitalism in North America is what I call social minimalism. Social minimalists accept certain principles of human rights wholeheartedly. They especially accept the principle of equality, and they encourage complete nondiscrimination and social mobility regardless of social status. But at the same time social minimalists eschew the principle of social obligation. They do not accept principles of responsibility to assist others to achieve material security, maintaining rather that everyone ought to be able to provide for her own security in a fair market system. North America is a class society and the poor suffer more violations of their human rights than the rich, regardless of other social statuses such as race or gender. Yet an ideology of social closure, based on the belief that anyone can rescue herself from poverty with enough effort, serves to exclude the poor from full enjoyment of human rights.

I will discuss social minimalism and social closure in Chapter 7. Before doing so, however, it will be necessary to dispose of the other four challenges to the ideal of human rights. These challenges emanate both from the Third World and from Western society, yet they overlap in their critique of the individualism inherent in human rights. All four are socially powerful belief systems that endanger the principle of human rights both internationally and in North America. All four exhibit different aspects of communitarianism.

The first of these four challenges is traditionalism, the contention that traditional societies should be permitted to violate human rights when those rights conflict with traditional rules for orderly social behavior. Traditionalists are particularly affronted by the idea that human rights should be universal and equal for all and frequently express a preference for group rather than individual rights. Traditionalists argue that their societies fully protect human rights within the confines of the group and, moreover, that traditional societies are more likely to protect economic rights than Western (capitalist) societies. This challenge is located within the international debate on the meaning of individual rights and articulated *inter alia* by scholars purporting to present uniform "African" and "Muslim" perspectives on human rights.

In the Western world, the traditionalist critique resonates with the second communitarian perspective, which I call reactionary conservatism. This perspective is concerned by what it views as the excesses of contemporary freedom, such as women's liberation, gay (homosexual and lesbian) rights, and the supposed breakdown of the family. Reactionary conservatives agree with traditionalists that excessive individualism is antithetical to social order. But they also agree with social minimalists that economic security is a matter for individual striving, not a matter that should be protected by the state as a human right.

The principle of universal, equal, and individual human rights is challenged not only by right communitarians but also by left communitarians. The third communitarian challenge is what I call left collectivism, which is the Third World nationalist position that the most important human right is to national self-determination and relief from the control of Western states and multinational corporations. To Third World left collectivists, the ideals of human rights are a form of Western cultural imperialism. The Third World left collectivist challenge is finding its way into recent discussions of peoples' rights or groups' rights as opposed to individual rights.[6] This position merges with traditionalism insofar as traditionalists also assert a nationalist right to be free of liberal pressures from imperialist societies that undermine their social values.

The fourth communitarian challenge, which also emanates from the left, is what I have dubbed status radicalism. It might be more familiar to readers in its guise as the politics of identity. Proponents of this position argue that in practice, certain categories of people are systematically denied their human rights on the basis of their social identity or status. Status radicals view the differences among categories of people variously positioned in the hierarchy of oppression as so large as to be insurmountable. Since the denial is systemic, it implies that liberalism has failed, in principle, by not recognizing that human rights are not available to certain status groups. In the Western world, some feminists and some black activists therefore argue that the individual's status membership is more salient than her individual identity. Human rights are available only for dominant status groups and are an irrelevant principle for subordinated ones.

I discuss the various individualist and communitarian positions described here in both theory and empirical practice. As a sociologist, I am interested in what ordinary people believe and value and in what motivates their interactions with others. There may or may not be sophisticated intellectual justifications for the way individualists or communitarians behave. But people will base their actions and judgments on their own beliefs about the correct way to live, even when there are no intellectuals who agree with them. Methodologically, I describe the holders of these various positions as ideal types. These ideal types illustrate social trends in both North American and Third World society, and demonstrate how the various critiques of human rights intersect.

Both right and left communitarians believe that materialism and social alienation are inherent in the individualism that human rights seem to encourage. Western societies, it seems to communitarians, encourage individualism to the point of social breakdown. Social minimalists, by contrast, rejoice in individualism and disregard its social costs. They attribute social breakdown not to materialist excess but to the unwillingness of some individuals to avail themselves of free-market opportunities for personal and material betterment.

The debate over the meaning of modernity is crucial to this debate on the value of individualism. "Modern" society seems to many of its critics to be characterized by materialism, competitiveness, excessive individualism, and the breakdown of community. If modern society does indeed encourage individualism at the price of responsibility to others, then both traditionalist and Western communitarians want no part of it. I believe that misinterpretation of the meaning and organization of the modern community contributes to much of the communitarian critique of individualism. There can be community in modern society, although it is weaker and thinner than community in traditional society.

I define a "community" as a group of individuals who have a sense of obligation toward one another. This obligation can be thicker or thinner, as one moves from smaller local communities to larger communities such as the city or nation. Community is not necessarily based on primordial ties of kinship, common religion, common language, or common ancestral origins—as much of the nostalgia for the supposedly lost, premodern community supposes. Modern community rests on secondary, not primary, associations and on voluntary rather than ascriptive memberships. Modern community is created by individuals acting out complex role-sets, not conforming to a limited and prescribed set of roles. Social obligation and commitment to the community are possible, and indeed are frequently found, in societies that value autonomy, privacy, and individualism.

Some communitarians view the principle of human rights and its social manifestation of individualism as a form of cultural imperialism. Traditionalists, left collectivists, and status radicals are all connected by relativism, the claim that the universalism implied by the international human rights documents is both unattainable in practice and unethical in principle. They are also connected by culturalism, the view that culture is the most important defining aspect of the human person's identity. For the traditionalist, culture is a holistic entity that is entirely unproblematic for the members of the society and must be preserved. For the left collectivist, the culture of oppressed national groups ought to be preserved against the onslaught of imperialism. For status radicals, a new kind of culture exists, the culture of oppressed social categories (for example, "women's culture" as opposed to that of men).

The radical capitalist challenge to human rights takes the opposite perspective on culturalism. For radical capitalists, culture is irrelevant, and there is no such thing as an oppressed group defined immutably by its status. The radical capitalist is a universalist, arguing for universal civil and political rights and discounting the need for relativistic adjustment. Radical capitalism is concerned only with individual achievements and interests: It is not part of radical capitalism's agenda to try to build a community in which all social categories are included.

By contrast, underneath both the right and the left communitarian challenges to the principle of human rights is the concern that community is disappearing. Traditionalists and reactionary conservatives alike worry that societies based on human rights produce anomie or alienation. They fear that the individualism inherent in human rights produces people withdrawn from their societies, people who suffer from normlessness and a lack of connection to others. Left collectivists join traditionalists and reactionary conservatives in their fear of the selfish individualism that they believe is exemplified in its worst form in the United States. Status radicals maintain that by retreating into their own cultural groups they will be able to create more caring societies in which individuals feel a sense of obligation to the oppressed.

I propose that both the radical capitalist and the right and left communitarian challenges to the principle of universal human rights are wrong. It is wrong to neglect economic rights as radical capitalists would do: Basic human needs must be provided so that people can stay alive and so that people can live in dignity. It is also wrong to ignore the necessity for individual civil and political rights, no matter how poor a society and how dominated it is by outside political and economic forces. If traditional societies, developing states, and oppressed social groups cannot pursue their collective goals without denying civil and political rights to individuals (whether their own members or outsiders), then they must be reorganized and new goals must be introduced.

The communitarian critics of modernity see only its bleakest aspects. But it is wrong to ignore modernity's many liberating benefits. Subordinated status categories do indeed experience dishonor, shame, and even social terror in contemporary North America (see Chapter 6). But the freedoms and legal equality now permitted women, blacks, and other subordinated status groups are major achievements of modern liberal life. Members of such status groups all have multiple identities and interests: They cannot be aggregated into one undifferentiated mass. Their class position especially will influence their life chances in modern society.

I agree with the critics of modern individualism that community is valuable. I am a white Western woman, living with my husband and son in a small city in Canada where communities are alive and well, embedded in strong family ties, ethnic and religious organizations, and volunteer community groups. Hamilton, Ontario, has approximately 91,000 volunteers in a population of 317,000 and 264 Christian churches, as well as many non-Christian houses of worship.[7] I think these aspects of my society enhance the quality of my life, even though I am an immigrant to Canada, with no religious or ethnic affiliations of my own and no kin besides my immediate family. My personal community is one of neighborhoods, sports teams, school events, my husband's church, casual chatting at local stores, and work-related social interaction. Many of my neighbors are actively involved in local, national, or international projects to enhance the common good.

My community is not, of course, a community of the kind lamented by traditionalists. Geographic mobility is high, and neighbors are usually not related to each other. By communitarian standards, community even in stable, prosperous Western towns and cities is thin and weak. Weakly embedded as I am in my neighborhood's social relations, I could easily pull up stakes, move elsewhere, and begin the process of establishing thin social relations all over again.

But communities are not always pleasant milieus. For many individuals, the community in which they are raised and live can be highly oppressive. Indeed, if I were to live in a community that did not tolerate atheists, people of mixed ethnic backgrounds, or women earning an income outside the home, I too would feel oppressed. Despite the value that I put on community, frankly, I am concerned that an overemphasis on it can carve away individual human rights. Human rights are absolutely necessary in the modern world, wherever one lives and whatever one's personal values. Human rights are meant above all to protect the individual against the state and the all-pervasive coercive power of which many modern states are capable. But human rights also protect people against society. Human rights give individuals the right to conduct their lives as they see fit, even when their choices challenge societal or community norms.

Individual choice undermines ascriptive restrictions on individuals' lives. Ascriptively based social categorization is characteristic of all societies. People are categorized as insiders or outsiders on the basis of race, ethnicity, nationality, or religion. People are also categorized by age, sex, and social status. Thanks to these categorizations some people are honored, some degraded. Others are considered completely beyond the pale. This categorization can be found in the smallest and least technologically advanced social units as well as in larger, more technologically advanced political states. For the dishonored, these categories mean restricted roles, privileges, and obligations in society (as is the situation of women virtually worldwide). Sometimes those restrictions, for example on outcastes in Hindu society, are so pernicious as to imply permanent social degradation, denial of social and political participation, and even denial of the right to food.[8]

A community that degrades some of its members is, in my view, a community in need of change. All communities should be based upon the free and equal participation of all their sane, adult members. In all communities the members should be citizens, not subjects governed by the whim of higher authorities. Citizens can actively participate in the decisions affecting their lives; subjects must hope that the decisions others make will be in their interests. Coercively organized communities, and communities that differentiate among members on the basis of their social status, adhere to a concept of social justice that is not based on human rights. Although social cohesion may be maintained and a form of unequal membership—at least of those insiders who obey the rules—may guarantee partial "rights," many individuals are repressed and degraded in such societies. The "rights" in these societies are actually privileges dependent on social status and conformity to group rules.

A human rights–based society presents opportunities for social membership not possible in status-bound communities that deny human rights. Human rights do not require reducing all members of definable social groups to atomized individuals. It would be ridiculous to advocate such reduction. Group identification is an extremely important part of most people's psychological makeup. The rituals, social support, and sense of belonging that ethno-religious groups provide for their members are an important check on the kind of social anomie now found in Western or Westernized societies. But when group cohesion is based on internal systems of invidious categorization and degradation, then social membership and human rights are incompatible. A culture and community based on systematic degradation must be challenged; if individual rights threaten such a society, so much the better. Human rights may sometimes require cultural rupture.

Nevertheless, it is possible to introduce human rights into a collectivity without destroying the group. For example, Jewish and Roman Catholic feminists who seek equality with men within their respective religions do so precisely because they value their group membership. If they did not, they could simply withdraw from their synagogue or church, convert to a more egalitarian religious denomination, or become atheists. For these feminists, not only their religious identities but also their ethno-cultural and social identities are bound up with their communities of worship. To grant equality to women is to change many customs within a group, but it does not follow that the group will be destroyed. Certain branches of Judaism now grant equal rights to women, as do certain branches of Protestant Christianity; in fact women who actively participate in these branches of their religious community contribute to their continued vitality in a secular society containing strong social forces that undermine religion.

Jewish and Roman Catholic feminists assert their right to be treated in a nondiscriminatory fashion regardless of the social group to which they belong. In modern complex societies individuals may be members of ascribed social categories based on gender, race, ethnicity, or religion. They may also be members of other groups. Memberships will be influenced by economic position, educational level, voluntary choice of friendship networks, and by individual decisions (such as the decision to join a different ethnic or religious community through marriage). In order for individuals to make choices about group and community memberships as active, participating citizens, they require the protection of nondiscrimination laws. All citizen must be treated equally regardless of gender, racial-ethnic, religious, or linguistic affiliation, regardless of economic status or class, regardless of voluntary memberships. Without the principle of nondiscrimination, modern societies perpetuate systems of status categorization and dishonor, allowing some citizens far more choice in social membership than others.

In modern liberal societies most discrimination on the basis of social status is illegal. But invidious distinction on the basis of social class is more difficult to eliminate, as class position is not always connected to status category. A status is an ascribed position, usually acquired at birth; class position is economic and can vary according to one's lifetime "achievements." The most important criticism of the principle of human rights remains the one made by Karl Marx: In unequal economic situations an "equal" right is a right of inequality.[9] Marx "condemned the capitalist system for what many would now call gross violations of fundamental human rights, the miserable living conditions of the workers, their subjection to capitalist tyranny in the factory, and brutal state suppression of working-class protests."[10] Marx, and his socialist and Communist successors, criticized liberalism for its failure to make the fulfilment of basic material needs a human right.

The most important aspect of social exclusion in modern North American society is disregard of the poor. They do not have full economic rights in practice; indeed very few economic rights are even acknowledged in principle. Both radical capitalists and right communitarians blame the poor for their incapacity to earn, whereas status radicals subordinate the needs of the poor to the pursuit of group goals that categorize people by ascriptive criteria rather than by actual social position. In many ways the human rights discourse of the late twentieth century has become a discourse of the privileged, of relatively well-off members of social categories that experience discrimination claiming the right to equal treatment in law and society. At the same time, the poor have little chance of using the human rights discourse to claim their fundamental rights in the economic sphere.

Social Construction of Human Rights

The legal standard of international human rights has been embodied since 1948 in the UN Universal Declaration of Human Rights, codified in 1966 in the International Covenant on Civil and Political Rights and the International Covenant on Economic, Social and Cultural Rights.[11]

Human rights are divided in the 1966 Covenants into two major classes: civil and political rights on the one hand and economic, social, and cultural rights on the other. Civil and political rights include first of all those that protect the individual against violation of her physical security by arbitrary execution, by torture, and by cruel, degrading, or inhuman treatment or punishment. Civil and political rights also protect citizens against abuse by state authorities through recognition before the law, the presumption of innocence, the guarantee of fair and impartial public trials, prohibition of ex post facto laws, and protections against arbitrary arrest, detention or exile. The rights to citizenship and to have a home in a defined country are also protected, by the rights to nationality, to freedom of movement, and to choose one's own residence.

Equality of status is protected in the UN human rights regime by the prohibition of all distinctions made on the basis of "race, color, sex, language, religion, political or other opinion, national or social origin, property, birth, or other status."[12] (There is, however, no prohibition of discrimination on the basis of sexual orientation; "other status" has yet to be interpreted at the international level to include sexual orientation.) One's right to privacy is protected by prohibitions against arbitrary interference with one's family, home, or reputation. Civil and political liberties also include rights that allow the citizen to participate in public and political life. Freedoms of thought, conscience and religion, opinion and expression, and peaceful assembly and association are protected. Finally, political rights include the rights to take part in government and to vote in periodic and genuine elections with universal and equal suffrage; these are not, however, required to be multiparty elections.

In the first section of this chapter I argue that radical capitalists disregard economic rights. Economic, social, and cultural rights recognized in the Universal Declaration of Human Rights include the rights to food and to a standard of living adequate for the health and well-being of oneself and one's family. They also include the rights to work, rest and leisure, and social security; and rights to education and to participation in the cultural life of the community. Some rights might be considered cultural: The right to speak one's own language, to practice one's own religion, and to practice one's own culture are included in the Covenant on Civil and Political Rights rather than in the Covenant on Economic, Social and Cultural Rights.[13]

Communitarian critics of human rights condemn the principle that individuals may assert claims against society and the state without obligations to either. Certainly, the idea of obligation is only weakly included in the International Bill of Human Rights. Article 29.1 of the Universal Declaration of Human Rights states, "Everyone has duties to the community in which alone the free and full development of his personality is possible."[14] The Covenants on Civil and Political Rights and Economic, Social and Cultural Rights contain identical clauses in their Preambles stating that the individual, "having duties to other individuals and to the community to which he belongs," is responsible to "strive for the promotion and observance" of human rights.[15] These weak statements of social responsibility, stressing the free development of the personality and the preservation of human rights, clearly cannot satisfy communitarian critics of the individualism inherent in human rights.

It is now generally agreed that human rights have the status of international law. Although they lack an enforcement mechanism, they provide a strong normative standard for the way states ought to treat their own citizens. The UN Covenants justify outside interest, on human rights grounds, in what had been formerly considered the exclusively internal affairs of a nation-state: "The failure of a government of a state to provide for its citizens' basic rights might now be taken as a reason for considering it illegitimate."[16] Whatever the force of claims of national sovereignty, the evaluation of national human rights practices from the perspective of the international standards of the Universal Declaration is now considered to be appropriate. Similarly, from a legal point of view, the claims of cultural uniqueness or traditional practices cannot be taken to imply the illegitimacy of outside concern with internal human rights practices. In 1992, military intervention in a sovereign state's internal affairs for purposes of humanitarian aid was given legitimacy when the UN sent troops into Somalia to organize the distribution of food.

The concept of human rights enunciated in the Universal Declaration reflects modern human thought about the nature of justice. Human rights have been removed from their earlier connection with "natural" rights, which are given by God. "Rights" in premodern Christian Europe were defined not by one's social relations with the state and society, but by one's relationship to God. Some protection from abusive acts of power was found in the belief that God had ordained some inviolable rights for individual human beings; these rights were therefore "natural" in a way that does not make intuitive sense for modern individuals accustomed to thinking of God and the divine as supernatural.

The idea that human rights are ordained by God is still attractive to many religious believers, and some human rights advocates still try to ground their beliefs in a religious rather than a secular worldview. This is the approach of the Muslim legal scholar Abdullahi Ahmed An-Na'im, who attempts to reconcile international human rights norms with Islamic principles. An-Na'im argued that all religio-cultural traditions, including Islam, share the principle of the Golden Rule, "the principle that one should treat other people as he or she wishes to be treated by them." All religions can use this principle to promote universal human rights.[17]

An-Na'im also contended that all religious traditions contain the essence of the world's consensus on human rights. I disagree. Human rights are a secular matter: They are derived from human thought about the nature of justice, not from divine decree. Although human rights might be better guaranteed in practice if they are also grounded in religious belief, it is not necessary to find a religious basis for them. Human rights are nothing more than what human beings proclaim they ought to be. They are universal in the sense that they ought to be universal, regardless of whether the great religions universally accept them as principles. Human rights principles are grounded not in religion but in secular society, in secularists' views of the rights that all humans need in order to live a life of dignity.

Among these essentially secular theories there are attempts to ground human rights in empirically verifiable facts about human needs or wants. Some theorists have attempted to divine such facts by seeking consensus among all societies about the values, needs, or desires of human beings. Such a consensus, they believe, could then be taken as a core list of what ought to be human rights. One might ascertain, for example, that there is a consensus across all societies that conforming members of the group should not starve. The job of the state, the lord, or the chief is at minimum to preserve basic economic security.[18] Yet even freedom from starvation is not a universal value. In many African and Asian societies men enjoy basic subsistence but women and children do not, even when they obey all social norms and do not resist any authorities. Women and children eat after the males of the families, and often eat less than they need; it is taken for granted that the paterfamilias can eat his fill without consideration of others' needs.[19] Cross-cultural research into social ideals might well reveal that there is none that is universal.

Arguing that there are naturally given requisites or needs for physical and mental health and well-being is another approach to defining basic human rights. This method seems reasonable at face value but can be challenged easily. Most thinkers would agree on minimal biological needs, mainly, to life, food, and shelter. Almost everything else, however, would have to be considered a socially generated want. Even health care can be considered a want rather than a need, since it is biologically "natural" for most people to die at relatively young ages after having completed their reproductive cycle. A needs approach to human rights limited to those absolutely necessary to keep human beings alive reduces human beings to their animal functions. But any other needs approach is actually a list of what its proponents think is necessary to be human. This is not, then, a list of needs in any empirically verifiable sense. Whatever list of needs is generated reflects the thinker's view of what it is to be a social being possessed of human dignity. The late philosopher Christian Bay, for example, included in his list of needs the right to self-respect.[20]

Some thinkers eschew the idea that human rights should be derived from human need, preferring instead to concentrate on basic human rights. The basic human rights approach combines two separate methods, one a sense of what is most important to human beings (either as wants or needs), the other a sense of what key human rights are strategically necessary in order that other human rights also can be protected.

Philosopher Henry Shue referred to security, subsistence, and liberty as a minimal, but not complete, list of basic rights.[21] Most people would agree that security (for example, the right not to be tortured) and subsistence are two values that every human being would want for herself. Liberty, on the other hand, is often debated; some critics argue that liberty is a culturally specific notion that does not reflect any necessary human need. Yet one can argue that liberty is strategically necessary: Only the free citizen can protect her rights to security and subsistence against the onslaught of societal and state forces.[22] Similarly, other human rights that Shue suggested might be basic, such as the right to freedom of movement, might be necessary to protect fundamental human needs.

Like Shue, the late R. J. Vincent derived his list of basic human rights both from a sense of fundamental human needs and from his theory of what is strategically necessary to protect human rights. He asserted that one basic right is the right to life "in the sense both of a right to security against violence and of a right to subsistence." He added to this a tentative right to liberty, "not in the heroic sense of liberty or death, but in the sense that it is essential to the enjoyment of all other rights, including the right to life. . . . Having a right to life means having at least the liberty to protest and mobilize opinion against its deprivation."[23]

Debates about basic human rights have produced a general consensus on what are considered to be gross human rights violations. Gross human rights violations are those that directly threaten a person's actual life or physical integrity. The Canadian political scientists Cranford Pratt and Robert O. Matthews have proposed as their minimal list of basic human rights freedom from detention without trial, freedom from torture, freedom from extrajudicial execution, and the right to subsistence.[24] This list is similar to that proposed by a Dutch working group, the Center for the Study of Social Conflicts based in Leiden. This group considered gross human rights violations to be such threats to one's life, liberty, and security as political murder, torture, and disappearances; it did not include threats to economic rights, even the right to subsistence, as gross human rights violations.[25]

Thus many contemporary social science approaches to human rights present opinions on what is minimally necessary to live one's life as a human being. All these arguments reflect perceptions (usually implicit) of human nature, of what human beings need and want to live a life of dignity. But human "nature" is a socially variable phenomenon; more than that, it is a social creation. Human nature is strongly affected by our biological needs for survival, but it is also affected by the norms, values, and desires that are internalized in the process of becoming a social being.[26] Human nature is also affected by human thought about what our nature is: Our norms, values, and desires reflect social ideals and teachings of what we are and ought to be. There are no basic human needs, human desires, or human rights separate from what human thought considers to be basic.

As Jack Donnelly put it, the concept of human rights is best interpreted by constructivist theory. Constructivist theory is a "moral theory of human nature" that acknowledges that rights are "not 'given' to man by God, nature or the physical facts of life." Rather, "human rights arise from human action [and] represent the choice of a particular moral vision of human potentiality and the institutions for realising that vision. . . . The evolution of particular conceptions or lists of human rights is seen in the constructivist theory as the result of the reciprocal interactions of moral conceptions and material conditions of life, mediated through social institutions such as rights."[27] Constructivist theory, then, accords with the sociological view that human rights are a social phenomenon, a creation of the human mind. Human rights are human rights because humankind has decided they are. Human beings create their own sense of a morally worthwhile life.

Moral Prerequisites for a Life of Dignity

The International Bill of Human Rights, then, embodies one constructivist theory of human rights. Its underlying moral conception is its particular interpretation of human dignity. The Preambles to both the 1966 International Covenants on Human Rights state that human rights "derive from the inherent dignity of the human person."[28] "All human beings are born free and equal in dignity and rights. They are endowed with reason and conscience and should act toward one another in a spirit of brotherhood."[29] In his analysis of religion, Emile Durkheim argued that man had created God as an embodiment of social morality.[30] Human rights are a modern secular version of our social need to have overriding, inviolable principles of morality. Whatever their origin, either in God's command or in the mind of humankind, human rights exist as a strong set of normative principles influencing the actions both of states and of citizens.

Human rights are now what Durkheim called social facts: "ways of acting, thinking and feeling, external to the individual, and endowed with a power of coercion, by reason of which they control him."[31] Without endowing it with heavily coercive powers, one can argue that the international consensus on human rights is a politically influential fact in its own right. In states that abuse human rights, citizens who discover this consensus are inspired by it, and use its existence to justify their claims for better treatment by their government. In 1988, for example, the citizens of Hungary were inundated with copies of the Universal Declaration of Human Rights during the "Human Rights Now!" concert tour organized by Amnesty International.[32] They based their claims for liberalization partly on this newly discovered consensus.

Morality does not need to be grounded in God's will. Nor does it need to be grounded in empirically verifiable facts about universal needs or wants. Morality is grounded in what human beings think is moral. As societies change, people's moral norms and values also change. Human beings construct their own theories of how they ought to live, of what their privileges and rights are, and of what their obligations ought to be to family, society, and state. The doctrine of human rights reflects and justifies the theoretical positions that many individuals have derived independently, the world over, whatever their cultures are claimed to dictate.

The social fact of human rights influences public policy, helps groups and individuals seek justice, and mobilizes shame among those who enjoy human rights but know that others do not. This secular consensus on the type of justice required to live a life of dignity in modern society affects social action in all parts of the world. In this sense it is a universal social ideology.

Nevertheless, the interpretation of human rights is debated by diverse social actors, many of whom dislike the way that human rights reflect the moral order of liberal Western society. One of the most hotly debated characteristics of the international consensus on human rights is the requirement of nondiscrimination. Another is the perceived lack of social obligation—to family, community, and the state. These debates reflect different views on what it means to live a life of dignity. Dignity is not defined in any of the international human rights instruments; rather, it is left to "intuitive understanding."[33]

In my view, dignity requires personal autonomy, societal concern and respect, and treatment by others in society as an equal.

Personal autonomy requires protection from those gross human rights violations that render one always subject to the arbitrary coercive powers of the state. The citizen who is constantly afraid of the police or army cannot conduct her life as she sees fit; she cannot fulfil even her minimum social obligations—to work, to raise her family, to honor her elders—in any sort of security. To have personal autonomy also means to have the freedom to act on one's decisions and to have one's decisions respected by the state and other citizens. To have autonomy, finally, means to have privacy—to think, to consider, to resist pressures from conformist social forces. The citizen who has privacy can act on her thoughts and considerations in the public arena.

Autonomy, however, does not mean complete independence or self-reliance. The autonomous individual does not live in a social vacuum, without connections with, obligations to, or claims on fellow citizens. Rather, all citizens ought to be concerned with the dignity of all fellow citizens. Ronald Dworkin maintained that the state should treat all its citizens with equal concern and respect; I extend this to argue that citizens must treat each other with concern and respect.[34] Citizens will not accord concern and respect equally to all fellow citizens: Their sense of obligation will normally extend outward, with progressively thinner connections, from family, kin, friends, and local community to the nation and the wider world. Nevertheless, societal concern and respect require that all citizens enjoy minimum economic rights. However thin one's sense of obligation may be to the stranger on the other side of the country, that stranger cannot be bereft of material security. Concern for another's dignity is meaningless if it is confined to the legal and political spheres but excluded from the economic.

Societal respect also requires that citizens treat each other in a nondiscriminatory and egalitarian manner. Nondiscrimination is a key human right for two reasons. One reason is strategic: Without equality before the law and in the political arena, an individual cannot easily claim her other human rights. The other reason is intrinsic to the type of human person that capitalism and modernity have created. In the world today, influenced as it is by the social ideology of human equality, not to be considered of equal moral value to all other human beings is to be profoundly hurt and degraded. Personal respect ought to be accorded to all individuals. No one should be raised or taught to feel that she or he is—by virtue of some categorical social marker such as race, gender, or inherited social status—a stigmatized and inferior human being. In modern society a sense of efficacy and usefulness is so intimately bound up with personal autonomy and societal respect as to obviate any possibility of finding contentment in subordination.

The concept of human dignity that I present here is not one that promotes anomic individualism or the breakdown of the community. My conception of dignity integrates the individual more fully into society, rather than removing her from it. If the individual human being is to function as a citizen, she must be accorded personal autonomy, societal concern and respect, and treatment equal to that afforded to everyone else. Inequalities and social degradation remove people from the larger social group, rendering them incapable of autonomous action in the public sphere, in the community, or even in the family. Material security, personal autonomy, and societal respect render one more, not less, capable of action on behalf of others. Enjoyment of human rights can enhance individuals' sense of responsibility to others.

This constructivist view of human dignity is one that links human rights to both individual freedoms and belongingness in the community. The communitarian challenge to Western individualism is a serious one. The accusation that human rights exclude economic rights has some justification, as also has the accusation that Western—or at least North American—society has destroyed the collectivity. The principle of human rights can be defended against the charge that it is responsible for these problems in Western society. Nevertheless, Western social practice does reflect a lack of concern with the human rights of all its members; until this breach of its own principles is remedied, the communitarian rejection of liberalism will have some justification.

Searching for Human Rights and Community

This book discusses in detail questions about the relationships among the individual, the community, and human rights that I have just introduced. I defend the individualism, equality, and liberty that the ideology of human rights promises and that is, to a significant if limited extent, available to residents of Western capitalist societies. At the same time, I argue that liberal society still excludes large categories of people partly on the basis of status and partly on the basis of class. The most significant form of social exclusion in modern society, that is, exclusion based on social class, is largely ignored in the liberal human rights debate.

In order to discuss criticisms of Western liberal society we must first understand its own social evolution. Chapter 2 considers the creation of the ideology of human rights within bourgeois capitalist society. I discuss the evolution of the social values of privacy and individualism and how they affect notions of individual autonomy and the right to respect. The human rights of the early capitalist bourgeoisie became human rights necessary for all other social groups wanting to act as citizens in modern society. Privacy of thought and action became a means of articulating and asserting the public interest. Thus autonomy is considered a key human rights value in the modern West. Objections to privacy and autonomy form the basis of the traditionalist and conservative reactions to human rights.

Traditionalists have a further objection to human rights, based in the notion of cultural autonomy. Left collectivists and status radicals join traditionalists in this objection, also arguing for groups or collectivities to be able to formulate their own ideas of human rights on the basis of their own social norms. Chapter 3 introduces the debate between universalism and relativism in the formulation of human rights principles. I argue that the relativist perspective on human rights is actually one that posits culture as the absolute ethical value, thereby superseding human rights; I illustrate this point with a (hypothetical) absolutist defense of a white Canada. The relativist argument is influenced by a romantic perception of exotic societies whose roots can be found in the nineteenth-century Euro-American contact with colonized Others. This romanticism, I believe, now infects people who themselves live in these societies.

Chapter 4 discusses the differences between liberal and other conceptions of human rights and of human dignity. I argue that there are many conceptions of social justice that do not accept that individuals should have human rights. In many societies, to be dignified means to accept one's subordinate status, not to insist on equal and autonomous human rights. Thus, I reject the fashionable idea that all systems of social justice are systems of human rights. To illustrate this point, I discuss contemporary arguments for uniquely African and Muslim conceptions of human rights. These arguments are rooted in part in the difference between religious and secular worldviews and more generally in the belief that assertion of individual human rights will destroy a community.

Both the relativist critique of human rights and the traditionalist critique are part of the larger communitarian disquiet with individualism, which I address in Chapter 5. Two competing views of society, one that stresses the collectivity and one that stresses the individual, are presented but with a warning that neither one can protect human rights. I argue that there is a modern community, based on voluntary associations and voluntary dedication to the good of others who may not share one's ascriptive or cultural characteristics. Modernity is a social fact: Both its liberating potential and its potential for social exclusion must be considered in contemporary accounts of community.

Chapter 6 turns to the criticism of liberal societies made by status radicals, and presents an analysis of the process of social degradation. I argue that the concepts of honor and shame are at the basis of how social groups are categorized. Despite their progress toward equality in modern North America, women and blacks remain dishonored, shamed groups. Some women and blacks accept their shame to such an extent that they actually engage in practices of self-mutilation that are designed to hide or control their perceived inherent imperfections. Women and blacks are also subject to noninstitutionalized violence that reinforces their status degradation. I call this violence social terror. I end Chapter 6 by arguing that the solution to the problems of shame and social terror is not to divide social groups into permanently irreconcilable categories. Rather, the complexity of individuals' lives in modern Western society gives them a multiplicity of social identities, some of which protect even women and blacks from shame and allow them to express interests in common with members of other status categories. In particular, status-based shame can be overcome by success in the capitalist marketplace.

Thus I turn to the most important aspect of social exclusion in modern North America: the continued inability of liberal society to deal with the problem of class distinctions. In Chapter 7 I argue that poverty is the primary and enduring form of social degradation in advanced capitalist states. In North America, especially the United States, disregard of the poor and abuse of their basic economic rights causes social breakdown. "Sub-welfare" and the social degradation of the poor are processes that maintain both the economic advantage and the status honor of more privileged social classes in North America. Two social trends, social minimalism and reactionary conservatism, encourage disregard of the poor. Both share the core value of economic autonomy, a value that excludes those who cannot achieve economic security on their own.

There is no easy answer to the question of how to integrate the poor more fully into the human rights contract. In Chapter 8 I argue that the conflict between communitarianism and individualism in modern society can be resolved only by respecting the entire range of human rights, especially economic rights. Social democracy is a neglected approach to human rights that attempts to do just that and is therefore compatible with community as well as with liberal individualism. Yet as the example of Canada shows, outsiders can still suffer discrimination in social democratic societies. Status radicals and left collectivists, observing such discrimination, argue that the philosophy of individual human rights is bankrupt and cannot protect members of degraded social groups. Nevertheless, I argue that human rights can be preserved and provide the best protection for degraded groups. If we are to reject individual human rights in the name of the search for community, then we must clearly define in our minds the type of community that a human rights–based society can generate at its best, not merely the type that radical capitalism has produced at its worst.

Notes

1. Rhoda E. Howard and Jack Donnelly, "Human Dignity, Human Rights and Political Regimes," *American Political Science Review*, vol. 80, no. 3 (September 1986), pp. 801–817; Neil Mitchell, Rhoda E. Howard, and Jack Donnelly, "Liberalism, Human Rights and Human Dignity [a debate]," *American Political Science Review*, vol. 81, no. 3 (September 1987), pp. 921–927; Rhoda E. Howard and Jack Donnelly, "Introduction" to Jack Donnelly and Rhoda E. Howard (eds.), *International Handbook of Human Rights* (Westport, Conn.: Greenwood, 1987), pp. 1–28.

2. Maurice Cranston, "Are There Any Human Rights?" *Daedalus*, vol. 112, no. 4 (fall 1983), p. 12.

3. Carnes Lord, "Human Rights Policy in a Nonliberal World," in Marc F. Plattner (ed.), *Human Rights in Our Time: Essays in Memory of Victor Baras* (Boulder: Westview, 1984), p. 132.

4. Nick Eberstadt, *The Poverty of Communism* (New Brunswick, N.J.: Transaction Publishers, 1990), part 1.

5. For lack of a better collective term I use "North America" to mean Canada and the United States, with apologies to the other countries in North America and their inhabitants.

6. E.g., Issa G. Shivji, *The Concept of Human Rights in Africa* (London: CODESRIA Book Series, 1989).

7. Number of volunteers from personal communication, Sheila Hagens, Hamilton-Wentworth Volunteer Centre, August 1993. Number of churches from a manual count in Hamilton, Ontario, telephone book, August 1993.

8. For a description of the life of one such degraded person, see James M. Freeman, *Untouchable: An Indian Life History* (Stanford, Calif.: Stanford University Press, 1979).

9. Karl Marx, "Critique of the Gotha Program," in Lewis S. Feuer (ed.), *Karl Marx and Friedrich Engels: Basic Writings on Politics and Philosophy* (Garden City, N.Y.: Anchor Books, 1959), pp. 118–119.

10. Richard Nordahl, "A Marxian Approach to Human Rights," in Abdullahi Ahmed An-Na'im (ed.), *Human Rights in Cross-Cultural Perspectives: A Quest for Consensus* (Philadelphia: University of Pennsylvania Press, 1992), p. 162.

11. These documents are easily available in many sources, for example, Center for the Study of Human Rights, *Twenty-Four Human Rights Documents* (New York: Columbia University, 1992), pp. 6–30. For a thorough discussion of both United Nations and regional human rights regimes, see Jack Donnelly, "International Human Rights Regimes," in his *Universal Human Rights in Theory and Practice* (Ithaca, N.Y.: Cornell University Press, 1989), pp. 205–228.

12. United Nations Universal Declaration of Human Rights, Article 2, in Center for the Study of Human Rights, *Twenty-Four Human Rights Documents*, p. 6.

13. International Covenant on Civil and Political Rights, Article 27, in Center for the Study of Human Rights, *Twenty-Four Human Rights Documents*, p. 24.

14. Ibid., p. 9.

15. Ibid., pp. 18 and 10 respectively.

16. R. J. Vincent, *Human Rights and International Relations* (Cambridge: Cambridge University Press, 1986), p. 127.

17. Abdullahi Ahmed An-Na'im, *Toward an Islamic Reformation: Civil Liberties, Human Rights, and International Law* (Syracuse: Syracuse University Press, 1990), pp. 162–163.

18. Barrington Moore Jr., *Injustice: The Social Bases of Obedience and Revolt* (White Plains, N.Y.: M. E. Sharpe, 1978), Chapter 1.

19. Amartya Sen, "More than 100 Million Women Are Missing," *New York Review of Books,* vol. 37, no. 20 (December 20, 1990), pp. 61–66.

20. Christian Bay, "Self-Respect as a Human Right: Thoughts on the Dialectics of Wants and Needs in the Struggle for Human Community," *Human Rights Quarterly,* vol. 4, no. 1 (winter 1982), pp. 53–75.

21. Henry Shue, *Basic Rights: Subsistence, Affluence and U.S. Foreign Policy* (Princeton: Princeton University Press, 1980), p. 9.

22. Rhoda E. Howard, "The 'Full-Belly' Thesis: Should Economic Rights Take Priority over Civil and Political Rights? Evidence from Sub-Saharan Africa," *Human Rights Quarterly,* vol. 5, no. 4 (November 1983), pp. 470–478.

23. Vincent, *Human Rights and International Relations,* p. 125.

24. Robert Matthews and Cranford Pratt, "Human Rights and Foreign Policy: Principles and Canadian Practice," *Human Rights Quarterly,* vol. 7, no. 2 (May 1985), p. 160.

25. Alex P. Schmid, *Research on Gross Human Rights Violations* (Leiden: Center for the Study of Social Conflicts [C.O.M.T.], 1989), p. 6.

26. On the biological influence on human nature, see Edward O. Wilson, *On Human Nature* (New York: Bantam Books, 1979).

27. Jack Donnelly, *The Concept of Human Rights* (London: Croom Helm, 1985), pp. 31 and 35.

28. In Center for the Study of Human Rights, *Twenty-Four Human Rights Documents,* pp. 10 and 18.

29. Universal Declaration of Human Rights, Article 1, in ibid., p. 6.

30. Emile Durkheim, *The Elementary Forms of the Religious Life* (London: George Allen and Unwin, 1968 [1st ed. 1915]), pp. 206–214.

31. Emile Durkheim, *The Rules of Sociological Method* (New York: The Free Press, 1938), p. 3.

32. Amnesty International, "Human Rights Now! Concert Tour 1988," *Bulletin,* Canadian Section (English Speaking), vol. 16, no. 1 (December 1988/January 1989), pp. 18–21.

33. Oscar Schachter, "Editorial Comment: Human Dignity as a Normative Concept," *American Journal of International Law,* vol. 77, no. 4 (October 1983), p. 849.

34. Ronald Dworkin, *Taking Rights Seriously* (Cambridge: Harvard University Press, 1978), p. 273, and Dworkin, *A Matter of Principle* (Cambridge: Harvard University Press, 1985), p. 190.

2 Liberal Society

The Central Park Thesis

Both right and left communitarian critics of human rights base their commentaries on their pictures of life in the modernized, capitalist West, particularly the United States. These critics hold to what might be called the "Central Park thesis," the logic of which is as follows.

The philosophy of human rights is individualist and anticommunitarian. Human rights are a Western concept. The United States is the West. The United States is characterized by very high crime rates. They are highest in New York City, a center of acquisitive materialism and greed. They are especially high in the notorious Central Park, which no decent person can ever enter. People who commit crimes in the United States are usually able to escape punishment because of exaggerated human rights to a fair trial. Therefore, human rights breed crime and disorder.

New York does seem to the unaccustomed foreign eye to be a city of enormous and immoral contrasts. To people accustomed to less violent cities, having to use caution on the subways and avoid certain parts of the city (white or black, depending on one's own color) are extremely unsettling experiences. So is the experience of encountering homeless people wandering the same streets as some of the richest people on earth. New York seems callous, cruel, an exaggeration of the right of the individual to disregard all others in pursuit of his own fortune.

The Central Park thesis is part of a larger conglomerate of stereotypes that traditionalist communitarians, in particular, hold of the Western world. All marriages in the West end in divorce, all aged people are abandoned, all children are latch-key children, homosexuality is rampant and flagrant. So goes the stereotype of Western individualist culture. Third World traditionalists thus reject human rights in favor of more familiar, safer, and socially cohesive models of society.

Traditionalist critics of human rights confuse the human rights of the individual with individualism—private materialism and abnegation of social responsibility. They have seen for themselves the kind of behavior they often decry. In the Western homes that they visit, children talk back to parents, elderly people are absent, and women refuse to subject themselves to the authority of their husbands. These patterns of intimate family behavior appear grossly selfish, especially to people who are used to living in three- or four-generational homes and assisting in the support of a wide network of kin and clients. Human rights appear to breed extreme selfishness and disregard for others.

This type of critique is common not only among traditionalist critics of human rights, but also among right communitarians. It is also the backdrop to the status radicalist desire to form new communities of shared values and social responsibility. Characteristics typical of the United States are assumed to exemplify all Western societies that protect human rights, and human rights protection is taken to be the cause of many social pathologies that can be found in the United States. But social pathologies such as high crime rates and the ghettoization of the black poor should be taken not as examples of protection of human rights but as examples of their abuse. Racism, poverty, and homelessness are not consequences of a surfeit of human rights. They are consequences of the absence of economic rights, which in the United States are not entrenched in law and are not part of the guiding social philosophy.

The Central Park thesis reflects a picture of individualism at its worst, of people who seek human rights, material wealth, and social privilege without concern for others. This critique of human rights is also a critique of modernity, of liberalism, and of the excesses of the capitalist marketplace. Crime in Central Park is the symbol of excessive protection of human rights, even as the homeless beggars outside it symbolize the excesses of a market economy that discards its own poor. In the absence of a liberal impetus to collective social responsibility, the critics are justified in rejecting the individualism that human rights imply in modern society. If human rights are not tied to social responsibility, they are easily perverted, in the social and economic realm, into human selfishness.

The picture drawn below is of ideal-type Western individualism. It focuses on those characteristics of Western social behavior that critics of liberal society find offensive. To understand the social trends that, at the

end of the twentieth century, constitute a serious threat to the maintenance of liberal society, we must first view it through the eyes of its critics.

The Social Evolution of Liberal Society

Several centuries of social evolution in the West have produced a type of
society that has not evolved autonomously anywhere else. As this type of
system spreads elsewhere, it produces a strong social reaction.
Concomitantly, there are strong reactions against it and what are perceived as its alienating tendencies within the West itself.

One characteristic of liberal society that makes it distinct from both
traditional societies and nonliberal societies is the high value that it
places on individualism and on privacy. "Privacy in its modern sense—
that is a sphere of thought and action that should be free from 'public'
interference . . . constitute[s] what is perhaps the central idea of liberalism."[1] This individualism and privacy seem to result in a society in which
each person seeks his own interest, disregarding the interests of others,
so that a highly abusive class system results. Liberal society also seems
to promote disconnection from those primary communities—family,
church, ethnic group—that make the living human being into a social
person and tie him to others. Instead, liberalism promotes secularism,
disconnection from God and all He stands for. It strips people of their
social attributes, leaving them only a formal citizenship in a remote
state.

Liberal society replaces gemeinschaft with gesellschaft, to use the
vocabulary introduced by the German sociologist Ferdinand Tonnies. A
gemeinschaft society is one in which people live together in primary
groups, tightly wound around the institutions of kin, community, and
church. There is little social change. Identity seems holistic: The individual's life is not fragmented into various parts unconnected from one another. The individual's work is passed on to him from his father, marriage partners are chosen either from within the group or from another
group recognized as the source of partners, and there is little if any social intercourse with strangers.[2] Rose Laub Coser called gemeinschaft
societies "greedy." By this she meant that they demand complete loyalty
from their members and discourage intercourse with outsiders.
Members experience few if any demands to reflect on their roles or on
the nature of their society; in return, their life is secure.[3]

In gesellschaft society, by contrast, people frequently leave their primary groups for association with people who may be strangers. One
chooses one's occupation, place of residence, and marriage partner. Ties

to primary kin, place of origin, and church are loose and may be cut off entirely. Life in a gesellschaft society is insecure and complex, and individuals must constantly reflect on their roles in it. According to Tonnies, gesellschaft life is unpleasant and alienating. "In the Gesellschaft . . . everybody is by himself and isolated, and there exists a condition of tension against all others. . . . Such a negative attitude toward one another becomes the normal and always underlying relation. . . . Nobody wants to grant and produce anything for another individual, nor will he be inclined to give ungrudgingly to another individual."[4]

Yet as Coser has pointed out, this unhappy picture of gesellschaft society obscures its advantages. The very insecurity and complexity it produces in individuals result in more complex mental abilities: "The ability to think conceptually is in large part an attribute of the social structure."[5] The individual in modern gesellschaft society exercises role distance and role choice. He can detach himself from his prescribed place in society and substitute for society's purposes his own. "Confronting all possible roles, [the individual] . . . may in principle adopt, perform or abandon any at will. . . . As sovereign chooser, he *decides* between actions, conceptions of the good, plans of life, indeed what sort of a person to be. The will, choice, decision, evaluation and calculation are central to this picture; and the individual to whom these features are essential thinks and acts as an autonomous, self-directing, independent agent who relates to others as no less autonomous agents."[6] The most outstanding change from gemeinschaft to gesellschaft, then, is the change from identity as bestowed by the community to identity as created by its own possessor.

Emile Durkheim made a similar distinction between gemeinschaft and gesellschaft societies, referring to societies based on community and those based on association. In Durkheim's view, one of the advantages of modernity is precisely that one can choose one's associations: occupation, marriage partner, religious affiliation. For Durkheim, the stuff of democracy is the social pattern of memberships in freely chosen associations. Liberal society protects individualism, not in the sense that the individual is removed from society, but in the sense that he leaves the communities given to him at birth for the wider community of choice, reflection, and participation.[7]

These typologies indicate the social rupture that modern, capitalist liberal societies exemplify. We are accustomed to discussing social change, the idea that societies change in reaction to a variety of influences, such as evolving economic forms, new political arrangements, and new ideals of proper social behavior. Yet social change makes many people uncomfortable. Although they have been urbanized for two centuries, many Westerners still harbor a nostalgia for a close, rural gemeinschaft society that they think existed before industrialization changed so many people's lives. In the rest of the world, modernization and industrialization have changed societies very rapidly, as a result both of colonization and the expansion of the world economic system. For non-Westerners, social change is often social rupture. It is dramatic, overwhelming, and frightening. "Collisions of consciousness" characterize the entry into modernity.[8]

Liberalism necessitates a new culture. Liberalism cannot preserve holistic cultures in their pure, gemeinschaft form: It must undermine them and introduce new ideas of the nature and value of the individual and the roles that individuals play in society. This rupture is one of the reasons for the current culturalist reaction against Western society. One aspect of this culturalist reaction is traditionalist defense of, and longing for, the social order that existed before the onslaught of imperialism and capitalism.

Liberal culture, with its stress on individualist achievement, also attracts the hostility of people such as women and blacks whose paths to achievement are impeded by the ascriptive categorizations that still underpin Western social structure. And it attracts the hostility of those who, though not blocked from success by their ascriptive memberships, nevertheless long for the security and belongingness of gemeinschaft societies. Thus even in North America, deep-seated communitarian social beliefs are continually at odds with the more recent, culturally novel, and perhaps less embedded liberal society that governs the official norms of political rules, legal rights, and egalitarian social intercourse.

The moral order of a society based on human rights is markedly different from that of other types of societies. In a society based on human rights, human dignity consists not of acquiescence to hierarchical order but of equality and assertion of one's claim to respect. The historical precedent for societies based on human rights is the liberal society of capitalist Europe. Both structural and cultural changes must occur for a society such as that which emerged in parts of Europe after the feudal period to appear. The values of autonomy, respect, and equality are key to the cultural underpinnings of a society in which the individual can make human rights claims not only upon the state but also upon society at large. For these values to have meaning, the notion must emerge of the individual as a private person, separated from the community and entitled to value such separation.

The Individual as a Private Person

Liberal capitalist society is based on a strong cultural element of privacy. The human being is an individual separate from his family, society, and the state. The individual is presumed to have a strong need for separation from the community.

Differentiation of the individual from his social relations has resulted in two new human "needs." The first is a psychological need for privacy—a "private space" in the current jargon. Early in the social evolution of capitalism, individuals were "created." They moved away from their natal communities to find work, they married strangers, they ignored their priests. Individuals found they could indulge in personal habits and desires without social censure from the new communities in which they found themselves. As individuals began to value these social freedoms, an ideology evolved that the freedoms were natural, an inherent part of what it meant to be human. To be human was to need not only social interaction and a sense of community, but also withdrawal from society, time for private pursuits and private reflection.

The second consequence of the differentiation of the individual from his social relations is the need to act as a private person in some political matters. The assumption is that politics are most fairly conducted when each person makes decisions and votes according to his private interest. As the invisible hand of the marketplace regulates economic relations, so the invisible hand of the voting booth regulates political affairs. It is in the nature of the human being in Western capitalist society to need to express his private political opinions even if they are unattractive to others and to participate in public affairs free from fear of coercion. Thus, in liberal capitalist society it is accepted that the individual needs bodily integrity, freedom from assault by the state, and freedom of speech, press, and association. The body is a private possession, the integrity of which must be preserved: The mind is a private attribute whose public expression must be permitted.

The value of personal privacy implies the individual's right, within the law, to do what he considers in his best interests, even if these interests conflict with those of larger social entities of which he may be a member. Such an individual is entitled to have a domain of personality and interest separate from that of kin or community. He is entitled to autonomy in his personal, social, and political relations with others. Conformity to the social norms of the group is no longer a necessary aspect of what it means to be human; rather, the possibility of individual difference and choice is introduced.

This core value of Western society did not spring full-blown from capitalism. Barrington Moore Jr. argued that there were strong elements of privacy in both the Greek and the Hebrew traditions from which Western philosophy and Christianity are drawn.[9] But the value of privacy deepened and spread as the capitalist system evolved. In part, the new stress on privacy reflected the key capitalist principle that the citizen has the right to own private property. In early capitalist Europe, land was privatized and used as a basis for investment and collateral. Enterprise became a matter of private initiative: The guilds and their artisan-led restrictions on production broke down. Every man became entitled to life, liberty, and estate: Property consisted not only of real goods, but also of mastery over one's own physical integrity and one's own fate in society.[10]

The social group that personified the evolution of private property and private life in Europe was the bourgeoisie, the new merchant and later capitalist class. The bourgeoisie as a class is generally thought to have stressed the classic human rights of Lockean liberalism; that is, civil and political rights and the right to private property.[11] These are private rights. Private property leaves the bourgeois free to exercise his rights of ownership without worry about sudden and arbitrary confiscation.[12] Civil and political rights permit the bourgeois to assert his interests in the public sphere. Civil and political rights are often interpreted as "negative" rights in the sense that they require, above all, noninterference by the state in the private affairs (religion, speech, association) of the citizen.[13] Thus in the evolution of capitalist society, the state was gradually obliged to honor not only a man's property, but also his life, his liberty, and his opinions.

The notion of privacy thus contributed to a new type of legal system that assumed anything not specifically forbidden was permitted, not only in the economic and political spheres, but gradually also in the social sphere. This in turn broadened the scope for individual deviance from social norms and thus the scope for creativity—in thought or the arts as much as in means of production or social arrangements. Individuals were not suddenly removed from their families and communities, nor did the pressures of church and society suddenly become irrelevant. But individuals were more easily able to withstand the pressures of greedy gemeinschaft institutions: Their thoughts became more critical, their deeds more innovative. Thus capitalism permitted the flowering of individual identity.

The new conception of the self that characterized capitalist society reflected more than freedom. The self that emerged in nineteenth-century society was not merely the consequence of the ideology of the independent bourgeois, asserting himself in control of his environment. As the capitalist classes retreated into the freedom and privacy of their everyday lives, they simultaneously set in motion the processes that wrenched peasants from their communities and transformed them into the proletariat of the new urban industrial centers. Under capitalism, property-based class relations become the principal form of social stratification. Peasants were transformed into propertyless wage workers at the mercy of capitalist property-owners.

The obverse side of the evolution of the free bourgeois in capitalist society is the tendency to treat the human person as a thing. Karl Marx argued that the worker in modern society is nothing but a productive commodity, a moving and thinking thing that could be used to produce other things. The only obligation that the employer had to the worker was to pay him the wage agreed upon in return for the labor provided. The bonds of the precapitalist system, in which lords had some obligations, however tenuous, to the peasantry, were replaced by strictly monetary links between the classes. Under the wage system, the worker— Marx's proletarian—sold his labor power, his capacity to work, to the bourgeois or capitalist employer for a set period every day. Thus, according to Marx, the proletarian was alienated from himself. Even if the hours were short and the conditions of work safe; indeed, even if the wages were high, the very act of selling one's capacity to work was personally degrading. The proletarian, according to Marx, became separated from his labor; his creative capacities alienated from the self as he became merely a human machine obeying the orders of his employer.[14] The proletarian was also separated from the land he used to own, or at least work, and he was separated from the community of kin and church that sustained him in his peasant existence. Thus he became triply alienated, from his own capacity to labor, from nature, and from community.

The Marxist thesis of alienation powerfully affects those who, from both right and left, criticize the individualist character of human rights. To Marx's concept of separation from self, community, and nature these critics add Durkheim's concept of anomie. Durkheim originally used the term "anomie" in his analysis of different forms of suicide. He called "anomic" that type of suicide that resulted from "man's activity's lacking regulation." When society did not properly influence and restrain man's "individual passions," suffering resulted.[15] More generally, the term anomie is now used to mean normlessless, a lack of connection to society and its values. Thus the capitalist world, in the modern critique of liberalism, destroyed both man's value in his own productive labor and his connection to the wider community. Marx's use of the term alienation and the Durkheimian definition of anomie join together in the sociologist's non-Marxist usage of "alienation" to mean "a generalized feeling of frustration that comes over a person who is expected to behave in a way that is experienced as not being 'meaningful.'"[16]

In the transition to capitalist society, critics of liberalism maintain, community is destroyed. The worker has no social identity outside of his role in the productive system to which he can refer as a guide to morals or as validation of his behavior. The worker as parent cannot fulfilll his obligations to his family, as such obligations interfere with the contract of sale of his labor power. The worker as aged person cannot expect the communal and family respect now given only to those who earn a wage. The worker as member of the community is valued only for the amount of money he earns and the material possessions he displays.

Thus the class-based stratification of capitalist society undermines the connection of the human being to his community. Part of the human being's link to his community is his link to the divine, which joins humans together in their shared moral code.[17] As the worker under capitalism cannot fulfill his obligations to his family, so he cannot, as parishioner, fulfill his obligations to his church and cannot, as adult male, fulfill his proper role in the social group. Capitalism ruptures those older social relations in which God instructed the wealthy to care for the poor: It leaves the poor reeling in a world emptied of social respect.

Shared membership in the community of God no longer binds landowner and peasant, capitalist and worker. The relation of the human to the spiritual world changes as the natural world loses its mystery. The development of science and technology allows men to control nature directly, without the continued mediation of God. A rupture between the individual human soul and the collective spirit occurs: The man in control of a machine no longer relies so clearly on his priest. This was an aspect of social change that Marx considered beneficial: He regarded religion as a means to deceive the people, their faith in a future reward blinding them to the realities of their hell on earth. As Marx so eloquently put it, "Religion is the sigh of oppressed creatures, the heart of a heartless world, just as it is the soul of soulless conditions. It is the opium of the people."[18] But for other social theorists, the elimination of faith, ritual, and the sense of community fostered by common membership in a church dehumanized Western man: It reduced him to a physical being seeking material survival and comfort in a world devoid of spiritual or ethical meaning.[19]

Marx did not idealize precapitalist social relations, as do many traditionalist and right communitarian critics of capitalism.[20] But for Marx, the commodification of workers in the capitalist system constituted a new and unprecedented system of exploitation and degradation. Marx's analysis is that of capitalism at its worst and most exploitative. The human being under capitalism is no longer a natural being. He loses connection to his own creative capacities and his intrinsic ability to combine labor and pleasure into one whole. He loses connection to the community around him that is now divided into exploited and exploiting classes. Finally, he loses connection to the natural world.

But Marx's interpretation of the new social degradation implicit in capitalist organization may well be exaggerated. In feudal, precapitalist

Europe, the obligations landlords held to their tenants may not have been much more than those of capitalists to workers. Feudal society, said Marc Bloch, was unequal: It "extended and consolidated [over earlier times] . . . [those] methods whereby men exploited men."[21] The day-to-day life of the peasant might well have been more a repetitive, back-breaking grind than a fulfilling communion with nature. Community and church might have provided a sense of security typical of gemeinschaft society, but they might equally have pressured the individual into strict conformity to social norms and roles from which there was no escape.

Nor may Marx's analysis apply to the modern era. The conditions of capitalism and of capitalist labor have changed drastically. Trade unionism and social democratic welfare policies have ameliorated the exploitative conditions of industrial production. There is far more leisure time during which people can, if they wish, exercise their creative capacities. Even the daily conditions of work itself have changed so that for some, if not all, industrial workers there is now some satisfaction on the job and a certain level of autonomy. Even at its zenith, the quintessentially alienating assembly line memorialized in Charlie Chaplin's *Modern Times* (1936) employed no more than about 5 percent of American manual workers.[22] Although some repetitive industrial jobs are boring, alienating, and destructive of an inner sense of self-respect, many other jobs in the complex late-twentieth-century division of labor require high degrees of autonomy, education, and responsibility. Workers holding these latter types of positions exhibit high degrees of job satisfaction.[23]

Nevertheless, Marx's analysis of the commodification and privatization of social relations during the early capitalist period is an important clue to the world the bourgeoisie made. This world simultaneously separated workers and the bourgeoisie itself from the primary gemeinschaft communities that had dominated rural peasant life. It encouraged the development of private social relations: It permitted private beliefs and private thought to flourish. The private property of the bourgeois was the key to other forms of privacy.

The European bourgeois privatized not only his material but also his spiritual relations with the rest of the world. Protestantism typified the spiritual attitude of the bourgeoisie, as Max Weber has permanently engrained upon our memory.[24] The Protestant had an independent, personal relationship with God, not a collective relationship bound up with and dependent on church ritual. Protestants rebelled not only against the political power of the Roman Catholic church and the corruption of the priesthood, but also against the priest's mediation between the individual and God. The Protestant preferred to communicate directly and silently with God in prayer: He no longer needed the priest to mediate for forgiveness of his sins. Indeed, the Protestant insisted on the right to rethink the nature of sin. Usury, prohibited by the Roman Catholic church, became permissible lending at interest, whereas waste of resources that could be invested became a new sin. In the capitalist world of wise savings and investment, ritual was abandoned as profligacy. Even while we acknowledge that there were Catholics as well as Protestants in the capitalist classes of Europe, we can recognize the Protestant spirit as the harbinger of the prudent citizen of the modern world.[25]

With the abandonment of ritual came the abandonment of the large families and communities that ritual held together through its collective affirmation of social values. In the precapitalist world, the wealthy supported many relatives, apprentices, servants, and hangers-on. Families were not privatized, property-ridden entities. Children were often exchanged among family groups: Boys and girls left their natal homes to become apprentices and domestic servants.[26] But at the same time, the norm of family living among the poor was the nuclear family.[27] The passing of family obligation was not as deep a rupture as nostalgic communitarians would have us think; nevertheless, a new type of family was created, closed in upon itself rather than open to inclusion of others. "In the eighteenth century [in France], the family began to hold society at a distance, to push it back beyond a steadily extending zone of private life."[28]

Under the new capitalist regime, the child became simultaneously more apart from and more a focus of the family's life. Childhood as a separate stage of life was, according to one influential account, discovered.[29] Instead of partaking in family productive activities, the child led a separate existence until such time as, if male, he could enter the bourgeois or professional world or, if female, she could be married. Children were no longer seen merely as miniature adults; they became the focus of sentimental familial affections in a manner that previous generations could not afford. Frederick Engels argued that in the new capitalist system, undisputed paternity of the (male) child was fundamental: As heir to property he deserved a special place, a special coddling.[30] But this is not a sufficient explanation for the intensification of nuclear family relations, as property relations had also existed in the prebourgeois world. Other factors were equally, if not more, important. One was the reduction in infant mortality that permitted parents to more safely invest their feelings in their children. Another was the extension of schooling that caused children to stay at home longer, thus developing stronger bonds of affection with their parents.[31]

As families removed themselves from the community, the home became, for the private bourgeois man, his inner sanctum, his castle, over
which he ruled as the medieval lord ruled his manor. Capitalist mass-
production techniques permitted the bourgeois class to become an acquisitive class with a large stock of personal goods stored in the home.
Wealth was invested in the private domain, inaccessible to the wider society but tangible and inheritable by one's own descendants. Objects
could now be produced and purchased through anonymous social relations; servants could be hired from outside the extended kin or village
society. Given the lessened need for cooperation among families, the
obligation to the group—to kin and community—faded: The obligation
to one's immediate family was strengthened.

Edward Shorter described this change in the role of the family as a
"surge of sentiment" and attributed it directly to the rise of market capitalism. Small-scale, economically self-contained units disappeared as
nation-states formed, yet simultaneously the material standard of living
improved. The proletariat, freed from its ties to the land, experienced, as
did the bourgeoisie, more freedom in everyday affairs; even women removed themselves from their rural communities in search of wage labor.
The logic of the marketplace demanded individualism and economic
egoism, an egoism that then spread to other aspects of daily life.
"Egoism ... became transferred to community obligations and standards, to ties to the family and lineage.... In the domain of men-
women relations, the wish to be free emerges as romantic love."[32]

Even within the home, the value of privacy influenced relations
among family members. Architecture was changed; instead of rooms
flowing open to one another, they opened off central hallways so that
once inside a room its occupant could effectively shut others out. The
first bourgeois paintings of modern capitalist Europe, the Flemish
(Dutch) school, reflected this change. These paintings commonly por-
trayed silent work performed by husbands or wives while alone in a
room. Different rooms had different functions: The entire household no
longer worked together in one great hall.[33] The ideal of comfort also
made its appearance. The home was no longer merely a functional productive place; it was also a place of consumption and pleasure.
Bourgeois comfort is rooted in the secure, private home, with excursions
outside carefully planned and regulated. Paintings of interior scenes
rather than public events reflected the new idea that life's meaning was
derived from private rather than public relationships.[34]

New social rites of civility defined the new bourgeois class. No
longer spontaneous, visiting was carefully regulated to protect not only

the homeowner's privacy but also his social status. Callers no longer dropped in but rather sent cards via their servants announcing their intention to visit.[35] Lower-class kin, employees, and hangers-on were no longer welcome in the bourgeois employer's home; instead, they used the kitchen entrance. Ritualized patterns of social interaction and of eating habits ("manners"), requiring long and assiduous training, separated the bourgeoisie from the lesser classes. The use of the fork, for example, separated polite society from those "cannibals" who continued to eat with their fingers.[36] With the focus on cleanliness, these rituals highlighted the polluting dirt and squalor in which the undisciplined lower classes were presumed voluntarily to live.

Thus the ideal bourgeois emerged as an individualized, private, autonomous creature. The bourgeois sought to make his own decisions on the basis of his own judgment: He objected to government restrictions on his autonomy even as he expected the government to safeguard his private interests. As his class became politically and economically dominant, his values spread to the entire society. Status-based distinctions gave way to a new stress on achievement that allowed individuals to demand respect for their accomplishments, regardless of their social origin. Earned money became more prestigious than inherited, and the social order of bequeathed status was turned upside down. In capitalist society "Profit [is] more in request than Honour," as one English ambassador observed of Holland in the seventeenth century.[37] Gemeinschaft society and its emphasis on status had given way to gesellschaft. Individual freedom was won at the price of capitalist social relations and alienation of many people from the new urban, secular mores.

The concept of individual privacy that originated within the bourgeois classes of Europe spread to other social classes and groups: The values of the bourgeois class quickly became the dominant values of all other classes. Prudence, financial rectitude, hard work, and the privatized comforts of home became the dominant values of the Western world. Philippe Aries lamented the loss of sociability that accompanied the emergence of the modern privatized family:

> This family has advanced in proportion as sociability has retreated. . . .
> Starting in the eighteenth century, people began defending themselves against a society whose constant intercourse had hitherto been the source of education, reputation and wealth. . . . Everywhere . . . private life [was reinforced] at the expense of neighbourly relationships, friendships and traditional contacts. The history of modern manners can be reduced in part to this long effort to break away from others, to escape

from a society whose pressure had become unbearable. . . . Professional
and family life have stifled . . . the activity of social relátions.[38]

Without community, social relations have changed from emphasis
on cultural and religious expression to preservation of family. Removed
from his community, the individual became free to pursue his own interests. Just as the invisible hand of the modern market economy symbolizes private interest and removal from economic obligation, so the
invisible spirit of bourgeois life has come to symbolize removal from social obligation. But if there is no social life, then there can be no public
interest. In the eyes of its communitarian critics, modern bourgeois life
has produced a society of self-interested automatons, unwilling to invest their energies in promotion of the wider social good. Capitalist society, communitarians argue, preserves individual human rights at the expense of social solidarity.

The "End" of Community and
the Creation of the Citizen

The communitarian critique assumes that there is only one type of social solidarity—that based on sameness or commonality of characteristics among a population occupying a given territory. Liberal society is
based upon a different kind of community—one that simultaneously
flattens out and celebrates difference. Political loyalties to substate entities are eliminated, but individuals are permitted to differ in myriad
ways from one another. All individuals share the status of citizen in the
nation-state, even as they choose the fellow citizens with whom to create a sense of community in their private lives.

The privatized life described in its ideal-typical form above is one
that communitarian critics take to be an accurate description of all
Western social relations. Right communitarians and traditionalists view
individualism as a removal of the person from the community and as a
focusing inward on private desires and gratifications. Both harken a
time when obligation to community took precedence over personal desire. Marx differed from the communitarians and traditionalists by
drawing our attention to the kinds of exploitation that can also take
place in noncapitalist societies.[39] In his view, one must look to the egalitarian socialist future, not to the hierarchical communitarian past, for
the true liberation of humankind from crass materialism. Thus left collectivists partially follow Marx's vision in their search for a new kind of
"people" freed from international capitalist exploitation and united in
pursuit of the common good. Status radicals also look forward to a new

kind of culture, one characterized by empathy and sharing among individuals of similar ascribed characteristics.

One of the key objections that both left and right communitarians have to modern liberal society is the destruction of peoples. Left collectivists overtly articulate this objection in their critique of colonialism and imperialism. Traditionalists and right communitarians articulate it implicitly in their concern about the breakdown of communities that are homogeneous, where social solidarity is the result of the similarities not only of individuals' social status, but also of their religious belief, customs, and values. Homogeneity of religion, customs, and values is most likely to be found in a society of individuals with similar ethnic backgrounds, which is harder to find in large-scale, mobile modern societies than in small-scale, status-bound premodern ones. To communitarian critics, the individuals who inhabit modern society seem denatured, removed from communities of kin and custom, inhabiting a world of existential nihilism in which values are mere expressions of the abstracted "self."

This existential nihilism that seems to pervade modern society reflects in part the replacement of religious commitment with a secular social order. Religion, like ethnicity, has become a discardable characteristic. Formerly part of the deep bond attaching individuals to their families and communities, religious belief is now a matter of individual choice. One can be religious or irreligious, one can attend church or not, one can change religions with each marriage partner. Indeed one's primary loyalties—to the group with which one shares ancestry or "blood"—disappear and with them a sense of rich cultural context.

Thus the thick ties of community seem to have disappeared as primary social relations disintegrate in modern society. Moreover, the impetus for social obligation and a sense of responsibility has also vanished, according to the communitarian critique. In effect, what Helen Fein called the "universe of obligation" is seen in this vision to comprise only those who are alike in ancestry, custom, and belief.[40] A strong community is a community of sameness; a community of the unlike must necessarily be weak.

Yet paradoxically, despite the social heterogeneity of many modern societies, homogeneity also exists. One major political feature of societies that protect human rights is a strong central state that rests on a politically created homogeneity of citizenship. This is a forced enclosure of all citizens within a common boundary of liberal beliefs that prescribe tolerance of the Other, even when the Other is demonstrably different in ethnicity, race, or religion. The modern Western state has forced its citizens to discard their identification with substate groups, in order that people from many groups can be incorporated into a common secular community.

Heterogeneous social membership makes protection of human rights difficult. If ethno-religious groups are fighting for political dominance within a state, then human rights cannot be protected: Civil war precludes human rights. If one ethno-religious group dominates all others in the state, certain communal or collective rights such as freedom of worship may be denied. Citizens who put their loyalties to ethnic group or religion above their loyalties to the state threaten its capacity to offer universal protection of human rights.

Forced homogeneity flattens out society, reducing collective attributes of ethnicity, language, and religious belief to personal choices of taste and discouraging their intrusion into the public sphere. Aspects of ethnicity or national identity are thus privatized, made matters of individual preference rather than corporate identity. They become transitory parts of the human identity to be discarded or adopted at will. This privatizing and individualizing of cultural characteristics makes protection of human rights easier in the long run, because no state or institutional boundaries need to be placed on such choices and because the state is not obliged to protect collectivities. One the one hand, a citizen can adopt any religion or ethnicity he chooses. He can convert to Baha'i, pretend to be Jewish, or wear African-American costumes. On the other hand, as long as individual human rights are protected, the state has no obligation to ensure that his community survives.

During the period of state formation in Europe, "nation"-states were created at the expense of politically defeated groups. Western European society passed through a phase in which violent creation of social homogeneity made it easier to agree that any person living within the physical borders of a certain society ought to be considered a citizen. Two centuries of civil wars between Protestants and Catholics, along with expulsions of Muslims and restrictions on Jews, ensured not only Christian but also sectarian conformity in Western Europe. Minority cultures and religions were outlawed; "national" languages were imposed on all regional groups. During the sixteenth century the English abolished both the Welsh language and the Welsh system of justice.[41] In the late eighteenth and nineteenth centuries, Paris forcibly imposed the French language on outlying regions; as late as 1863 over 10 percent of the nation's schoolchildren spoke no French at all.[42] The cultures of the politically victorious groups became the dominant cultures. Later, once their defeat had been assured, minority cultures were tolerated as collective expressions of individual choices. Minority customs stripped of political content became manifestations of interesting diversity, improving the texture of national life without threatening the overall homogeneity of liberal society.

Relegation of primary collective characteristics to the private sphere has created a "negative" equality of all citizens in modern nation-states. Everyone is equal in the public realm but without, some critics argue, rich cultural context. "The liberal, individualist ideology of the nineteenth-century bourgeoisie sought to integrate all people under the mantle of civil equality.... The competitive labor market of the strengthening capitalist economic system created a negative common equality for all the dispossessed. The ground was laid for the idea of civil equality in a 'public' sphere, weakening the moral divisions among people of the feudal period and 'privatizing' religious [and] cultural ... distinctions."[43]

The management of ethnicity is a perpetual problem in any state containing more than one ethnic group. It is easier when members of ethnic groups are geographically dispersed within the state than it is when they occupy definable territories that could relatively easily be carved into a separate state (as in the case of Canada's Quebec or the former region of Slovakia, now a state separated from the Czech Republic). In Western European societies ethnicity was managed from the early modernizing period to World War II by the simple expedient of brute force. The slaughter of the Jews was one of the most effective European projects of homogenization, following the "unmixing of peoples" in the Balkans after World War I and preceding the ethnic cleansing in the former Yugoslavia during the 1990s.[44]

The homogenization of the populations of Western Europe allowed the fiction that left collectivist advocates of group rights now find so offensive; namely, that citizens live in states merely as individuals, that no intermediate loyalties to substate entities interfere with their loyalty to the state itself. The state in modern Europe became the nation; the language of whichever group had won the struggle to dominate became the national language. Substate national loyalties were officially eliminated. As the worker confronted the capitalist with nothing to sell but his labor power and no claim to make except to a wage, so the citizen confronted the state with no human rights but those granted him from above and no means of membership and redress except formal equality under the rule of law.

Status radicals also object to the forced homogenization of populations. In North America today, there is an increasing push for state recognition of multiculturalism. After two centuries of promoting a common vision of what it is to be an American or an English-Canadian, governments are faced with a demand that resources be devoted to preserving the diverse cultural heritages of their citizens. For blacks and aboriginal Americans, this amounts to a demand to salvage and re-create cultural heritages that have been deliberately withheld from them or destroyed. For the many white groups and for nonwhite groups other than blacks, multiculturalism symbolizes a need to differentiate oneself from the wider social whole. By retrieving one's Ukrainian "heritage," by defining oneself as Italian rather than as Canadian, one obtains a sense of special identity denied in a social marketplace based on individual attributes of achievement. Multiculturalism is meant to combat racism, insofar as its official acceptance conveys the principle that no one (Euro-American) culture is superior to any other. But it is also meant to combat social alienation by permitting ordinary whites, who have no racial distinctiveness, to remove themselves from the larger society by creating communities based on the remnants of languages, religious ritual, and custom that their ancestors brought with them when they migrated to North American shores.

But multiculturalism in practice obscures a new reality: The modern liberal society produces its own ethnicity. If ethnicity is defined in large part by common customs, beliefs, and values, then secular liberal society is a form of ethnicity. In Canada, for example, except for some aboriginals there are "no ethnic differences . . . about the desirability of the bourgeois-democratic way of life."[45] Bourgeois-democratic practices and values are the core of the nondiscriminatory, liberal ethnicity. For example, a young woman born in North America who has internalized its concomitant social values will demonstrate this hidden ethnicity when she travels abroad. She will be shocked by religious discrimination, by ethnic warfare, by social customs demanding that women be subservient to men. She will be upset that in some societies one's ascribed status precludes the chance to show what one can achieve. She will be a liberal missionary, trying to persuade others of the importance of values deeply ingrained in her. Such a young woman will carefully pick and choose the multicultural values to which she "returns"; she may dance her ancestral dances but she is unlikely to adopt the ancestral veil. Her principal cultural heritage is that of the secular, urban, and modernized society into which she was born; her ancestral cultural remnants are an interesting gloss that can be discarded easily should they prove unwieldy.

Thus the homogeneity promoted in modern Western society is no longer merely fiction: A new secular, egalitarian, and individualist culture has been created. This new homogeneity has a positive as well as a negative side. Primary communities are not necessarily communities in which people feel contented or respected, despite their deep bonds of language, culture, tradition, and ancestry. The idealization of the purported peace, calm, and unity of primary social relations that characterizes the late-twentieth-century reaction to excessive individualism overlooks the early liberal fear of closed, suspicious communities unwilling to accommodate to change in a modernizing world. Without the fiction of group belongingness, the new state society prepared the conditions for human equality solely on the basis of being human, without status distinctions. Social individuals were created in part by the centralizing European state's coercive elimination of primary groups that offered a corporate, rather than a personal, identity. The new society freed individuals from community bonds: It permitted individual identity to emerge and it permitted all human beings to demand egalitarian treatment in the wider national society.

It is possible in modern liberal democratic states both to create a universal sense of citizenship and to permit, even encourage, the symbolic aspects of group membership that are valuable parts of most people's cultural identities. This can be done by permitting freedom of association; that is, of ethnic association as well as associations based on interest, profession, or any other criterion. That the older European liberal democratic states destroyed or suppressed minority ethnic groups does not mean that contemporary or future states that wish to protect human rights cannot permit voluntary ethnic group memberships and rituals while they promote individual equality and autonomy. The legally binational nature of the Canadian state as well as the opportunities for ethnic affirmation afforded to immigrant groups both in Canada and the United States show that homogeneity, though it eases the path to a centralized state that enforces equality of its citizens, is not a necessary aspect of it. Multiculturalism can also be encouraged, as long as the element of choice is retained and no one is compelled to be part of a particular cultural group.

Under the rule of law individual human rights can be protected without destruction of group membership. Such legal rules, however, are predicated on the assumption that group membership is a matter of private, voluntary choice. No one can be compelled to be a member of a group other than the legal state. Anyone may reject his religion; anyone may abandon his ancestral language and customs. The liberal state promotes collective membership in a noncoercive manner that permits loosening of primary ties. A strong central state carries with it the connotation that all other identities are weaker than the identity of citizen. Ethnic identity can be maintained, resurrected, or re-created, but it is always a matter of voluntary membership and private choice.

Critics of individual human rights reject this conception of ethnicity. For the critics, to render community identity a matter of private choice is to threaten the collectivity. An individual is by definition his collective identity, his culture. Traditionalists and right communitarians agree that liberalism either has destroyed or is in the process of destroying valued relations among family, kin, and communities of people sharing similar racial, ethnic, and cultural characteristics. Left collectivists and status radicals criticize individual human rights for depriving members of minority ethnic groups and races of the right to celebrate their difference. They do not wish to be flattened-out, legally equal citizens of a homogenized capitalist state. They wish to reclaim the integrity of corporate membership, even when they are members of immigrant groups far from the shores of their ancestral homes.

This claim is made not as individuals banding together under the right to freedom of association but rather as corporate groups of suppressed cultures claiming collective rights against the dominant ethos of homogenized capitalist social relations. As is the case in corporate claims to collective membership of First Nation groups (aboriginal societies) in Canada, some even go so far as to claim that individuals socially acknowledged to be members of the collectivity may not opt out of its customs. In 1992, aboriginal leaders in British Columbia were outraged when a British Columbia Supreme Court judge ruled that it was illegal for tribal elders to forcibly subject a member of the tribe to an initiation ritual. The initiate had laid charges of force, assault, battery, and wrongful imprisonment against the elders.[46] Although this claim for corporate group rights is an extreme rejection of the individual's right to remove himself from his society, it illustrates the evolving conflict between group rights claimed on the basis of shared primary characteristics such as ancestry and individual rights based merely upon common humanity.

The community that communitarians mourn has indeed been undermined by modern society. In modern society the similarities that create community can be based on far more than ancestry, religion, or language: They can be based on any number of common interests or merely on the belief that all human beings are equal. On the one hand, modern society has homogenized its population. By reducing the political salience of substate entities, the modern state has limited their powers of coercion and persuasion over members. It has created a thin community of citizens rather than a thick community of people sharing ancestry, religion, and custom. On the other hand, it has created the possibility for a new kind of community, one that transcends antagonistic divisions among ethnic and religious groups.

Individualism and the Public Interest

In the communitarian view, the liberal society that flattens out community reduces citizens to people whose lives are ruled by their individual wants and desires. Without obligation to any form of collectivity, individuals selfishly compete for social resources without regard for the compelling needs of others, whether they be their own children or parents, other families, or members of the community in distress. There is no overriding public interest; social life is reduced to fragmented, anarchic expressions of private interest. The citizen is naked against the state; expressing his own private interest, he is incapable of realizing that his interests might better be protected by embeddedness in a community.

But the picture presented above is only a partial description of the social evolution of Western society. Although the old order may have gone and old communities have disappeared, a new order has emerged and new communities have been created. Individualism does not necessarily mean abstracted privacy: It can also indicate a new mode of expression of concern for the public. Civil society in modern capitalist states does exist: Governments are constantly lobbied not only by private corporations but also by a dense, complex mixture of organizations representing citizens in all their social aspects. Governments in democratic societies must respond to the concerns of religious groups, ethnic groups, professional associations, and groups comprised of members who have common interests of all sorts, from Mothers Against Drunk Driving to those who want increased foreign aid to the developing world.[47] Civil society "penetrates deeply into . . . [political] power, fragments and decentralizes it."[48] The emphasis on human rights that evolved within Western civil society strengthens that society against the state, permitting the constant expression of interest by myriad groups of citizens.

This happy picture of civil society, however, omits one of its central features: It is class biased. Those who actively participate in civil society, who join organizations or pressure for recognition of their collective interests, tend to be disproportionately from the middle and upper classes. They have the education, funds, leisure time, and self-confidence to challenge their rulers and demand resources and policy changes. The middle class is the carrier of the ideology of proper behavior and attitudes in the Western world. Much maligned by Marxists, communitarians, and traditionalists alike for being immodestly materialistic, the middle class also incarnates some of the most basic processes of political democracy. It forms most of the voluntary groups that are the mediating institutions between citizen and state in contemporary Western society.

By contrast, the poor languish in a society in which the expression of collective interests of all kinds is permitted but also in which the resources for that expression are inequitably distributed. Material comfort has become the key to effective citizenship in the modern world. A minimum amount of property—whether real property or a secure job—appears to be a prerequisite to a citizen's full participation in society on equal terms with other citizens.[49] In late capitalist society those who are truly alienated from the social bargain of wealth and human rights are the working poor, the chronic unemployed, and welfare recipients condemned to a minimal level of income at the mercy of the state. Even the stable working class is becoming more alienated from the social bargain as highly paid, secure industrial jobs give way to low-paid, service jobs all over the Western world.

In the liberal worldview, each individual qua individual is in principle entitled to make his autonomous human rights demands on the state and society, regardless of status, rank, or wealth. The ideology of privacy implies that each individual is a distinctive being in his own right. Each individual thinks for himself about what is the best way to live and to conduct social, economic, and political relations with others. Each distinctive individual is entitled to put forth his private viewpoints in public debate, in the marketplace of ideas. All ideas are entitled to equal respect and must be rebutted only by reason, not by tradition. The freedom to conduct one's affairs as one privately sees fit is to be limited only by the possibility that, in so doing, one might adversely affect others' freedoms. Thus in principle the ideology that everyone is allowed to conduct public matters according to private beliefs permits everyone who is capable of reflective thought to be a citizen. A citizen ought to be a member of society, equal to all other members in legal standing, exercising rights of autonomous participation, his dignity fully respected.

One of the great achievements of middle- and working-class social movements in the nineteenth- and twentieth-century Western world has been to expand the boundaries encompassing those who are considered to be full, participating members of society. Having articulated the ideal of human rights both in response to social change and to further it along, the bourgeoisie and middle class became victims of their own success: Human rights became so patently valuable that all other sectors of society wanted them. This is the key to the social movements that began to free previously subordinated people. But the battles were hard fought, and class membership was still a significant feature determining success or failure in attaining equal human rights. Liberal and social democratic Western societies that have articulated the principles of universal human rights are still far from practicing them.

During the evolution of Western capitalist society, the social value of privacy also became the social value of the intrinsic worth of the citizen. If the citizen was now to be protected against the state, one major reason was that he (later she) was a person of value in his own right, regardless of status or of connection to state rulers. Once accepted as a value for the bourgeoisie, by logical extension some bourgeois came to the conclusion that members of the proletariat were as valuable, autonomous, and meaningful as the bourgeoisie themselves. Many mem-

bers of the bourgeoisie also advocated, or joined with workers to espouse, what are now considered "socialist" economic rights. Utopian
and Fabian socialists in Britain, for example, favored reform of the exe-
crable working and living conditions of the poor.[50] Middle-class women
in Britain, the United States, and Canada were prominent in social
movements that demanded equality of rights for all women and antici-
pated some special protections for working-class women. They joined
with the working classes and subordinate status groups to promote further reforms in the twentieth century. From these movements came the
origins of social democracy, a neglected variant of liberalism that attempts, as radical capitalism does not, to protect the entire range of human rights as posited in the Universal Declaration of Human Rights.

Individual privacy, personal autonomy, and active citizenship are
the stuff of liberal society. Joined together into active respect by all for
all, they impel concern for economic well-being as well as for protection
of the individual from state political abuse. Social democracy is the logical extension of belief in the real value of every human being. The social
inclusiveness that provision of economic security for all entails acts
against the alienating effects of modernity. Those who live secure lives
can join the political arena as active citizens. They can join together as
individuals to promote the public interest.

Yet to liberalism's critics, the values of individualism and autonomy
now appear to leave the individual adrift in an empty sea, without family
or community as guides to shore. Both in popular discussion and in
communitarian and traditionalist critiques of liberal human rights, the
autonomy of the individual is often assumed to mean anomie. Without a
set of moral beliefs and codes by which to live, the individual is thought
to withdraw into private gratifications and private pursuits. But privacy
does not mean the same thing as anomie. Privacy means that the individual, in and of himself, became a person of value, regardless of status.

Bourgeois individualism is fashionably derided by Marxists and left
liberals alike as possessive individualism, concerned only with individual possession of private property. "The individual in a possessive market society *is* human in his capacity as proprietor of his own person; his
humanity . . . depend[s] on his freedom from any but self-interested
contractual relations with others; his society . . . consist[s] of a series of
market relations."[51]

But the individualism of modern liberal society can also be ethical.
Ethical individualism can mean more than that; as Steven Lukes put it,
the individual is the source of morality.[52] Ethical individualism posits the
intrinsic value of the human person—of any and all human persons. The
possessive, materialistic attributes of the bourgeois class and later of
Western materialist culture as a whole do not obviate the moral worth of

a philosophy that values the individual person simply because he is human, hence worthy of respect. What Guy Haarscher dubbed "ethical-universal individualism" means that "every individual has to be respected as a person . . . : this is a duty, a categorical imperative, an unconditioned value."[53]

Privacy does not necessarily mean selfishness. There is another kind of privacy that sociologist C. Wright Mills identified several decades ago. One can be private in a manner that ties one to society rather than removing one from it. This kind of privacy is that of the autonomous individual, the person who is able to think about, reflect upon, and act to change his society. Such an individual does not withdraw from society; he is a constitutive and valuable part of it. As Mills put it,

> Men in a mass society are gripped by personal troubles which they are not able to turn into social issues. . . . The knowledgeable man in a genuine public . . . understands that what he thinks and feels to be personal troubles are very often also problems shared by others . . . capable of solution . . . only by modifications of the structure of the groups in which he lives and sometimes the structure of the entire society. . . . Men in publics confront issues, and they usually come to be aware of their public terms. . . . Democracy implies that those vitally affected by any decision men make have an effective voice in that decision.[54]

The citizen, for Mills, is the person capable of seizing upon the public meaning of a private concern and acting to modify public life for the benefit of all sharing his worry. Writing in the 1950s and 1960s, Mills thought that such a public man had existed in the United States at one time (among white males, though this was not specified) but was disappearing. Mills was worried about the decline of democracy in the United States as a consequence of the rise of the military-industrial complex and of the white-collar conformist. He warned his readers that a true democracy requires independent, thinking citizens. For Mills, the private man was the member of the public as opposed to the mass.

The reflective individual is the public person, the one prepared to act as a citizen in the public domain and to realize the commonality of his interests with the interests of others. "The creation of a public sphere comes about through the creation of a wider sphere of social networks [than merely the family]. . . . Public concern implies the capacity to put oneself in another person's position, to identify with other persons. The public is a generalized self in the form of the other. Its existence presupposes shared moral standards and a sense of moral community."[55] The public in the modern sense, then, requires the private individual who steps outside the closed boundaries of family and primary community to connect himself with others, to understand their concerns.

Richard Sennett described the ideal public man of Western capitalist society as cosmopolitan; he uses the city as a place to interact with strangers in commerce, politics, and the pursuit of the common good. He understands that privacy gives him the right to resist the pressures of the crowd but he also understands that it gives him the obligation to participate in public life, even if this means forgoing some personal pleasures. He realizes that he is a member of a larger society to whom he is obligated to give his best.[56] "The great civilizing achievement in the concept of privacy," said Barrington Moore Jr., "has been its questioning of social concerns."[57] The public man, used to expressing his private thoughts about social concerns, can question the power of the state or the corporation to decide on the contours of his life: Privacy means "private rights against holders of authority or other members of the same society."[58]

Sennett's public man or citizen, whom he lamented as disappearing in the late twentieth century, is key to a society that protects human rights. He is the product of specific structural changes in economic and political organization that have resulted in a new type of culture, one that values individual privacy, equality, and autonomy. If every citizen in modern society were to act as Mills or Sennett suggested they ought, then a community in which all members felt an obligation to each other would emerge. But this would also mean that all social classes would have to possess enough resources to participate in civic life, that no one could be left out because society had failed to provide him with that minimal security necessary both for self-respect and the respect of others. As Lukes argued, "Workers . . . are denied respect to the degree to which they are denied possibilities of real participation in the formulation and taking of major decisions affecting them, for they are thereby denied the opportunity to develop the human excellence of active self-government."[59]

Clearly, citizens in modern liberal societies are not always public men or women in the manner that Mills, Sennett, and Lukes envisaged. In the twentieth century, privacy has become for many people merely the expression of individual desire. Materialism has permeated Western culture and appears to have replaced social needs for dignity and community. Hedonism as a social value has peaked in the late twentieth century with its extreme stress on the self and the belief that one's first responsibility is to one's own person rather than to family or community. The promise of liberal individualism seems to many people to have fractured society and fragmented community. Individuals themselves seem to have interiorized their identity to the extent that they are now monads.[60] Thus critics both from within and without Western society now reject liberalism in favor of revival or re-creation of new, nonliberal communities.

48   *Liberal Society*

Notes

1. Steven Lukes, *Individualism* (Oxford: Basil Blackwell, 1973), p. 62.
2. Ferdinand Tonnies, *Community and Society* (New York: Harper and Row, 1957), pp. 33–102.
3. Rose Laub Coser, *In Defense of Modernity: Role Complexity and Individual Autonomy* (Stanford, Calif.: Stanford University Press, 1991), chapter 4, pp. 71–93.
4. Tonnies, *Community and Society,* p. 65.
5. Coser, *In Defense of Modernity,* p. 85.
6. Steven Lukes, "Conclusion," in Michael Carrithers, Steven Collins, and Steven Lukes (eds.), *The Category of the Person: Anthropology, Philosophy, History* (New York: Cambridge University Press, 1985), p. 298, emphasis in original.
7. Emile Durkheim, *The Division of Labor in Society* (New York: The Free Press, 1933).
8. Peter Berger, Brigitte Berger, and Hansfried Kellner, *The Homeless Mind: Modernization and Consciousness* (New York: Vintage Books, 1973), title to chapter 6.
9. Barrington Moore Jr., *Privacy: Studies in Social and Cultural History* (Armonk, N.Y.: M. E. Sharpe, 1984). See also Lukes, *Individualism,* chapter 9, "Privacy."
10. John Locke, "Second Treatise of Government: Of Political or Civil Society" (1690), excerpted in Walter Laqueur and Barry Rubin (eds.), *The Human Rights Reader* (New York: New American Library, 1989), p. 62.
11. This is the usual interpretation of Locke in the human rights literature; for an alternative Lockean interpretation of what are now called economic rights see Jack Donnelly, *Universal Human Rights in Theory and Practice* (Ithaca, N.Y.: Cornell University Press, 1989), chapter 5.
12. Michael E. Tigar and Madeleine R. Levy, *Law and the Rise of Capitalism* (New York: Monthly Review Press, 1977).
13. Isaiah Berlin, "Two Concepts of Liberty," in his *Four Essays on Liberty* (New York: Oxford University Press, 1970), p. 122.
14. Karl Marx, "The Meaning of Human Requirements," in *The Economic and Philosophic Manuscripts of 1844* (New York: International Publishers, 1964), p. 159.
15. Emile Durkheim, *Suicide: A Study in Sociology* (New York: The Free Press, 1951), p. 258.
16. Coser, *In Defense of Modernity,* p. 31.
17. Emile Durkheim, *The Elementary Forms of the Religious Life* (London: George Allen and Unwin, 1968).
18. Karl Marx, *Critique of Hegel's Philosophy of Right,* Joseph O'Malley (ed.) (Cambridge: Cambridge University Press, 1970), p. 131.
19. E.g., Tonnies, *Community and Society.*
20. On exploitative relations in precapitalist societies, see Karl Marx, *Pre-Capitalist Economic Formations,* Eric J. Hobsbawm (ed.) (New York: International Publishers, 1965).

21. Marc Bloch, *Feudal Society*, Volume 2: *Social Classes and Political Organization* (Chicago: University of Chicago Press, 1961), p. 443.

22. Kai Erikson, "On Work and Alienation," *American Sociological Review*, vol. 51, no. 1 (February 1986), p. 4.

23. Coser, *In Defense of Modernity*, part 1.

24. Max Weber, *The Protestant Ethic and the Spirit of Capitalism* (New York: Charles Scribner's Sons, 1958).

25. For criticisms of Weber's connection of capitalism with Protestantism, see Kurt Samuelsson, *Religion and Economic Action: A Critique of Max Weber* (New York: Harper Torchbooks, 1957), and R. H. Tawney, *Religion and the Rise of Capitalism* (Harmondsworth, England: Penguin, 1969 [1st ed. 1926]).

26. Peter Laslett, *The World We Have Lost—Further Explored* (London: Methuen, 1983), chapter 1.

27. Ibid., chapter 4.

28. Philippe Aries, *Centuries of Childhood: A Social History of Family Life* (New York: Vintage Books, 1962), p. 398.

29. Ibid., pp. 128–133.

30. Frederick [Friedrich] Engels, *The Origin of the Family, Private Property, and the State*, trans. Robert Vernon (New York: Pathfinder, 1972).

31. Aries, *Centuries of Childhood*, pp. 369–370.

32. Edward Shorter, *The Making of the Modern Family* (New York: Basic Books, 1977), pp. 5 and 259.

33. Witold Rybczynski, *Home: A Short History of an Idea* (New York: Viking, 1986), p. 18.

34. Aries, *Centuries of Childhood*, p. 347.

35. Ibid., p. 399.

36. Anonymous, *The Habits of Good Society* (1859), cited in Norbert Elias, *The History of Manners: The Civilizing Process*, vol. I (New York: Pantheon, 1978 [1st {German} ed. 1939]), p. 126.

37. Rybczynski, *Home*, p. 61.

38. Aries, *Centuries of Childhood*, pp. 406–407.

39. Marx, *Pre-Capitalist Economic Formations*.

40. Helen Fein, *Accounting for Genocide: National Responses and Jewish Victimization During the Holocaust* (Chicago: University of Chicago Press, 1979), p. 4.

41. Prys Morgan, "From a Death to a View: The Hunt for the Welsh Past in the Romantic Period," in Eric Hobsbawm and Terence Ranger (eds.), *The Invention of Tradition* (London: Cambridge University Press, 1983), p. 44.

42. Eugen Weber, *Peasants into Frenchmen: The Modernization of Rural France, 1870–1914* (Stanford, Calif.: Stanford University Press, 1976), p. 67.

43. Barry D. Adam, *The Survival of Domination: Inferiorization and Everyday Life* (New York: Elsevier, 1978), p. 28.

44. On the post–World War I Balkans, see Michael R. Marrus, *The Unwanted: European Refugees in the Twentieth Century* (New York: Oxford University Press, 1985), pp. 40–50; quotation is from p. 40.

45. Howard Brotz, "Multiculturalism in Canada: A Muddle," *Canadian Public Policy*, vol. 6, no. 1 (winter 1980), p. 41.

46. Robert Matas, "Native Ritual Ruled Subject to Law," *The Globe and Mail* (Toronto), February 8, 1992, p. A6.

47. Robert N. Bellah, Richard Madsen, William M. Sullivan, Ann Swidler, and Steven M. Tipton, *Habits of the Heart: Individualism and Commitment in American Life* (New York: Harper and Row, 1985), chapter 7, "Getting Involved," pp. 167–195.

48. Charles Taylor, "Civil Society in the Western Tradition," in Ethel Groffier and Michel Paradis (eds.), *The Notion of Tolerance and Human Rights* (Ottawa: Carleton University Press, 1991), p. 134.

49. Alan Walker, "Poverty and the Welfare State: Can Poverty Be Abolished?" public lecture, McMaster University, March 6, 1990, p. 20.

50. For descriptions of working-class living conditions, see Frederick Engels, *The Condition of the Working Class in England* (London: Panther, 1972), and Karl Marx, *Capital: A Critical Analysis of Capitalist Production*, Volume I (New York: International Publishers, 1967), chapter 10.

51. C. B. MacPherson, *The Political Theory of Possessive Individualism: Hobbes to Locke* (New York: Oxford University Press, 1962), pp. 271–272, emphasis in original.

52. Lukes, *Individualism*, p. 101.

53. Guy Haarscher, "European Culture, Individual Rights, Collective Rights," in Jan Berting et al. (eds.), *Human Rights in a Pluralist World: Individuals and Collectivities* (Westport, Conn.: Meckler, 1990), p. 151.

54. C. Wright Mills, *The Sociological Imagination* (New York: Oxford University Press, 1959), pp. 187–188.

55. Moore, *Privacy*, p. 27.

56. Richard Sennett, *The Fall of Public Man: On the Social Psychology of Capitalism* (New York: Random House, 1978).

57. Moore, *Privacy*, p. 275.

58. Ibid., p. ix.

59. Lukes, *Individualism*, p. 135.

60. Charles Taylor, "The Person," in Michael Carrithers, Steven Collins, and Steven Lukes (eds.), *The Category of the Person: Anthropology, Philosophy, History* (Cambridge: Cambridge University Press, 1985), p. 281.

3 Cultural Absolutism and Nostalgia for Community

Cultural Relativism as Cultural Absolutism

Of the four communitarian positions outlined in Chapter 1, three refer explicitly or implicitly to the principle of cultural relativism in their critique of individual human rights. Traditionalists reject universal human rights in large part because they fear such rights will undermine their own cultural practices. Left collectivists argue that universal human rights focus too much on individual rights at the expense of peoples and their cultures in the Third World. Status radicals object to the rationalist, competitive, individualist culture that they say human rights impose on members of status groups whose cultures might be better realized in a more empathetic, cooperative, and collectively oriented environment.

Thus the concept of cultural relativism is used by many communitarians as a defense of their idealized way of life against the individualism and alienation that liberal human rights are thought to imply. The underlying theme of the relativist critique is a nostalgia for the lost simplicity of communitarian society. This nostalgia is compounded by a general romanticization of the primitive that fulfills the function of alleviating the alleged mass alienation of modern society.

The relativism implicit in such arguments is actually a concept of cultural absolutism. Cultural absolutism declares a society's culture to be of supreme ethical value. It advocates ethnocentric adherence to one's own cultural norms as an ethically correct attitude for everyone except loosely defined "Westerners." It thus posits particular cultures as of more ethical value than any universal principle of justice. In the left-right/North-South debate that permeates today's ideological exchanges, cultural absolutists specifically argue that culture is of more value than the internationally accepted (but Western in origin) principle of human rights.

Cultural absolutism evolves from, but is not synonymous with, cultural relativism. Cultural relativism is a method of social scientific analysis "whereby social and cultural phenomena are perceived and described in terms of scientific detachment or, ideally, from the perspective of participants in or adherents of a given culture."[1] This method of analysis evolved in the early twentieth century to counteract Westerners' nineteenth-century belief that their own white, Christian society was morally superior to all others. During the colonial period, belief in Western moral superiority justified anthropological study of "primitive" or "native" cultures in order to assist the imposition of missionary and "civilizing" values. Anthropologists who clearly held to visions of white superiority abetted Western imperial conquest. Given the many attempts by Western powers to destroy indigenous societies, cultural relativism was and remains a valuable defense against attack and destruction by colonialists, missionaries, and others.[2]

Cultural relativism is not only a method, it is also an ethical stance. Relativism assumes that there is no one culture whose customs and beliefs dominate all others in a moral sense. One cannot set up a hierarchy of cultures, naming some as more advanced or more civilized than others. There is no model for which all cultures should strive; certainly the West is not such a model. Cultural relativism, therefore, is a stance that obliges Westerners to transcend their own values and prejudices and look at other cultures through the eyes of their participants.

But there is a difference between cultural relativism and the principle that no outsider may ever criticize any practice of a culture not her own. Relativism is now sometimes taken to such an extreme that any practice of an indigenous society can theoretically be defended merely on the grounds that it is a local custom. Outsider discussions of local violations of human rights are criticized as unwarranted ideological interference. When taken to this absolutist extreme, the term "cultural relativism" implies that no outsider should be permitted to make judgments of any social institution or practice that is culturally grounded. Jack Donnelly referred to this ethical position as radical cultural relativism, which holds that "culture is the sole source of the validity of a moral right or rule."[3] I call this position cultural absolutism.

The absolutist school claims, in effect, that human rights are not relevant to cultures that do not share Western customs, norms, beliefs, and values. Human rights are a notion culturally specific to the Western world. Different societies have different cultures that are not comparable. Because cultures are not comparable, human rights are not and should not be universal, and no Westerner has the right to discuss ways that other cultures could or should reorient their ethical systems. Human rights, in a now famous phrase coined by Adamantia Pollis and Peter Schwab, two leading relativists in the international human rights debate, are a "Western construct with limited applicability."[4] They are not and cannot be universal.

The absolutist argument against universal human rights has three separate components.

First, the absolutist argument confuses principle with practice. The principle of universal human rights is untenable because, in practice, human rights are not protected worldwide. For example, in 1980 Pollis and Schwab noted that human rights took second place to states rights in many African countries; they therefore concluded that what was not practiced was not relevant in principle.[5] This position confuses the immediate existence of human rights with their possible legal and practical relevance. The illogicality of this argument can be made clear by a medical analogy: One would not argue that lack of access to health care in Third World societies means health care is irrelevant. In fact, the argument against universalism usually is made with reference to civil and political rights, not to economic rights such as medical care. The fallacy of confusing practice and principle pervades a 1990 volume that presented a political economy (left collectivist) critique of human rights in Africa. "For countries that have known no peace, stability or progress since their contact with the forces of Western imperialism, civil and political rights have no meaning."[6]

Apparently, something that one lacks is not meaningful: One is not capable of speculating on what the quality of one's life would be if one had that which one lacked. Yet social movements for political change arise precisely because people do envisage a life in which more of their rights are protected. International human rights are a standard to which it would not be necessary to devote so much effort if they were already firmly protected everywhere. Those who advocate human rights as a universal principle do so precisely because they are not universally respected. To claim that what is not present is irrelevant assumes that those who are denied rights do not have the intellectual capacity to articulate their suffering and to grasp the fundamental principles of justice that human rights imply. Such a claim reinforces the stereotype of the "native" as a nonthinking, primitive being whose pain is part of the oneness of his existence. Thus the celebrated Danish writer Isak

Dinesen, without any self-consciousness whatsoever, romanticized the story of Kitosch, a "native" of her acquaintance who awaited the death brought on by a beating from his colonial master.[7]

The second absolutist argument refers not to practice but to principle. Universal human rights are untenable because, in principle, human rights are not a universal cultural ideal. This argument usually applies to the content of particular rights such as equality for women. "The belief that women are entitled to equal status as citizens . . . is not universally accepted in African, Islamic or Western societies."[8]

Yet cultural absolutists simultaneously argue that human rights *are* a universal ideal. The concept of human rights is universal, but the content (what, substantively, are or ought to be rights) varies among different societies. All cultures, absolutists claim, have some ideals of human rights, although these ideals may seem strange to Western eyes since they do not include norms such as equality that are basic to the UN human rights framework.

For example, several authors described the Hindu caste system as a system of human rights. "The fact that certain groups [in India], the lower castes, for example, the untouchables, are denied human rights in no way proves that the society lacks a concept of human rights."[9] "If by 'human rights' one means minority rights, then Hindu society can be said to have a human rights tradition, for it has always had a way of incorporating the poor and socially ostracized into the social whole."[10] Both these quotations explicitly deny that equality is a necessary aspect of human rights. Hierarchy is accepted as part of the Hindu "human rights" tradition, as in Max Stackhouse's claim that rights in traditional societies can be exemplified by the "social spirituality" of Hindu India, "centered institutionally in the hierarchies of kinship and caste."[11]

This approach argues that all systems of social justice are systems of human rights. It is more important to give all systems of social justice the attractive label of human rights than to differentiate among such systems and discover which ones allocate substantive and equal rights and dignity to all individuals purely on the basis of their humanity and which ones allocate only privileges and duties contingent on unequal social status.

The third absolutist argument is that universalism is untenable because (it is argued implicitly) indigenous cultures supersede human rights as a social good. As the Argentinean legal scholar Fernando Teson explained, "cultural relativism [absolutism] may be defined as the position according to which local cultural traditions (including religious, political, and legal practices) properly determine the existence and scope of civil and political rights enjoyed by individuals in a given society."[12]

This is the key to the absolutist perspective. For absolutists, culture is the supreme ethical value, more important than any other. Human rights, in particular, should not be promoted if their implementation might result in a change in a particular culture.

But cultural absolutists do not fully reject universalist ethics as they claim to do. Cultural absolutists actually posit one universal ethical law, that: "a) there are no universal moral principles; b) one ought to act in accordance with the principles of one's own group; and c) (b) is a universal moral principle."[13] This law carries more moral weight for absolutists than the law of universal human rights, although it is itself a principle that cannot be located in all cultural systems. If one were to look for it, one would probably find instead that most cultures believe their own moral principles ought to be universal. "The individual cannot but be convinced that his own way of life is the most desirable one. . . . Despite changes originating from within and without his culture that he recognizes as worthy of adoption, it becomes equally patent to him that, in the main, other ways than his own . . . are less desirable."[14]

The logical position that most people embedded in their own cultures will take is: a) there are universal moral principles, b) our own culture embodies these principles, and c) everyone else ought to follow our principles even if this means abandoning his or her own culture. Thus, the circumcised fight the uncircumcised, Christians and Muslims slaughter each other, vegetarians despise meateaters, and so on all over the world. It is precisely because of each society's tendency to think its own culture the best that we need a basis for judging social justice that is not culture-bound. To judge particular practices within cultures does not, however, mean judging or ranking cultures as a whole: Such judgment does not release the sensitive outsider from her obligation to transcend her own cultural background when observing others.

The third absolutist argument, that indigenous cultures supersede human rights as a moral good, is the major theme of a book by Alison Dundes Renteln, an exemplar of the cultural absolutist school of human rights.[15] Renteln believed that the 1948 Universal Declaration of Human Rights was so heavily influenced by Western thought that it had no pertinence to non-Western societies; indeed, human rights are an ethnocentric value of Westerners. But she simultaneously argued that in fact all societies do have their own human rights standards. In order to avoid ethnocentrism, she proposed that the only universal human rights standards be those empirically shown to be universal cultural ideals. Thus in practice Renteln did not completely reject universality. But she argued for additive, rather than ethical, universality; only a principle shown to be universal once we have found it in all cultures is legitimate. The only principle that is universal on an ethical basis alone is that all societies ought to (ethnocentrically) adhere to their own cultures.

Renteln believed that one can discover human rights, or their "homeomorphic equivalents," in all societies.[16] As an example she used the international legal prohibition of genocide. She reviewed anthropological studies of retribution, feuds, and vendettas that, she argued, show there are cultural rules of vengeance in most societies that limit the number of deaths permitted. Renteln contended this is evidence of a universal standard against genocide that is culturally entrenched and not dependent on a Western ethical norm.

One can certainly accept Renteln's view that international human rights standards have a better chance of being put into practice if they also reflect cultural ideals. This is a position that the Muslim legal scholar An-Na'im also espoused in his search for Qur'anic justifications for equal rights for women, better treatment for religious minorities, and the end of the notion of *jihad* (holy war) as a basis for relations between Muslim and non-Muslim states.[17] But An-Na'im was unable to find any internal Muslim precept that could be used to abolish outright the *hudud* punishments (amputation of limbs for theft) currently prescribed in his native Sudan.[18] This illustrates the difficulty of limiting ethical principles to those extant in particular cultural traditions rather than acknowledging the legitimacy of abstract, philosophical consideration of ethical questions that is transcultural and denies the preemptive claim of cultures to a superior moral status. In fact, An-Na'im, when he referred to the Golden Rule as a principle for international human rights, adopted just such a transcultural, abstract approach.[19]

Internal cultural buttresses to international human rights standards can be located partly because, despite Renteln's interpretation, cultures are not homogeneous entities. Underneath the official cultural positions espoused by powerful spokespersons there are often unofficial beliefs about the nature of right and wrong. In traditional societies lacking either ethical articulation or legal institutionalization of international human rights norms, individual disagreement with cultural norms of behavior is exemplified by religious conversion or by migration to areas more compatible with the individual's notion of how she should be treated. In hierarchical Confucian China, for example, conversion to Taoism was a means of being treated more equitably, much like conversion to Islam, Christianity, or Buddhism for low-caste or untouchable Hindus in India.[20] The fact that so many individuals do try to avoid cultural prescriptions that condemn them to lives of subordination and inequality suggests that cultures are not monolithic and that cultural underpinnings for human rights can be located in very many places, if one looks hard enough and talks to the downtrodden as well as to officials. Untouchables generally have very different views on human rights in India than do members of higher castes.[21]

But cultural absolutism is not an argument for searching out the subversive elements that undermine official culture; rather, the absolutist position accepts official versions of cultures at face value. In the world of cultural absolutism ethical debate in universalist terms is simply not countenanced; particularist cultures are all-encompassing. Yet if culture is as all-encompassing as absolutists contend, it ought to be impossible in practice for philosophers, lawyers, human rights activists, or indeed ordinary citizens to transcend culture-boundedness or to make ethical judgments of their own customs. All we can do to promote universal human rights is to wait until cultures evolve internally (but not in reaction to the stimulus of thoughtful human agency). This flies in the face of all empirical evidence. The great Prophets—Moses, Jesus, Muhammad—were all critics of their own cultures, as are the many social activists such as Gandhi of the contemporary era. Despite the cultural absolutist belief that abstract, transcultural ethical discussions are impossible, all sorts of people insist on holding them. Cultural absolutists thereupon maintain these discussions may not be impossible but are nonetheless illegitimate.

Teson referred to the idealization of culture as elitist. He disputed the position that

> countries that do not spring from a Western tradition may somehow be excused from complying with the international law of human rights. This elitist theory . . . holds that human rights are good for the West, but not for much of the non-Western world. . . . Relativist [absolutist] scholars . . . wish to respect the autonomy of individual cultures. The result is a vague warning against "ethnocentrism" and well-intentioned proposals that are deferential to tyrannical governments and insufficiently concerned with human suffering. Because the consequence . . . is that certain national or ethnic groups are somehow less entitled than others to the enjoyment of human rights, the theory is fundamentally immoral and replete with racist overtones.[22]

Moral discourse, contended Teson, is indeed universalizable.[23] It is perfectly legitimate for a Westerner to advocate universal human rights and to discuss the possibilities for their protection worldwide. Human rights are about protection of people's lives, safety, and individual freedom. They are a supreme universal value in the sense that most people, deprived of these protections, want to have them—regardless of the culture in which they live. And most people, even the most uneducated, are capable of stepping outside their own cultures and societies to discuss right and wrong in abstract terms. Ideas must and can be evaluated on their own terms. "Unauthentic" Third World thinkers who favor human rights should not be rejected as betrayers of traditional cultures. Without such betrayal, their cultures may very well stultify in the hands of self-serving elites.

The Concept of "Culture" in the Absolutist Viewpoint

I define "culture" as a system of customs, norms, beliefs, and values shared by a group of people who frequently speak the same language, adhere to the same religion, and share the same (real or mythical) ancestors, and who frequently also live in or originate from the same territory. My definition thus has two parts. The first pertains to the social meanings of a society's culture, those commonly shared beliefs and values that both reflect and are reflected by the norms (approved behavior) and customs (actual behavior) of the society. The second pertains to the actual social group that claims to be culturally specific. This is usually a group sharing the same language and religion, with a claimed commonality of history frequently identified as a common real or mythical ancestry and usually, though not always, tied historically or actually to a specific territory. Thus the term *culture* describes the values and social practices of national or ethnic groups.

For example, Serbians in Canada, originating from the former Yugoslavia, speaking Serbo-Croatian, adhering to the Serbian Orthodox church, and sharing many customs, norms, beliefs, and values, are perceived to be a cultural group. On the other hand, English-speaking Canadians as a group have difficulty identifying themselves as a cultural unit because they originate from so many different parts of the world and are of different religious and linguistic backgrounds. Their "historic" ethnicity (or ancestry), as it were, obscures their perception of the common culture—common beliefs and values, common living patterns and social arrangements—that most people brought up in Canada share. In fact, the Canadian government expects all Canadians to be able to identify their historic ancestry on census forms, regardless of the number of generations a citizen's family might have resided in Canada or of the number of different ethnic groups from which a citizen might be descended.[24] On the 1991 census, however, 2.8 percent of Canadians (about 764,000 people) refused to do this, identifying themselves solely as "Canadian," perhaps reflecting a new sense of social identity.[25]

Cultural absolutists assume that culture is a unitary and unique whole; that one is born into, and will always be a part of, a distinctive, comprehensive, and integrated set of cultural values and institutions that cannot be changed incrementally or only in part. Because in each culture the social norms and roles vary, so, it is argued, human rights must vary. The norms of each society are held to be both valuable in and of their own right and so firmly rooted as to be impervious to internal challenge. Nevertheless, it seems, these norms are highly vulnerable to external challenge to the extent that even an abstract discussion of human rights could rend the social fabric. The universal standards embodied in the main UN human rights documents really apply only to certain Western societies; to impose them on other societies from which they did not originally arise would do serious and irreparable damage to their cultures. As one Nigerian commentator stated, "The language of 'right' appears to be most used where there is a breakdown of relationship, a conflict of interest, or a dispute."[26] Human rights, in this view, do not hold together the social whole; they fragment it.

In fact, though, people are quite adept cultural accommodationists. They are able to choose which aspects of a new culture they wish to adopt and which aspects of the old they wish to retain. The child of a Serbian immigrant to Canada may choose to adopt Canadian dating and marriage patterns but continue to attend the same church her parents do. She might marry someone of Italian background yet identify herself as of Serbian origin on census forms for the next fifty years, even though her children attend her church only for increasingly exotic ceremonials and understand only a few words of Serbo-Croatian spoken by their grandparents.

Cultures are not the holistic entities that absolutists make them out to be. To believe so in the modern era is to be locked into nineteenth- and early-twentieth-century anthropological functionalism. Functionalist anthropology perceived societies as integrated wholes, whose equilibrium could be severely disturbed if one part or another changed. But culture, like the individual, is adaptive. Customs, values, and norms do indeed "glue" society together, and elements of culture do have a strong hold on people's individual psyches. But they are also permeable and changeable. Indeed, change is part of the nature of cultures, which are above all social creations. "Culture must be continuously produced and reproduced by man. Its structures are, therefore, inherently precarious and predestined to change."[27]

A corollary assumption of the absolutist school is that cultures are unaffected by social structure. Social structure is the complement of social institutions—the political, legal, educational, religious, economic, and other institutions—that organizes a society. Structure affects culture. To a significant extent norms, customs, and values reflect the basic economic and political organization of a society. For example, societies such as the newly industrializing countries of the Pacific Rim of Asia, which moved from peasant agriculture to industrial economies within a very short period, also experienced many changes in personal values. Women are freer, and members of outcaste groups such as the Japanese *burakumin* (descendants of occupational outcastes) are more anxious to be treated like all others in society.[28] Similarly the amalgamation of many different ethnic groups into one nation-state inevitably changes the way that individuals view themselves. For example, state-sponsored retention of ethnic customs, as under Canada's multicultural policy of preserving ethnic communities, cannot mask the fact that most of those communities are merging into the larger Canadian society.

Similar changes have taken place all over the world. Whether their social institutions changed over the last two centuries because of voluntary choice or because of colonial imposition is of only minor relevance in understanding many Third World cultures today. The changes have occurred, individual lives have been transformed, and fundamental beliefs and customs have altered accordingly. All across Africa, individuals move to modern cities not only because of the push of economic crisis in their natal villages but also because of the urban pull, the excitement of traffic, music, crowded meeting places. The reaction against the tensions of the modern city, the unemployment, crowding, and disease, may invoke a nostalgia for the old ways and a desire to return to the natal village where customs have been preserved and where everyone is known and events are predictable. But this gemeinschaft society is more and more a socially created myth, not a reality. In any case, those who mourn the loss of community also value their new personal freedom; short visits back home are easier to handle than permanent return migration.

This is not to argue that *all* cultural change is benign. In the past, forcible change was imposed on many indigenous cultures that came under colonial rule. Well into the twentieth century in Canada some indigenous peoples were forbidden to perform their ceremonial dances, to worship as they wished, and even to speak their own languages in residential schools.[29] Forcible cultural change is still a pattern in new nation-states. In Brazil, entire cultures have been irreparably damaged by forcible relocation into tiny reserves or by compulsory proletarianization.[30] In many other cases, encounters with Western society have unanticipated consequences that are detrimental to indigenous cultures.

My concern here is not with rights-abusive cases in which conquest destroys entire societies or in which all local customs are wiped out in the cause of socialist uniformity, as happened to Ukrainian culture in the late 1920s and early 1930s.[31] I am debating the extreme argument that any exogenously induced cultural change is inherently destructive of a society's fundamental norms and values that, in their turn, are inherently worth preserving. A corollary of this extreme argument is that the very concept of human rights is an exogenous imposition on the internal fabric of non-Western societies.

Cultures certainly do change as a result of exogenous or foreign influence, but exogenous influence is not always detrimental or of hostile intent. Cultural compulsion (imperialism) has certainly been a feature of all Third World societies that have had any contact with Europeans; it is especially typified in the propagation of Christian missionary beliefs. But cultural diffusion, the willing adoption of foreign ideas, values, and artifacts, is also a feature of most if not all Third World societies. Cultures can also change endogenously without any foreign influence whatsoever. They frequently do so as a result of internal conflicts over what are the most valuable prescriptive norms (for example, the Protestant revolution in Europe).

Cultural absolutists lament the changes that human rights might wreak on non-Western societies. Ignoring the existence of state structures with extensive coercive apparatuses in the non-Western world, they confuse Asian, African, and Central and South American states with indigenous societies. They then romanticize the integrated wholeness of these supposedly indigenous societies, a wholeness that Westerners in their individualized world appear to have lost. But when cultures are integrated wholes, this is often a result of their coercive as well as their cooperative capacities. Even in societies without states, collectively imposed punishments of deviants and elders' control within the household ensure conformity, frequently in violation of the material interests or individual preferences of that society's members.

Cultural practices are not neutral in their impact. Very few social practices, whether cultural or otherwise, distribute the same benefits to each member of a group. In considering any cultural change it is certainly useful to ask who benefits from its introduction. But similarly, in considering any unchanged cultural practice, it is useful to ask who benefits from its retention. Those who speak for the group are usually those most capable of articulating the group's values to the outside world. But in their articulation of group values such spokespersons are likely to stress those particular values that are most to their own advantage. Both those who choose to adopt new ideals, such as political democracy or atheism, and those who choose to retain old ideals, such as a God-fearing political consensus, may be doing so in their own interests. Culture is both influenced by, and an instrument of, conflict among individuals or social groups.

Quite often, absolutist arguments are adopted principally to protect the interests of those in power. The Native Women's Association of Canada (representing some, but not all, aboriginal women) objected strongly to the reassertion of aboriginal tradition on precisely these grounds: Male-dominated organizations do not necessarily represent women and have been known to expel from the reserves women who complain about abuse by their husbands.[32] The "traditional" (actually imposed by European fiat) culture preserves male privilege at the expense of women's rights.

Thus the argument that human rights cannot be applied across cultures violates both the principle of human rights and its practice. Human rights mean precisely that: rights held by virtue of being human. Cultural variances that do not violate basic human rights undoubtedly enrich the world. It is pleasant, exciting, and enriching to encounter differences in dance and music, dress and art, food preparation, and architecture. But to permit the powerful to masquerade behind spurious defenses of cultural relativity is merely to lessen the chance that the victims of their policies will be able to complain. In late 1989, Kenyan president Daniel Arap Moi expelled from its offices an environmental group that had protested the construction of an expensive high-rise building in downtown Nairobi. He contended that under "African tradition" the group's leader, well-known woman environmentalist Wangari Maathai, had no right to criticize policies devised by men.[33] In the modern world, concepts such as cultural absolutism that deny individuals the moral right to make comparisons and insist on universal standards of right and wrong are happily adopted by those who control the state.

The cultural grounding of human rights abuses is not a sufficient reason to excuse or, indeed, to condone them. But it is possible to be sensitive to cultures in applying or advocating human rights. Some human rights officially prescribed by UN documents, such as the prohibition of child marriages and child betrothals, do violate internal cultural norms.[34] It would be unwise for outsiders to advocate the blanket prohibition of such norms and customs without considering both how the social structure would change and how people inside the society would react. Cultural sensitivities arise particularly with regard to the question of nondiscrimination. For example, many countries view equality of the sexes differently from the liberal West.[35] Whatever one's analysis might be of the origins of the inequality of the sexes, it would be unwise to try to impose equality of the sexes on other countries, for example via manipulation of aid policies rather than to merely discuss one's views of gender subordination with citizens of other societies.

In their attempts to be sensitive to matters of culture, Western commentators should differentiate among practices initiated and employed by governments and those that do reflect culture or custom. Child betrothal and child marriage are rooted in culture and custom. One way to discover whether culture is really the root cause of a human rights violation is to consider the role of the government in upholding the violation. Does it promote the violations; does it tolerate them although they are not prescribed in law; or does it attempt—perhaps unsuccessfully because of insufficient resources—to stop them? When there are real cultural forces behind the violation of human rights, one ought to be able to locate strong sentiments favoring the violations among the population at large or among its opinion leaders.[36] In particularly clear cases of cultural norms underlying human rights violations, such as that of female genital mutilations in Africa, the government will have tried to eradicate the violations, only to find that there is too much popular support for it to be successful in its efforts.

Thus cultural relativity and cultural sensitivity are not prohibited by the principle of universal human rights. But the universality of human rights does mean that cultural absolutism must be rejected. If culture is the absolute value, then the fundamental characteristics of human rights, such as nondiscrimination and equality, must bow before it.

An Absolutist Defense of a White Canada

The absolutist position maintains that human rights are a Western cultural imposition on the rest of the world. It posits a very limited understanding of how culture and politics interact. The culturalist arguments underlying the absolutist position are usually made with respect to the former colonized nations of the world or to indigenous peoples in settler states. But to be consistent, culturalist arguments should also apply to large-scale, Western societies. All large political units have internal cultures, although they may not be identified as such because internal conflicts and expressions of nonintegrative particularist interests will be more obvious than in the small-scale, homogeneous communities that anthropologists have usually studied. If indigenous and Third World cultures are to be allowed the complete play of their values, beliefs, norms, and customs regardless of whether or not they conform to international human rights standards, then the cultures of other societies should have the same privileges. Any society should be permitted to retain its culture regardless of human rights considerations. If absolutists reject this position then they are arguing that some cultures (in practice, indigenous and Third World ones) are more absolute than others, that some are absolutely worth preserving, whereas others can be changed or destroyed. They thus reverse the cultural imperialism that, they contend, characterizes the universal human rights documents, giving greater weight to non-Western than to Western ethical beliefs.

If culture is a preemptive social good, with a higher moral standing than human rights, and if the only universal rule is that one ought to act in accordance with the principles of one's own group, then no cultural absolutist should find the following argument about the nature of Canadian society shocking.

> Canada is a white Protestant society of British origin (excepting Quebec). Its values are honesty, hard work, attachment to family, social rectitude, and loyalty to the monarchy. Canadians are a quiet people, not given to displays of emotion or unbridled festivities. They are sexually restrained.
>
> Immigration to Canada must be very carefully controlled so that these values are not destroyed. People of Slavic or Latin origin have different social values than Northern Europeans—they tend to be noisier and less restrained and have larger families. Jews are known to be merchants of questionable ethics; they are not capable of real attachment to the land or to the monarchy. The Chinese and Japanese are good workers but their culture is incompatible with ours because they are neither British nor white; they must not be allowed to stay in Canada except on short-term work permits. No decent Canadian would want to live in the same community as blacks, who are noisy, smelly, sexually unrestrained, and criminal, so they should not be allowed to enter Canada either.

The above is not a quotation but my own summary of a position with which, obviously, I disagree. Nevertheless, it is a fair representation of dominant social attitudes in Canada well into the 1950s. Many Canadians would even contend that it is an accurate representation of their society's cultural values today, and some would be willing to stop all further immigration of non-Europeans. In 1993, 26 percent of Canadians responding to a national poll agreed that "the fabric of Canadian Society is being threatened by non-white minorities."[37]

Preservation of white and Christian Canadian culture keeps the community close and promotes the security of its members by not exposing them to different people with different customs. As Michael Walzer stated: "The right to choose an admissions policy [to one's country] . . . is not merely a matter of acting in the world, exercising sovereignty, and pursuing national interests. At stake here is the shape of the community that acts in the world, exercises sovereignty, and so on. Admission and exclusion are at the core of communal independence. They suggest the deepest meaning of self-determination. Without them, there could not be *communities of character,* historically stable, ongoing associations of men and women with some special commitment to one another and some special sense of their common life."[38] Communities of character with a special sense of common life are a morally valuable social good. To belong to a community that shares your values, in which you feel at ease and in which everyday social intercourse is based on commonly acknowledged rules and customs, is to find social life pleasant rather than confusing or shocking. Canada is a typical Western society insofar as its immigration is carefully controlled to maintain its community of character in ways that, until very recently, violated international human rights norms.

Canada has a long history of exclusion of nonwhite, non-Christian immigrants. Immigration policy has favored people of British or Northern European origin. In 1914, a boatload of Sikhs attempting to immigrate into Canada via Vancouver was turned back.[39] They were only one of many groups historically excluded. Chinese laborers were enticed to Canada to build the Canadian National Railway, but once it was completed most of them were deported; those few permitted to stay were not allowed to sponsor their wives and children into the country until well after World War II. Canada did not open its doors to refugee Jews during the Nazi period.[40] Both noncitizen and citizen ethnic Japanese were subjected to mass internment during the war.[41] After the war, about 4,000 people of Japanese ethnic descent, including Canadian citizens, were deported to Japan.[42] Legislation passed in 1923 to stop Chinese immigration was revoked in 1947,[43] but the racial basis of Canada's immigration policy was not fully eliminated until 1967, when a nonracial point system based on such criteria as wealth, occupation, education, language skills, and entrepreneurial abilities was adopted for independent immigrants not sponsored by family members already in Canada. By 1991 about 7.5 percent of the residents of Canada were of non-European, nonindigenous origin.[44]

These nonwhite immigrants, known as visible minorities, certainly do not conform to the earlier image of Canada as a whites-only country (indigenous peoples having been regarded for decades as anomalous and irrelevant, if not inexorably doomed to extinction). Yet their aspirations and lifestyles fit very closely with Canada's community of character. In most cases, immigrants had fully adopted so-called Canadian values such as hard work, capital accumulation, and investment in home and family before they arrived in the country. They are also eager to adopt the Canadian social values of individual freedom of choice in occupation, religion, and politics. Aside from skin color, they are distinguished from Euro-Canadians only by language retention by first-generation immigrants and by some symbolic aspects of culture such as religion and ritual behavior.

Nevertheless there has been a great deal of public hostility in Canada to the new nonwhite immigrants. During the 1970s, physical attacks on Asian immigrants were frequently reported; in Toronto, a Tanzanian Asian was permanently crippled when he was pushed onto the subway rails.[45] In 1979, a major television news program, CTV's "W5," broadcast an inflammatory report on how Chinese foreign students were taking up an inordinate number of places in university professional schools; further investigation revealed that almost all of the people filmed were Canadian citizens of Chinese ethnic descent.[46] In 1989–1990, public ire was aroused by a proposal that Sikhs in the Royal Canadian Mounted Police should be permitted to wear turbans. Many Canadians argued that to permit turbans would attack the prized tradition of the red Mountie jacket and broad-brimmed hat, and a petition of over 125,000 signatures opposing the change was presented to Parliament. Racist pins and calendars were produced in the Canadian West, including one calendar featuring a Sikh Mountie with the words "Sgt. Kamell Dung" written on it.[47] The prime minister's statement that such objections resembled the behavior of the Ku Klux Klan annoyed many Canadians who defended "tradition" while asserting that they were not bigots.[48]

That Canada's official non–racially based immigration policy arouses so much hostility and opposition is not surprising. For many Canadians of European extraction, community of character is possible only among people who share the same racial characteristics, if not the same Christian religion. If culture is an absolute social value, then those who kept Canada closed to non-European and non-Christian immigrants for so long acted ethically. Those who pressured Canada to open its doors undermined its culture and were unethical. They should have recognized that immigration threatened Canada's basic social values, its very culture as a society of descendants of British, French, and Northern European Christian immigrants. The introduction of liberal, nonracist social values into Canadian public policy in the 1960s destroyed this previous cultural unity.

Cultural absolutism is the antithesis of human rights. Positing culture as the highest social good, it permits among many other human rights violations the exclusion of outsiders from the pure and inviolable community. This contradiction cannot be resolved by making the false claim that all societies' systems of social justice are systems of human rights, even when they violate such basic tenets of human rights as the principle of nondiscrimination. The belief that all systems of social justice are equally good reflects both Western romanticism of primitive societies and an unwillingness to acknowledge the social changes that have occurred in non-Western societies over the past several centuries.

Relativism, Primitivism, and Romanticism

In traditional societies principles of social justice are based not on equal human rights but on unequal social statuses and on the intermixture of privilege and responsibility. Cultural absolutists refer to the existence of such traditional societies to argue against any presumed universality of human rights. Often anthropologically anachronistic pictures are presented of premodern societies, taking no account whatsoever of changes that might have occurred. Pictures constructed by anthropologists of how societies might have behaved "before the white man came" are presented as accurate descriptions of how those societies still behave, decades if not centuries later. Yet the great anthropologist Claude Levi-Strauss actually had to persuade the remnants of the Tupi-Kawahib tribe in Brazil, whom he had set out to study, to return to the bush with him, as they were just about to collectively join a Western settlement. Levi-Strauss was obliged to persuade his primitive community to stay primitive; his research plans were upset by the conscious decision his objects of study had taken to modernize.[49] The use of anachronistic (literally, out of time) pictures of "native" societies to illustrate so-called cultural principles airbrushes out history, to use James Clifford's provocative phrase.[50]

Westerners often want native societies to stay pure because they believe that natives are their cultural ancestors. Natives represent a pure, idealized state of harmony and peace to which, someday, Westerners may return. In these societies human rights are unnecessary because conflict is unknown. These societies show that the anxieties of modern civilization are not inevitable: They are a contingent accompaniment to modernity that Westerners may be able to eliminate if they can find the true path back to communal living. Yet the ethnographic studies on which cultural absolutists rely are not neutral, objective pictures. Contemporary anthropologists sympathetic to the cultures they study are as likely to overdraw their pictures as were their earlier, arrogantly colonialist forebears. Anthropological conclusions about both the substance of cultural values and the integrative, unchanging nature of cultural norms are drawn from highly questionable data that reflect both the arrogance and the romanticism of Western observers.

Many of these pictures of indigenous cultures are a right-side-up version of what Edward Said called "Orientalism." Said used the term to refer to a pejorative view of the Orient, or more particularly, of the Middle Eastern Islamic world. In the Orientalist perspective, according to Said, the presentation of Islamic societies as unchanging, holistic entities is used as evidence of their incapacity to adapt to ethically superior modern ways. "Islam is a unitary phenomenon, unlike any other [Western] religion or civilization. . . . [It is] monolithic, scornful of ordinary human experience, gross, reductive, unchanging. . . . [For Orientalists] there are still such things as *an* Islamic society, *an* Arab mind, *an* Oriental psyche. . . . 'Arabs' are presented in the imagery of static, almost ideal types, and neither as creatures with a potential in the process of being realized nor as history being made."[51] Cultural absolutists often present the inverse of Orientalism, not a pejorative picture of the societies they discuss but a complimentary, romanticized picture. In so doing, however, they use the same idiom of unchanging societies unaffected by human history. And they often attribute these characteristics to entire geographical regions or religions, as if a culture can be completely identified by its location or its religious beliefs. Said commented on this tendency to attribute cultural characteristics to entire regions of the world: "'The Orient' is itself a constituted entity. . . . The notion that there are geographical spaces with indigenous, radically 'different' inhabitants who can be defined on the basis of some religion, culture, or racial essence proper to that geographical space is . . . a highly debatable idea."[52]

In academic discourse racial stereotypes are no longer used, yet in human rights debates commentators persist in stereotyping all the inhabitants of non-Western geographical regions with the religio-cultural beliefs they assume must define their lives and dominate their thoughts. Thus Robert Traer referred to the religious traditions of "Africans" and "Asians" as if there were only one religion on each of these continents.[53] Vincent also referred to Africa and China as places having unitary cultural traditions of human rights.[54] Unwillingness to acknowledge difference and conflict in these exotic (to Western eyes) areas undermines the capacity to view their inhabitants as individuals needing the classic protections of individual human rights.

Many Westerners—explorers, anthropologists, culturally sensitive analysts of human rights—impose on the "traditional" societies they encounter their own desires to find a romantic, rustic original state in which social harmony prevails. This romanticization of "backward" or "primitive" cultures is a right-side-up Orientalism, not criticizing but idealizing. The absolutist denial of universal human rights revels in the romantic mysticism of primitive society. "The relativist [absolutist] . . . often defines the interests of a people in mystical or aggregative terms that ignore or belittle individual preferences. Such mystical definitions may be articulated in the form of axiomatic 'true' interests of peoples, as opposed to real or expressed interests."[55]

Cultural absolutism, then, is in part a spinoff of Western primitivism, the simultaneous idealization and denigration of the primitive that has characterized Western culture since the mid-nineteenth century. Primitivism as an ideal began with the early European explorations to such remote places as "darkest" Africa where, it was thought, man was his true natural self—at one with nature, sexually free, yet simultaneously violent and depraved until civilized by the white man. "Primitives are our untamed selves, our id forces—libidinous, irrational, violent, dangerous. Primitives are mystics, in tune with nature, part of its harmonies. Primitives are free."[56] Contemporary idealization of Third World cultures is a new version of that same trend.

Denial of the individuality of members of these societies merges them into one amorphous whole, in which cultures are at risk of being destroyed (for example, by introducing new norms of human rights) but actual human beings are not. When the people who comprise these romanticized cultures are considered not real individuals with their own needs, wants, and desires but rather living anthropological exhibits, then their human rights can go unheeded. The primitive by definition is natural and cannot have the socially constructed desires for human rights that Westerners have as refined, alienated social beings. The primitive is not capable of abstract thought, of stepping out of her environs to consider the nature of social life or the ethics of her group. Thus to introduce the ideal of human rights even into verbal discourse with a primitive is to be an imperialist, to set off a process of social change that may well wreck the indigenous social order.

That Westerners themselves might once have been primitives whose societies underwent centuries of social change is of no consequence here. Those primitive societies that still exist are taken to be the psychological ancestors of modern man. Westerners need primitives, even when their social organization may well be exploitative of, or cruel to, many of their members, so that they can enjoy a mythic past of purity. Primitives' organic wholeness, their oneness with nature, their repression of individual choice appeals to a Western desire for an imagined simpler world. Primitives are communitarians par excellence, unpolluted by ideas of individualism or competition. In their societies no one questions the rules; everyone, even the lowliest, lives in harmony with others and with authority. Thus is the appeal of the primitive not only to left romanticizers, but also to right traditionalists.

The cultural absolutist critics of universal human rights look for a world that no longer exists, if it ever did: a world of community, of integrative membership of the individual in the group, and of a wholeness and unity with nature. The absolutist defense of indigenous cultures against universalized human rights is to a large extent a consequence of their concern that human rights will encourage the emergence of an individualized, atomistic, and competitive social world. Absolutists idealize the Third World community, which exemplifies for Western culture the primitive arcadia it has lost—even as the Third World displays some of the worst human rights abuses of early modernization. "Is the present too materialistic? Primitive life is not—it is a precapitalist utopia."[57]

In the absolutist perspective, preserving the corporate entity of the community in Third World societies will do more to preserve human rights than introducing the principle that the individual may make claims against society and the state. This corporate community, a product of over two hundred years of romantic reaction to the individualizing and liberating tendencies of modern capitalist society, is completely unproblematic. In its romantic rendering, internal inequities, power relationships, and brutalities disappear in a foggy haze of mythological collectivity. The "traditional" way of life beckons to Westerners' anxious citified psyches, reminding them of the pristine collective origins from which they spring.

Individuals living in primitive, precapitalist communitarian societies, like the people Levi-Strauss begged to stay in the bush, are not permitted to change or to think about what they would like from life. Certainly, they are not permitted to deny the dream of Utopia by adopting Western artifacts or ideas. The Tasaday of the Philippines, for example, were accused by two anthropologists of being fake primitives when they started to wear Western dress and eat cheese crackers.[58] In a similar vein, the contemporary primitives of Third World societies are not permitted to be attracted to, adopt, or advocate individualist ideals of personal autonomy or human rights. Those who do are quickly dismissed as "Westernized"; that is, as unauthentic, undermining the psychological role they play for Westerners. . . . "It is critical to realize that the

Western-based notions of human rights, to the extent that they are articulated by Third World political elites, reflect these elites' 'Westernization.'"[59] Thus even as Westerners value intellectual independence in their own tradition they refuse it to intellectuals in others; intellectuals in other traditions are supposed to be conservative exemplars, not radical challengers, of their own traditional values.

Cultural Absolutism and the Conservative Reaction

The absolutist critique trumpets the right to community over individual human rights, but only for people in other societies for whom critical and abstract thought is unauthentic. Thus in the culturally differentiated Third World the individual is not permitted to claim fulfilment of her human rights from the state or society: She renounces her human rights for the greater good of the collectivity. This renunciation is costless to her because her identity is merged with that of the group, so that human rights on an individual basis would seem not only irrelevant but laughable. She is merged with her family and society in an organic oneness that fulfills both her creative and her social needs. And, since in this rendering she either does not live in a state or class society or is untouched by the state's or the ruling class's political and economic interests, she is entirely without need for the classic civil and political rights.

In the communitarian view of individualist rights–protective society, autonomy is seen as alienation. Pollis, for example, referred to the Western view of man as an "isolated, autonomous individual."[60] As I have already discussed, autonomy does not necessarily mean alienation from the community. Autonomy does mean that the individual makes decisions for herself and may well refuse socially prescribed roles in favor of other roles that seem preferable. The autonomous individual in Western society is frequently one who is connected to the community through freely chosen associations and friendships as well as through continued family ties. The autonomous individual is not necessarily an alienated individual; she can rather be the public man (person), actively involved in the community and participating in political decisions.

This does not mean that the tension between individual and community in contemporary North America does not need to be examined. Some of the absolutists' concerns about modern liberal society are justified, even if the culturalist conclusions they draw do not solve the problem. The materialistic culture that became characteristic of some sectors of the North American population in the 1970s and 1980s is an antisocial phenomenon. But it is not an argument for reducing autonomy, reimposing communitarian controls that limit individual choices, or eliminating the principle that individuals may make claims for their human rights on society and the state.

Arguments for the absolute value of culture and for the importance of the petrified community over the individual result in political conservatism. The cultural absolutist approach to human rights has real political implications. Communitarianism denies the existence of status degradation and oppression within all societies. The romanticization of "primitive" and "traditional" societies by traditionalists, left collectivists, and status radicals exacerbates this trend.

The absolutist perspective meshes culture with tradition and with the past. It ignores the existence in the Third World of disparate political regime types and the modern repressive philosophies that many espouse. Cultures in the twentieth century are very much determined by the capacities of political elites to influence values through the educational system, the mass media, and political incorporation. We are not our ancestors, either our mythic, prehistoric ancestors or our immediate ones. Every individual and every cultural group is now influenced by a central state apparatus adhering to one or another political ideology. To espouse cultural absolutism as if these political regimes do not exist is, in effect, to espouse political relativism and to argue that all regime types possess ethically equal "cultures" of human rights.

Romantic communitarianism now buttresses many of the criticisms of liberal individualism made by political regimes on both the left and the right. On the left, the Communist criticism of human rights as bourgeois and individualist was picked up in the 1970s by left collectivists who still sometimes argue that their communities, struggling against imperialism for self-determination, have no room for individual claims against society or the state. On the right, recourse by traditionalists to the myth of a golden arcadian past prevents discussion of the human rights abuses perpetrated by twentieth-century political regimes. Romanticizing non-Western societies as embodiments of the values that Westerners have lost, or never had, does not solve the problems of the West; it merely obscures problems elsewhere.

Reliance on myths of communal living avoids discussion of serious ethical questions of how to ensure justice in the contemporary world. That much of the world was recently subjected to Western imperialism does not mean it is now exempt from international ethical debate. Those who work for change within their own societies, and those who suffer both modern state-generated brutality and traditional human rights abuses, are done a disservice by some Westerners' willingness to dismiss such suffering as culturally authentic and thus impervious to criticism from other cultural (philosophical, political) traditions.

Serious critical analysis of the human rights abuses that exist in non-Western parts of the world does not necessarily imply imperialist policy recommendations. To criticize another society or political system because human rights abuses are intrinsic to its practices is not to advocate that one's own society should therefore take it over and rearrange matters. Contemporary human rights advocates are not the equivalent of nineteenth-century Christian missionaries; that their principles are sometimes co-opted by self-serving political rhetoric does not mean that they are the de facto agents of their governments. Nor does ethical criticism of a society, whether one's own or another, imply that one regards all of its culture as unworthy. Many human rights–abusive practices that do exist are not matters of culture; rather they are consequences of economic or political interest.

Many critics of universal human rights from less-developed societies want to preserve their social values and are afraid that human rights will undermine them. But many aspects of culture, such as kinship patterns, art, or ritual, have nothing to do with human rights and can safely be preserved, even enhanced, when other rights-abusive practices are corrected. These include many aspects of public morality. The existence or abolition of polygynous marriage, for example, is not an international human rights issue, despite feminist objections to it in the West. Nor is the proper degree of respect one should show to one's elders or the proper norms of generosity and hospitality. The apparent Western overemphasis on work at the expense of family is a cultural practice that Third World societies can avoid without violating human rights. Many other such matters, such as whether criminal punishment should be by restitution or imprisonment, can be resolved without violating international human rights norms.

Cultural absolutism forgives cruelty on the grounds that acting in accordance with the customs of one's own group is a universal moral principle. The actual values of various groups are brought to our attention when they seem to be universally good, as when Renteln highlighted tendencies to limit retribution in small-scale societies, even though principled universality is rejected and only additive universality is accepted.[61] But when the principles of such groups would seem to be bad, when they condone denial of food to the weak or denial of respect to those ritually impure, they are ignored. Traer, for example, managed to gloss over Christian, Jewish, Hindu, and Muslim discrimination against women in his anxiety to prove that all religious traditions show equal respect for human rights.[62] In their longing for the good, cultural absolutists overlook evil, and claim they are doing so in the name of nonimperialist relativism.

Cultural absolutists are the real ethnocentrists. They not only argue that no one's sense of justice can transcend the boundaries of her own culture, they also argue that one ought not to transcend them. For citizens of the underdeveloped world, abstract discussion of norms of human rights that do not reflect one's cultural embeddedness is a form of cultural betrayal. Nevertheless, the West is expected to adhere to such abstract notions when in contact with the rest of the world. It is expected to compensate for its past colonial depredations, act in a nonracist manner in both international and domestic politics, and respect other cultures. This is a double standard. Cultural absolutists applaud ethnocentrism in underdeveloped societies, yet they expect the West to behave in ways that respect human rights and thereby do not adhere to many of its own cultural norms, which include racism, sexism, and religious prejudice. And they consider the standards of human rights, to which some Westerners and some thinkers and activists from the Third World want their own society to adhere, to be cultural impositions or imperialism. This denies to citizens of the underdeveloped world the right to use their reason to consider transcendent ethical norms which, if implemented in their own societies, might well result in the betterment of their own lives.

Notes

1. David Bidney, "Cultural Relativism," in David L. Sills (ed.), *International Encyclopedia of the Social Sciences* (New York: Crowell Collier and Macmillan, 1968), vol. 3, p. 543.

2. On the destruction of indigenous (Fourth World) societies, see John H. Bodley, *Victims of Progress*, 3rd ed. (Mountain View, Calif.: Mayfield Publishing, 1990).

3. Jack Donnelly, *Universal Human Rights in Theory and Practice* (Ithaca, N.Y.: Cornell University Press, 1989), p. 109.

4. Adamantia Pollis and Peter Schwab, "Human Rights: A Western Construct with Limited Applicability," in Pollis and Schwab (eds.), *Human Rights: Cultural and Ideological Perspectives* (New York: Praeger, 1980), pp. 1–18.

5. Ibid., pp. 10–12.

6. Julius O. Ihonvbere, "Underdevelopment and Human Rights Violations in Africa," in George W. Shepherd Jr. and Mark O. C. Anikpo (eds.), *Emerging Human Rights: The African Political Economy Context* (New York: Greenwood Press, 1990), p. 57.

7. Isak Dinesen, *Out of Africa* (New York: Vintage Books, 1972 [1st ed. 1937]), pp. 278–283. For discussion of Dinesen's colonialist views, see the Kenyan writer Ngugi wa Thiong'o, *Detained: A Writer's Prison Diary* (London: Heinemann, 1981), pp. 35–37.

8. Alison Dundes Renteln, "The Unanswered Challenge of Relativism and the Consequences for Human Rights," *Human Rights Quarterly*, vol. 7, no. 4 (November 1985), p. 534.

9. Ibid., p. 527.

10. Mark Juergensmeyer, "Dharma and the Rights of the Untouchables," unpublished essay, March 8, 1986, p. 1. Cited in Robert Traer, *Faith in Human Rights: Support in Religious Traditions for a Global Struggle* (Washington, D.C.: Georgetown University Press, 1991), p. 129.

11. Max L. Stackhouse, *Creeds, Society and Human Rights: A Study in Three Cultures* (Grand Rapids, Mich.: William B. Eerdmans, 1984), pp. 259–260.

12. Fernando R. Teson, "International Human Rights and Cultural Relativism," *Virginia Journal of International Law*, vol. 25, no. 4 (summer 1985), p. 870.

13. Ibid., p. 888.

14. "Statement on Human Rights," submitted to the United Nations Commission on Human Rights by the Executive Board, American Anthropological Association, in *American Anthropologist*, new series, vol. 49, no. 4 (October–December 1947), p. 540.

15. Alison Dundes Renteln, *International Human Rights: Universalism Versus Relativism* (Newbury Park, Calif.: Sage, 1990).

16. Ibid., p. 11.

17. Abdullahi Ahmed An-Na'im, *Toward an Islamic Reformation: Civil Liberties, Human Rights, and International Law* (Syracuse: Syracuse University Press, 1990).

18. Abdullahi A. An-Na'im, "Toward a Cross-Cultural Approach to Defining International Standards of Human Rights: The Meaning of Cruel, Inhuman, or Degrading Treatment or Punishment," in An-Na'im (ed.), *Human Rights in Cross-Cultural Perspectives: A Quest for Consensus* (Philadelphia: University of Pennsylvania Press, 1992), p. 36.

19. As quoted in Chapter 1. See note 17, Abdullahi Ahmed An-Na'im, *Toward an Islamic Reformation: Civil Liberties, Human Rights, and International Law* (Syracuse: Syracuse University Press, 1990).

20. Traer, *Faith in Human Rights*, p. 133. See also Zuhair Kashmeri, "Segregation Deeply Imbedded in India," *The Globe and Mail* (Toronto), October 13, 1990, p. D3.

21. Barbara R. Joshi, "Human Rights as Dynamic Process: The Case of India's Untouchables," in Claude E. Welch Jr. and Virginia A. Leary (eds.), *Asian Perspectives on Human Rights* (Boulder: Westview, 1990), pp. 162–185.

22. Teson, "International Human Rights," p. 895.

23. Ibid., p. 889.

24. Statistics Canada, *1991 Census Dictionary* (Ottawa: Supply and Services Canada, 1992), p. 26.

25. Statistics Canada, *Ethnic Origin: 1991 Census of Canada* (Ottawa: Industry, Science and Technology Canada, 1993), table 1A, pp. 12–27.

26. Nienanya Onwu, "Theological Perspectives on Human Rights in the Context of the African Situation," in George W. Shepherd Jr. and Mark O. C. Anikpo (eds.), *Emerging Human Rights: The African Political Economy Context* (New York: Greenwood, 1990), p. 73.

27. Peter L. Berger, *The Sacred Canopy: Elements of a Sociological Theory of Religion* (Garden City, N.Y.: Anchor Books, 1969), p. 6.

28. On *burakumin* see Lawrence W. Beer, "Japan," in Jack Donnelly and Rhoda E. Howard (eds.), *International Handbook of Human Rights* (Westport, Conn.: Greenwood, 1987), p. 219.

29. Celia Haig-Brown, *Resistance and Renewal: Surviving the Indian Residential School* (Vancouver: Tillacum Library, 1989), p. 53.

30. Anonymous (Brazilian anthropologists), "The politics of genocide against the Indians of Brazil" (Pamphlet) (Toronto: Brazilian Studies, 1975).

31. Robert Conquest, *The Harvest of Sorrow: Soviet Collectivization and the Terror-Famine* (Edmonton: University of Alberta Press, 1986).

32. Native Women's Association of Canada, "Aboriginal Women and the Constitutional Debates: Continuing Discrimination," *Canadian Woman Studies*, vol. 12, no. 3 (spring 1992), pp. 14–17; and Donna Sinclair, "In Search of an Equal Voice: Native Women and the Constitution," *The Nation* [United Church Observer], vol. 56, no. 2 (August 1992), pp. 14–15.

33. Jane Perlez, "Kenya's Plan for Tower Annoys Aid Donors," *New York Times* (International Edition), December 29, 1989, p. A5.

34. United Nations, Convention on Consent to Marriage, Minimum Age for Marriage and Registration of Marriages (1962), Article 2 (United Nations, *Treaty Series*, vol. 521, 1964), pp. 232–239. Interestingly, this prohibition is not included in the Convention on the Rights of the Child (1989), in Center for the Study of Human Rights, *Twenty-Four Human Rights Documents* (New York: Columbia University, 1992), pp. 81–93.

35. Rebecca J. Cook, "Reservations to the Convention on the Elimination of All Forms of Discrimination Against Women," *Virginia Journal of International Law*, vol. 30, no. 3 (spring 1990), pp. 643–716.

36. Rhoda E. Howard, "Practical Problems of Monitoring Human Rights Violations," in Alex P. Schmid and Albert J. Jongman (eds.), *Monitoring Human Rights Violations* (Publication no. 43, Center for the Study of Social Conflicts, Faculty of Social Sciences, Leiden University, 1992), p. 79.

37. The Angus Reid Group, "The National Angus Reid Poll: Tolerance and the Canadian Ethnocultural Mosaic," April 10, 1993, p. 3.

38. Michael Walzer, *Spheres of Justice: A Defense of Pluralism and Equality* (New York: Basic Books, 1983), pp. 61–62, emphasis in original.

39. Hugh Johnston, "Komagata Maru," in *The Canadian Encyclopedia* (Edmonton: Hurtig, 1985), vol. 2, p. 948.

40. Irving Abella and Harold Troper, *None Is Too Many: Canada and the Jews of Europe 1933–1948* (Toronto: Lester and Orpen Dennys, 1983).

41. Ken Adachi, *The Enemy That Never Was* (Toronto: McClelland and Stewart, 1979).

42. Ellen Baar, "Issei, Nisei, and Sansei," in Daniel Glenday, Hubert Guindon, and Allan Turowetz (eds.), *Modernization and the Canadian State* (Toronto: Macmillan, 1978), p. 348.

43. E. B. Wickberg, "Chinese," in *The Canadian Encyclopedia* (Edmonton: Hurtig, 1985), vol. 1, p. 336.

44. Calculated from Statistics Canada, *Ethnic Origin,* table 1A. European origins calculated by adding single and mixed origins.

45. "Racial Attacks Concern Toronto," *Canadian News Facts,* vol. 11, no. 1 (January 19, 1977), p. 1699.

46. Sol Littman, "'W5 Generation' changing Chinese," *Toronto Star,* April 19, 1980, p. B4.

47. "Prairie Backlash: Anti-minority campaigns cause heated debate," *Maclean's,* March 19, 1990, pp. 18–19.

48. E.g., three of five letters on this subject in *The Spectator* (Hamilton, Ontario), March 28, 1990, p. A6.

49. Marianna Torgovnick, *Gone Primitive: Savage Intellects, Modern Lives* (Chicago: University of Chicago Press, 1990), pp. 180–181.

50. James Clifford, *The Predicament of Culture: Twentieth Century Ethnography, Literature and Art* (Cambridge, Mass.: Harvard University Press, 1988), p. 202.

51. Edward W. Said, *Orientalism* (New York: Vintage Books, 1978), extracts from pp. 296, 299, 301, 321, emphasis in original.

52. Ibid., p. 322.

53. Traer, *Faith in Human Rights,* chapters 9 and 10.

54. R. J. Vincent, *Human Rights and International Relations* (Cambridge: Cambridge University Press, 1986), pp. 39–42.

55. Teson, "International Human Rights," p. 882.

56. Torgovnick, *Gone Primitive,* p. 8.

57. Ibid.

58. Seth Mydans, "20th-Century Lawsuit Asserts Stone-Age Identity," *New York Times,* October 29, 1988, p. 4; cited in Torgovnick, *Gone Primitive,* p. 259, n. 58.

59. Pollis and Schwab, "Human Rights: A Western Construct," p. 12.

60. Adamantia Pollis, "Human Rights in Liberal, Socialist and Third World Perspective," in Richard Pierre Claude and Burns H. Weston (eds.), *Human Rights in the World Community: Issues and Actions,* 2nd ed. (Philadelphia: University of Pennsylvania Press, 1992), p. 148.

61. Renteln, *International Human Rights.*

62. Traer, *Faith in Human Rights.*

4 Rights, Dignity, and Secular Society

Rights and Dignity

The cultural absolutist argument holds that there can be different conceptions of human rights in different societies.[1] In effect, all systems of social justice in all known societies can be viewed as systems of human rights. Yet among societies there are great variations in what is considered to be just, reflecting fundamental conflicts in worldviews or weltanschauung. The concept of weltanschauung implies a particular social way of viewing the world, "the total structure of the mind of . . . [a] group."[2] A group's weltanschauung includes beliefs about the correct and proper way for people to interact with each other and with society in general. Thus a group's weltanschauung includes notions of morality, justice, and human dignity.

To confuse all worldviews of morality and justice with the human rights worldview is to erode the meaning of the latter. The principle of human rights represents one particular way of looking at morality, justice, and human dignity. The Preamble to the Universal Declaration of Human Rights obscures this fact by implying that human rights and human dignity are, if not synonymous, then at least very closely linked. "Recognition of the inherent *dignity* and of the equal and inalienable *rights* of all members of the human family is the foundation of freedom, justice and peace in the world."[3] Human rights, in fact, imply a particular form of relation of the individual to society and the state that differs from what most cultures mean by human dignity.

A weltanschauung of respect for human rights deems all human beings to be equal in legal status. Every human being holds human rights equal to those of any other human being merely by virtue of being human. Human rights are inherent, individual, and autonomously exercised. They inhere in the human person himself, unmediated by social relations. They are consequently individual; an isolated human being can in principle exercise them. And they are exercised autonomously because, again in principle, no authority other than the individual is required to make human rights claims.

Human rights are an egalitarian means of allocating membership in a collectivity to all physical persons. Everyone has human rights: Children, prisoners, the mentally ill, the intellectually impaired, foreigners, all categories routinely denied human rights even in those advanced capitalist societies that view themselves as protective of human rights, must be included. These human rights are also institutionally protected. They are not merely a set of values expressed in religious or secular culture but also a set of rights that the law, government, and all other social institutions are organized to defend.

The weltanschauung of human rights presumes egalitarian and autonomous relations among all individuals in any society. It also presumes tolerance of a variety of religious beliefs. Secularism is an important characteristic of the human rights worldview. Religion or irreligion is considered to be a private choice, even by individuals whose belief in human rights is inspired by their own religious predispositions. This worldview is at odds with many traditionalist views of how human society ought to be ordered, as traditionalists tend to locate morality in religious beliefs, not in secular principles of the right and the good. Religion, moreover, often validates the stratification of a society's members into categories enjoying greater or lesser respect.

In many cultures the social order stratifies "individuals" in ways that enhance dignity for some categories of people but leave other categories dishonored, without dignity or respect. Certain members have a higher moral worth than other members. Although some deserve honor, others do not. Such different conceptions of human dignity are rooted in particular understandings of the inner moral worth of the human person and his proper relations with society. These social evaluations are part of the cultures of each society; they reflect, and in turn shape, the values, norms, and customs that regulate people's lives.

Most cultures give precedence to the community or the collectivity over the individual. The human being as such is regarded not as an individual but as a member of a social group, and individual desires are considered to be illegitimate claims upon the group. In this view, the notion that individuals might be private beings whose private desires constitute legitimate moral claims upon the group is incomprehensible. Most people's claims, privileges, powers, and obligations (not human "rights") are dependent on their social status, reflected in ascribed social roles.[4]

In many societies past and present, particular roles are ascribed by sex and age. In some Asian and African societies, for example, children are expected to show deference to adults. In North American society children look adults in the eye while talking to them and even call adults by their first names, something that strikes some outsiders as shameful. Gerontocracy, or rule by elders, is more common than the egalitarianism among age cohorts found in liberal Western societies. It is not surprising, for example, that the leadership in China should have reacted so adversely in 1989 to students who demonstrated in Tienanmen Square. In China, the value of respect for one's elders is still very strong; Confucian relations of authority did not disappear in 1949.[5] The student rebellion was therefore perceived not only as an expression of political dissent, but also as socially unacceptable criticism of elders by young people.

The status of women worldwide is an almost universal illustration of the different levels of respect accorded to different categories of people. In most societies the dignified woman willingly subordinates herself to the authority of father, husband, brother, or son. The woman who makes individualistic personal demands or resists such subordination is castigated as a shrew or witch. We can see this underlying social belief even in modern North America in the reaction of many men and women to feminists. Women making claims for equal human rights against state, society, and family are frequently depicted as shrill, shrieking, or strident. Such depictions emphasize the undignified way in which they are behaving—refusing to bear injustice as a properly socialized woman should.

It is now fashionable in anthropological circles to look to "primitive" hunting and gathering societies as examples of arcadian social equality that preceded the days of status divisions. But even here there are status-based hierarchies of authority. Among the !Kung San of southern Africa, frequently idealized as a completely egalitarian society, rudimentary political roles as chiefs are held by males, not females.[6] Thus the society as a whole differentiates among its members as to approved relations with others. These relations are not only cultural, but also political. They shape one's privileges, perquisites, obligations, and duties. They give some people categorical power over others.

Different societal conceptions of dignity also shape different views of whether human rights ought to be balanced by social duties. A common criticism of the "Western" concept of human rights is that fulfilment of duty by the rights-holder is not required; even criminals and social misfits, those who attack core social values, are permitted to have human rights. In other societies one is entitled to respect only if one fulfills certain duties and obligations. An elder male in an African village, for example, is entitled to power and privilege over his juniors, but only if he fulfills his obligation to make fair decisions and to equitably distribute collectively owned goods. To critics, human rights held without concomitant duties seem to result in a society that permits the competitive assertion of rights-claims, regardless of the costs of such competition to society as a whole.

Thus the contiguity and concurrence of the concepts of human rights and human dignity in the Universal Declaration of Human Rights reflect one particular substantive conception of human dignity, but they do not reflect the many other substantive conceptions rooted in principles of social obligation rather than individual claims against society. In most societies one cannot claim that one is worthy of respect merely because one is a human being. Rather, dignity is something that is granted at birth or upon incorporation into the community. It is usually a concomitant of one's ascribed status. It also accumulates or is earned during the life of an adult who adheres to society's values, customs, and norms: the adult, that is, who accepts the cultural constraints on his behavior.

As Pollis and Schwab noted, "Traditional cultures did not view the individual as autonomous and possessed of rights above and prior to society. Whatever the specific social relations, the individual was conceived of as an integral part of a greater whole, of a 'group' within which one had a defined role and status."[7] As one Indian philosopher once put it, "An individual is an isolated knot: a person is the entire fabric around that knot."[8] In most past and many present societies, the social fabric is considered to be more valuable than the knot: Social personhood is what makes one human. To call the social organization of dignity in such societies a system of human rights is erroneous. The individual is not entitled to make private, autonomous claims, solely on the basis of his abstract human rights, against the family or the collectivity.

The modern ideal of human rights implies equality among all individuals regardless of their status or group membership and implies that there is no "natural" (ascribed) hierarchy. In many societies such an ideal sits uneasily, regardless of the stated norms in political constitutions or in formal adherence to UN human rights documents. The ideal of human rights is associated with the individualism of North American political culture, which in turn is perceived as an abnormal social phenomenon. The insistence that age and sex do not imply differences in duties and privileges is seen as a principle bound to undermine family relations. Competitiveness in the marketplace is thought to undermine all relations of respect and deference and to permit those who are wealthy to rule regardless of their concern for the social group. In North America, it seems, one can have human rights without human dignity.

Thus the emptying of mental hospitals in the United States and Canada in the 1970s to accommodate the human rights of the patients to freedom (but also to save tax money) resulted in an increased number of homeless people on urban streets.[9] Disputes over the "right" of a New York City schizophrenic to defecate on the street due to an absence of public toilets strike many observers as shameful.[10]

To visitors from more communally oriented societies in which extended-family structures frequently (but not always) care for the mentally ill, the disabled, and the incapacitated elderly, it appears that North Americans have completely abandoned the unfortunates in their midst. "Justice" in North America seems to consist of formal equality for everyone—whatever the real social and economic inequalities that might exist. The flattening-out of status distinctions subjects everyone to the same legal rules, whereas in other societies a person's particular circumstances might be taken into account in applying the rules to him.

What is conceived of as "justice" does indeed vary from society to society. A society that protects human rights requires a particular type of justice, which distinguishes it from other societies in which justice is based on principles other than human rights. The concept of justice does not imply either the same rules of fairness in every society or the same rules for everyone within each society. The debate over the universality or particularity of the concept of human rights is, in fact, in large part a debate about different paths to social justice. Different conceptions of social justice can be identified through the different values that societies place on equality, autonomy, and respect for the individual.[11] In some societies equality detracts from the respect due to the aged, to males in general, or to those deemed to be worthy of deference by virtue of outstanding attributes such as leadership in warfare. Nor is autonomy a universal social value: Both traditional and communistically inclined societies deny autonomy. In some liberal societies such as the United States, equality and autonomy imply that no one deserves unearned respect; indeed, one's entitlement to respect must be demonstrated and can be denied by any fellow citizen.

One standard definition of justice is "the constant and perpetual will to render to everyone his due."[12] But frequently what is due to one person or set of persons differs from that due to another person or set. Michael Walzer maintained that "a given society is just if its substantive life is lived in a certain way—that is, in a way faithful to the shared understandings of the members."[13] But such shared understandings change from society to society and frequently permit inequality of treatment and assertion of collective claims over individual claims. Fairness does not necessarily imply equality of social status. Status differences mean differences in dignity, the respect to which one is entitled, and the type of justice one can therefore expect.

In modern liberal-democratic societies based on respect for human rights, the idea of different rules of justice for different categories of persons is anathema, at least insofar as such rules are formally institutionalized in law. All individuals are subject in principle to the same laws (although practice varies for different social categories and classes). But in many early Western societies laws varied depending on one's social status. The exercise by a European lord of his *droit de seigneur* over a peasant woman (the right to have sexual intercourse with her on the first night of her marriage) was not considered rape, whereas presumably a sexual advance by a peasant male to a noble's daughter ran the risk of severe penalty.[14] Criminals of different social statuses received different punishments for identical offenses. The relatively humane hanging (as opposed to torture) was first tried in England in 1760 in the execution of one Lord Ferrier.[15] Even clothing was regulated by sumptuary laws in order to ensure that everyone's social status was readily apparent.[16]

Not all cultures, then, value human equality. But even if value is placed on equality, the adversarial assertion of individual human rights may not be viewed as the fairest path to social justice. "Human Rights," said R. Panikkar, "are [merely] one window through which one particular culture envisages a just human order for its individuals."[17]

In the U.S. liberal tradition social justice is attained if all citizens have equal opportunity to seek out what they, as individuals, define as necessary for their own happiness. The goal is to make sure everyone starts the race for (material and other) happiness without disadvantages (to use a common metaphor); the outcome of the race is left to individual effort and capacity. In other societies such individualistic striving is seen as a recipe not for social justice but for social chaos. Moreover, it is seen as disrespectful for society as a whole to neglect the needs of those who, through bad luck or lesser ability, have not emerged among the winners of the race. An ordered distribution of economic benefits and relations of authority is seen as more respectful, and the assumption that all individuals can be deemed equal at the start of the race is seen as absurd; for example, the aged or mothers with children are assumed to be unable to compete. The human person is not deemed to be innately competitive or so separate from society as to be entirely responsible for his own fate.

In many lexicons of dignity and justice, to be human is a social attribute. The human being is the person who has learned and obeys the community's rules. A nonsocial, atomized individual is not human: He is a species of "Other," perhaps equivalent to a (presocialized) child, a stranger, a slave, or even an animal. There is very little room, in most so-cieties, for what the sociologist George Herbert Mead dubbed the "I"—the individual, self-reflective being—to emerge over the "me"—that part of a being that absorbs his community's culture and faithfully follows the rules and customs expected of a person of his station.[18] The human group takes precedence over the human person. The notion that a fully socialized human person is one who has reinterpreted social norms be-fore incorporating them into his own psyche is, in this sense, modern and unusual.[19] Individualist reflection by the adult on the meaning and personal applicability of the rules that the child learns is not generally considered to be socially desirable. The type of human being that liberal capitalist society has created—frequently highly individualistic and self-seeking, alienated by choice from family and community—is not valued.

The concept of honor is a better descriptor of fundamental social values in many societies than the concept of human rights. The hon-ored person is someone who is integrated into the social group in a manner befitting his status, who conforms to the rules and roles pre-scribed by society for persons occupying that status. Honor simultane-ously varies by and protects categorical distinctions among individu-als. "Honor is a direct expression of status, a source of solidarity among social equals and a demarcation line against social inferiors."[20] The im-portance given in Muslim law to protection of reputation is an indica-tion of the salience of honor in Islamic society. One of the most basic rights that all descriptions of Islamic "human rights" mention is pro-tection of one's name. The penalties for making false accusations are severe.[21]

Honor can support justice, equality, and redistribution. For exam-ple, the honorable Saharan nomad gives shelter and food to passing strangers, even to the neglect of his own needs. In societies based upon honor, one's self-respect requires fulfilment of obligations to those less well-off than oneself, an obligation that extremely competitive or liber-tarian advocates of Western capitalism frequently ignore. But honor has its obverse side too. During the Civil War in Spain (1936–1939), Peter Berger has observed, General Francisco Franco's troops fought for "faith, honor and manhood."[22] They wanted to preserve the remnants of a hier-archical and feudal society that, by the turn of the twentieth century, condemned the masses to degraded, humiliating poverty.[23] Honor pre-serves status inequalities; human rights overturn them.

In the modern world, it seems to many critics, the homeless mind has displaced the concept of honor. The price of individualism is anomie, a normless abstraction from social values. The individual whose capacity for reflection causes him to examine the order into which he was socialized, and who goes so far as to impose his own desires over that social order, denies honor; in so doing he denies society itself. In the eyes of critics the existential shift from communitarian orientation to individual privacy and autonomy means a removal from values that guide human beings toward the social good and reward them with honor when the good is pursued and maintained. Often, this also means a rejection of the religion of one's ancestors and a turn toward a selfish, alienating secularism.

Thus for many communitarian critics of modern Western society, human rights imply disorderly, selfish, and antisocial individualism. This perspective is evident in both the African and the Muslim claims to conceptions of human rights superior to the conception found in the West.

The African Critique of Individual Human Rights

The African traditionalist school of thought exemplifies communitarian criticisms of individual human rights.[24] There are several schools of thought about human rights among African intellectuals, only one of which is traditionalism; I focus on the latter in this section not only because traditionalism is still influential in Africa, but also because it has influenced the way left collectivists and status radicals think about non-Western societies and their attitudes to human rights. The traditionalist school stereotypes African societies, but since the stereotype conforms to the Orientalist perceptions of the "primitive" I discussed in Chapter 3, it is attractive to those Westerners looking for a less individualistic, competitive approach to justice than the one that seems to characterize individual human rights.

The African traditionalist school implicitly adopts the position that all systems of social justice are human rights systems. It rejects the "Western" (liberal) school of individual human rights and substitutes a mythical communitarian view of social justice as its own indigenous variety. This traditionalist perspective paints the African world before colonialism as peaceful, cooperative, and fulfilling. Order, authority, and hierarchy, in this vision, created families and communities without discord, unhappiness, or alienation. Thus the right traditionalist perspective joins the left collectivist in a vision of precolonial society as one that satisfied all human needs without social conflict.

Even in the late twentieth century, this perspective implies, Africans continue to live in a communal setting and are community or group oriented rather than individualistic. The human rights of the individual are inappropriate and irrelevant in a communal setting. Since human rights are grounded in individual claims against the state or society, and since people in Africa do not normally view themselves as individuals, human rights are not relevant to Africa.

Spokespersons of this viewpoint focus on the alleged alienation of the individual in Western society to promote a picture of the greater social integration of traditional society. They also focus on the selfish materialism that they perceive to be characteristic of Western individualism. Fasil Nahum, for example, argued that Africans do not alienate the individual by viewing him as an entity all by himself, having an existence more or less independent of society. "The individual does not stand in contradistinction to society but as part of it. Neither should he be considered as alienated from and at war with society."[25] Similarly, Asmarom Legesse claimed that "No aspect of Western civilization makes an African more uncomfortable than the concept of the sacralized individual whose private wars against society are celebrated."[26] Olusola Ojo agreed that "The Africans assume harmony, not divergence of interests . . . and are more inclined to think of their obligations to other members of society rather than their claims against them."[27]

On the whole, the argument that Africans are more communally inclined than Westerners is correct, despite massive social change in the Africa of the late twentieth century.[28] To acknowledge the continuation of a communal orientation in Africa, however, is not necessarily to acknowledge the corollaries of the argument for African collectivism. These can be summarized as having three strands: that African economies were and are redistributive, not acquisitive, in orientation; that African politics were and are consensual, not competitive; and that there was and is no social stratification in Africa. Such corollaries are both factually questionable and irrelevant to the argument that Africans do not need human rights. As societies change and political elites affect everyone's life, so everyone needs protection against the state and the new social structure.

The first assertion about the nature of African collectivism is that African economies are redistributive, and that individuals work for the common good, not in order to maximize their own capacities to acquire material goods. Legesse, writing about the Anuak of Ethiopia and Sudan, stated that peasants could not be deprived of their land and that kings or chiefs had the obligation to share their wealth with their subjects.[29] Yet Legesse, writing in 1980, ignored contemporary political and economic realities in Africa. The belief that economic values in Africa are unchanged even as economic relations are severely ruptured, both by capitalism and, in the case of Ethiopia in the 1980s, by Soviet-style Marxism, permeates the romanticized Orientalism not only of traditionalists, but also of left collectivists and status radicals.

The second traditionalist assertion about the nature of African collectivism is that African politics were and are consensual. Dunstan Wai noted the example of Ashanti chiefs, who could be deprived of their power if they abused their authority.[30] Benoit Ngom agreed that African societies were founded on consensus and group cultural values. Ngom, however, at least added the qualifier that consensual politics could work only for small-scale polities.[31] Indeed, this is the case. In Africa as in Europe, newly emergent large-scale polities rely on arbitrary authority and political dictatorship, not on democratic consensus.

The third assertion about the nature of African collectivism is that there was and is no indigenous system of social stratification in Africa. A number of authors noted that most African societies were gerontocracies based on the rule of elders but contended that there was otherwise little stratification. The rule of (male) elders is not seen as stratificatory in itself.[32] Further, other indigenous means of stratification, such as by lineage (membership in large kin groups) or differentiation among slaves and free subjects, is ignored. Ngom did mention slaves, but argued that even they were not excluded from the consultative process.[33]

Taken together, these three propositions about the nature of African collectivism are an accurate depiction of the values held by some societies in Africa in the past. These values still exist as part of the dominant social ethic today.[34] As such, description of these values provides an accurate picture of the ethic that still guides much of African thinking. But they are an incomplete picture of the practice. The picture does not take into account the existence of expansionist African states and of caste-stratified societies in the past. It is, in fact, a version of the "myth of Merrie Africa," cited by John Iliffe as a cause of the "widespread belief that until recently there were no poor in Africa, because economic differentiation was slight, resources were freely available, and the 'extended family' supported its less fortunate members." In fact, Iliffe argued, there were many poor in precolonial African societies, especially incapacitated people who had no family support; slaves and pawns (debt-peons); outcasts of various kinds; and unsupported women, especially childless women and widows in Islamic society.[35] Chris C. Mojekwu indirectly confirmed this viewpoint when he noted that "the concept of human rights in Africa was fundamentally based on ascribed status. . . . Only those who 'belonged' to the community would have their human rights protected by the kinship authorities."[36]

In general, status differentiation based on age and sex pervaded all African societies; some societies further differentiated between freemen and slaves and between insiders and aliens. The traditional African society to which proponents of the African concept of human rights refer is partly an ideological creation by the more powerful groups in African societies to justify their own authority and control. Tradition has been "created" in Africa. "Elders tended to appeal to 'tradition' in order to defend their dominance . . . against challenge by the young. Men tended to appeal to 'tradition' in order to ensure that [there was no] diminution of male control over women. . . . Paramount [supreme] chiefs and ruling aristocracies . . . appealed to 'tradition' in order to maintain or extend their control over their subjects. Indigenous populations appealed to 'tradition' in order to ensure that the migrants who settled amongst them did not achieve political or economic rights."[37]

Reliance on tradition among authors who argued against the relevance of human rights to Africa obscures the actual practice of modern societies. Perhaps the greatest weakness of the myth of Merrie Africa is not exaggeration of precolonial democracy and egalitarianism but rather unwillingness to acknowledge contemporary social change. Rising rates of landlessness coupled with burgeoning populations have impelled permanent urbanization and reliance on nonagricultural employment. These new social changes are accompanied by social-psychological aspects of modernization, especially an increasing trend toward individualism. Young people, women, and members of former slave lineages are no longer willing to accept the authority of elders, male relatives, and former slaveowners. They go to the city and they seek individualism precisely to free themselves from such constraints.

This social change is largely a consequence of imperialist penetration and colonialism. Nevertheless, today it is a social fact that strongly influences the lives of most contemporary Africans. The ethic of communalism still has a strong hold, as witnessed for example by urban hometown associations dedicated to funding improvements such as schools and clinics in members' home villages. Yet social attitudes are changing as a consequence of economic crisis, urban under- and unemployment, and highly inegalitarian social stratification. Social custom is also affected by the political reality of frequently abusive personal dictatorship, one-party rule, or military regimes. Nothing in the present political economy of Africa suggests that a move back to a simpler, more communitarian time is possible.

Nevertheless, some African thinkers still maintain that human rights are inappropriate for Africa insofar as social change has not (yet) converted it into a mainly urbanized, industrialized society. It is certainly true that the majority of sub-Saharan Africans still live in rural areas (71 percent in 1991) and still have ties to the land, although the rate of urbanization (5.8 percent in 1991) is very high.[38] It is also certainly true that Africans are as a whole more tied to their extended family and kinship groups than are Westerners. But the continued existence of a communitarian ethic among many (not all) Africans does not obviate the relevance of human rights to Africa. Human rights are meant to protect individuals—either on their own or in groups—against such abuses as state-induced starvation, deprivation of one's means of livelihood, or torture. These protections are necessary in any state society. Communally oriented systems of social justice, based upon ascribed and differentiated memberships in small-scale pastoral or agricultural societies, unfortunately cannot be transferred to the modern, large-scale state arena.

The African concept of "human rights" is actually a concept of human dignity. It does not protect the individual against society and is not meant to. African communalism, stressing the dignity of membership of, and fulfilment of one's prescribed social role in, a group (family, lineage, tribe), still represents accurately how many Africans view their personal relationship to society. Membership in a group means that protection against that group is seen as absurd.

This conception of dignity implies a different notion of justice than does the version based on human rights. The African traditionalist concept of justice is one that is rooted not in individual claims against the state but in the physical and psychic security of group membership. In such societies in the past, social justice was based on the premise that responsibility in fulfilling one's role carried certain privileges: Privileges were contingent upon fulfilment of responsibility. These were certainly not societies based on human rights, yet both dignity and justice were served. For many Africans, unequal allocation of responsibility and privilege according to age, gender, or social status is still a fundamental and valued way of ordering their world. For such people, to assert their human rights as individuals would be unthinkable, as to do so would be to undercut their dignity as group members. Thus many African women, even when aware of their own severe burden of agricultural work, domestic duties, and child care, prefer to stress family problems instead of their own.[39]

The cultures and values characteristic of indigenous African societies do not negate the need for human rights in Africa today; rather, they point out the need. Human rights can protect families and communities by promoting the right to food, protecting individuals against torture and execution, and protecting the rights of minorities to speak their own language and practice their own religion. Immediate attention to the full range of human rights in Africa, while it is in the process of modernizing, might stem the emergence of some of those anomic characteristics of Western social psychology that some ethnic African critics of human rights have observed to be characteristic of capitalist societies.

Certain aspects of the African ethic of communalism could be used to buttress human rights. An-Na'im stressed the need for human rights to be grounded in the indigenous cultural traditions of every society.[40] The Nigerian scholar G. O. Olusanya made the same point: "For any law to grow and be productive, it must be rooted in the culture and tradition as well as the realities of the people for whom it is made."[41] In African communal societies there were many features well worth preserving and many that could buttress the present international consensus on human rights. The Mossi of West Africa, for example, practiced a "palaver" political system in which the monarch routinely consulted with chiefs, who were "endowed with great power to brake, hinder, oppose or even to effectively veto" his wishes.[42] Both these practices provide an ethical support for the right to political participation. With regard to economic rights, in many societies chiefs were responsible for food storage to protect their communities against famine. The ethic of sharing among family and offering hospitality to strangers also protected unlucky individuals against hunger. These practices could strengthen the right to food. And they serve as an example to Western societies in which collective or community responsibility for the economic rights of others has fallen into abeyance.

The communal concept of social justice had many elements that could support human rights and could be adapted to fit the need for the individual to make enforceable claims against new, often politically and economically abusive, African states.[43] But human rights–based protections of African individuals against the state will also mean protections against the group, which is idealized in the traditionalist argument that human rights are not relevant to Africa. The social values of precapitalist communities in Africa, as elsewhere, contain elements that both support and undermine individual human rights. Communities in Africa, like communities in the Western world, can be repressive and inegalitarian as well as supportive and egalitarian. The same applies to Muslim communities, whose customs tie certain individuals to the collectivity, even as they exclude others in the name of adherence to a traditional moral code.

The "Muslim" Approach to Human Rights

The Salman Rushdie affair is often taken to exemplify the two world-views that are at conflict in the individualist and the communitarian (traditionalist) perceptions of human rights and social justice. The drama and immediacy of the Rushdie *fatwa* has focused world attention on the differences between "Western" and "Muslim" perceptions of human rights. At the same time, however, the mythologized Muslim perspective on Rushdie reinforces Orientalist stereotypes of Islamic society. Muslims, like Africans and Westerners, are split among many different approaches to human rights: Many Muslims advocate the civil and political rights considered most exemplary of the "Western" perspective.

On February 14, 1989, Ayatollah Ruhollah Khomeini, the head of state of Iran, pronounced a death sentence on Salman Rushdie.[44] Rushdie is a British author of Indian origin and of Muslim religious heritage. The Ayatollah accused Rushdie of heresy that, he claimed, permeated Rushdie's novel, *The Satanic Verses*.[45] The Iranian regime offered a large reward to anyone who would assassinate Rushdie, who immediately went into hiding under the protection of the British police. Although the Ayatollah Khomeini died in June 1989, as of January 1995 the death sentence remained in effect, supported by the Khomeini's successors in Iran.

In making the death threat (and continuing it even after Khomeini's death), Iran in effect claims to represent not only the ethno-religious nation of Iranian Muslims (but not, presumably, Iranian citizens who are Christians, Jews, Baha'i, or members of other groups such as Zoroastrians) but also the entire cultural group of Muslims wherever they may live. This ignores the fact that Iranian Muslims are members of the minority Shi'ite group, whereas 90 percent of the world's Muslims are estimated to be members of the majority Sunnite branch; there are also numerous smaller Muslim groups such as the 2 million Ismailis.[46] Thus Ayatollah Khomeini, as a political leader, took it upon himself to falsely imply that he was a spiritual leader of the internally divided Muslim world.

The death threat, issued by a head of state against a citizen of another country, violates international law. It also violates Muslim law.

First, assuming that Khomeini is [was] the undisputed ruler of an Islamic state . . . his jurisdiction under Shari'a [Islamic law] does not extend to a non-Islamic state. . . . Second, even if Khomeini were to have jurisdiction over Rushdie on the absurd ground that the ruler of an Islamic state has universal jurisdiction over Muslims anywhere in the world, Shari'a requires that a person be charged with an offense and allowed a chance to defend himself before he may be punished. Third, repentance and recantation of heretic views is always a complete defense against a charge of apostasy *(ridda)*, which is presumably the offense Rushdie is supposed to have committed.[47]

Islam is a written religion that contains rules for the organization of society. Islam was and remains an evangelical religion that seeks converts, sometimes by force. It shares this evangelical bent with Christianity, also a religion historically imposed on others by force. The final defeat of Islam in Europe was only three centuries ago; indeed, even more recent if one considers the influence of the Ottoman Empire in the Balkans until early in this century. Many Muslims believe that Islam has been humiliated not only by European conquest and imperialism, but also by the modern liberal ideology of human rights that claims to be more just and righteous than Shari'a law.

In the traditionalist conception of "human rights" presented by some scholars purporting to represent Islam as a whole, the Qu'ran is taken as the unchallengeable basis of justice. "Human rights" must conform to those duties, privileges, and obligations enjoined upon believers in the Qur'anic verses, in the practice of the Prophet Muhammad and in Shari'a law. According to traditional interpretations, Islam excludes entire categories of people, most notably women, slaves, and non-Muslims, from equality under the law, although it does set out careful rules for their unequal protection.[48] Yet this is not to say that Islam, especially at the time of its inception, was a particularly unjust system of ethics, even in modern liberal terms.

Although it permitted slavery, Islam at its inception enjoined merciful treatment of slaves and envisaged a future society in which slavery would be abolished. Slaves in Islamic societies had more opportunities for manumission (freedom) than slaves in the capitalist West, and children of mixed slave–free marriages might become free.[49] Islam also specifically forbade racism, noting "Allah says . . . a coloured man has no superiority over a white man, nor a white man over a coloured man, nor an Arab over a non-Arab, except for righteousness."[50] Muslim women had some unequal legal rights. They were, in fact, granted more legal rights of inheritance (one-half the inheritance rights of a male of equivalent degree of kinship to the deceased) than women had in the Christian world until well into the nineteenth century. In Victorian Britain, for example, women could inherit property, but there was no obligation upon their male relatives to leave it to them, and primogeniture favored oldest sons.[51] Islam also enjoined compassion and charity to the poor: Alms-giving was a holy act and the state was obliged to set aside some of its spoils from warfare for support of "the poor, the orphans and the way-farers."[52]

Even in criminal law, Shariʻa law was until fairly recently more humane than law in some Western societies. The *hudud* punishments (like amputation for theft and stoning for adultery), currently practiced in a very few Muslim countries including Sudan and Saudi Arabia, seem barbarous to Western eyes. Yet until fairly recently, European criminal law might have seemed barbarous to Muslims. In England, between 1660 and 1819 "187 new capital statutes became law"; this was in response to urbanization and the creation of a mass proletarian society.[53] Under Islam, even an act of murder punishable by death can be commuted as an act of charity by the family of the victim (which can also, however, demand "eye for an eye" retribution).[54]

Finally, until quite recently Islam was much more tolerant of some religious minorities than was Christian Europe of any. Although only Muslim males enjoyed full rights, *dhimmi* (People of the Book, namely Christians and Jews) were granted legal protections at a time when Christian Europe was torturing, expelling, and burning to death Muslims and Jews. Catholics and Jews in Britain did not obtain full civil or political rights until well into the nineteenth century; the great Jewish Prime Minister of England, Benjamin Disraeli, was a convert to Christianity.[55]

Thus, compared with Europe until barely a century and a half ago, Islamic societies might well be characterized as far more just in the modern sense of protecting human rights. The West's anti-Islamic and anti-Arab racism since the 1973 oil confrontation with the Organization of Petroleum Exporting Countries, a prejudice that was reinforced by the 1991 Gulf War, has meant that the worst features of Islam are played up in Western eyes; its more humane, protective aspects are forgotten. Nevertheless, however superior some of its substantive content may have been in the past to the then-applicable Western rules of justice, the Islamic conception of justice is not one of human rights. While the Western world shifted from a communitarian, hierarchical, and religion-centered conception of social justice to an individualist, egalitarian, and secular conception, the Islamic world has not, by and large, done the same. However humane and just some of its principles may be, Islam is pervaded by anti-individualist and hierarchical ideas, and it forbids freedom of thought. Heretical ideas and outspoken atheism are condemned.

The Ayatollah Khomeini's condemnation of Salman Rushdie thus opportunistically took advantage of the split between Western liberalism and Third World communitarianism over the issue of individual human rights. The political protection to which Rushdie is entitled as a

British citizen was interpreted by pro-Ayatollah forces as an instance of Western cultural imperialism, the protection of a Muslim heretic by secular Western society. In the eyes of some Muslims, under the rubric of freedom of speech Rushdie is being permitted the freedom to blaspheme.

The Rushdie affair represents a serious clash of two worldviews. These two worldviews, however, are not monolithic either on the Muslim or the Western side; rather, they represent different points of view within Islam and within the West. The Ayatollah's *fatwa* is an extreme representation of a theological worldview that demands religious orthodoxy of all believers or indeed of all those "born into" the Faith, even though they might never have considered independently whether or not they were actual believers. Western analogues to this religious worldview, with greater or lesser degrees of repressive intent, are easy to find. The Christian expulsions and burning of heretics, including Muslims, in the early modern period in Europe are the most obvious example. So are the Rabbinical laws of the state of Israel that create a partial theocracy, insofar, for example, as the religious authorities control marriages and divorce.[56] Indeed, the resurgent Christian fundamentalist movement in North America that advocates the erosion of freedom of speech and of women's rights also suggests a theocratic bent.[57]

Most people—Muslims or others—who advocate full or partial theocracies are not, of course, suggesting execution of heretics. But they are disturbed, as was the Ayatollah Khomeini and his supporters, by the secular worldview. Secularism is a point of view that advocates the separation of church and state, the legal tolerance of heresy, and equal rights to people of various religions, including atheists. Such a worldview appears by definition to advocate or support the breakdown of community. Religious heterogeneity undermines coherent state-ethno-religious groups. Toleration of heresy and atheism portends the breakdown of common moral values represented, in almost all societies, by religious belief-systems. In secular societies religion is viewed as a private matter completely separable from political authority; though a heretic Catholic may be excommunicated by the church, he is not punished by the state. In religiously based societies the heretic is also punished by the state because his views threaten community or national coherence.

This conflict between religious and secular worldviews is rooted in the social changes consequent on the transition from traditional to modern societies. Insofar as modernity has been at least partially imposed on non-European societies by imperialist Western powers, the conflict is bound to intersect with nationalistic reactions against the former practice of colonialism. Many Muslims regard Islam not only as their sacred belief, but also as a social bulwark against the decadence, family disintegration, individualism, and materialism that they believe exemplify Western society. In this they are joined by many Westerners who have returned for the same reason to orthodox or conservative versions of Christianity or Judaism or indeed who have converted to Islam.

To a person holding a religious, traditional worldview, laws permitting unfettered freedom of speech are deeply offensive. The Rushdie affair encapsulates and exemplifies extreme views of what the relationship of the individual to his ethno-religious group ought to be. Those who agree with the Ayatollah's death sentence in effect contend that not even the most basic human right, the right to life, is more important than the collective right of the community to protect its core values. Those who hold to the liberal, individualist view of human rights advocate complete protection of the entire range of Salman Rushdie's rights, not only to life and to freedom of movement, but also to publish what he sees fit in both the Western and the Islamic worlds, even if it is blasphemous.

Westerners wishing to be sensitive to what they sometimes perceive as a monolithic Islamic worldview might be tempted to offer a compromise on the issue of Rushdie's right to freedom of speech. Such a compromise might defend all of Rushdie's individual rights in the Western, more secular society but agree that his right to publish might be limited by a banning order within the Muslim world. In secular human rights terms, religious belief is a private cultural matter. It is not imposed by the state. The state has an obligation to permit practice of the religious customs and beliefs that are central to the community's culture but not to impose them on minority groups or individuals. But in the Islamic world, religion shapes morality, relations between the sexes, and relations between rich and poor; it provides comfort and ritual and a sense of belonging. The idea of religion as a private cultural matter is not tenable in this type of society; religion is public and collective, and adherence to it is required.

Thus there is a compromise position on the current conflict: Since Rushdie's book is indeed culturally, if not politically, offensive, it should be banned in Muslim state societies. In secular Western societies the culture views religion as a private matter and accepts freedom of speech even when blasphemy is the result. If Muslims live in Western society, then they must be prepared to encounter blasphemy against their religion.

Such a compromise, however (even if advocated for reasons of cultural sensitivity rather than mere political expediency) would in practice ignore the diversity of religious views among Muslims of different stripes. It would also ignore the move to modernity that creates nominal

Muslims, or indeed outright atheists, of many in the Islamic world. Further, the possibly liberating and politically progressive role of literature and freedom of speech as a whole would be denied in the Muslim world. In 1989, Salman Rushdie joined a long list of Muslim authors banned in their own countries, often for reasons of political repression rather than to uphold the Faith. Censorship of newspapers, banning of books, and imprisonment of writers and intellectuals are common events in the Muslim world.[58] If the price of freedom of speech is some blasphemous utterance, the prize is political openness and an enhanced possibility of democratic rule. In theocratic states preservation of religious orthodoxy in the name of community is in practice preservation of political dictatorship.

The Western world modernized and became (in some places at some times) protective of human rights partly as a result of religious debate, the Reformation split of Protestants from the Roman Catholic church, and the ultimate separation of church and state. Although one might agree that such religious freedom of speech in the Muslim world will have to result from internal social change rather than from Western insistence on its own principles of human rights, a culturally relativist stance that supports internal Muslim censorship merely out of respect for a different way of life will seriously discount the fact that, in practice, that way of life has changed or is changing for many Muslims.

Modernization, the combination of the processes of secularism, individualism, materialism, and urbanization, is exerting its pull everywhere, even in the most backward of villages and on the most remote of peoples. In reaction to such change, a return to the old ways, a reinforcement of respect for tradition, exerts a powerful appeal on societies that feel besieged by outsiders and by ways of life that threaten their cohesiveness. Thus, the eminent scholar of Islam, Bernard Lewis, explained (some) Muslims' anti-Western feelings. "Ultimately, the struggle of the fundamentalists is against two enemies, secularism and modernism. . . . Islamic fundamentalism has given an aim and a form to the otherwise aimless and formless resentment and anger of the Muslim masses at the forces that have devalued their traditional values and loyalties and, in the final analysis, robbed them of their beliefs, their aspirations, their dignity, and to an increasing extent even their livelihood."[59]

Taking a similar perspective to Lewis's, Benjamin Barber wrote of the phenomenon of "Jihad versus McWorld."[60] *Jihad* (referring to Islamic holy wars against infidels) is Barber's shorthand expression for the rest of the world's traditionalist reaction against the onslaught of capitalist and commercializing modernity, represented by McDonald's hamburgers, or McWorld. This reaction is against individualism, egalitarianism, and autonomy in private and public life. Like Christian fundamentalists, Muslim fundamentalists want to return to or preserve a collectivist, nonegalitarian, and guided human existence. Such a philosophy of life, from wherever it emanates, denies human rights as the UN documents define them.

Underneath the African and Muslim criticisms of the particular Western and individualist formulation of human rights is a reluctance to admit that the critics, in fact, do not accept human rights at all. The cachet of international respectability and legitimacy that accompanies formal ratification and acceptance of the international human rights documents renders it difficult, if not impossible, for Muslim, Hindu, Christian, or Jewish traditionalists to say what they really believe: that they are against human rights; that they disagree with the ideals of equality, autonomy, and respect for all; and that they prefer societies in which certain categories of people are considered unequal and undeserving of respect, in which the assertion of human rights would be punished.

Since the Khomeini takeover in 1979, Iran has been one of the few countries (perhaps the only one) to actually take this position in UN debate. It argued in 1984 that the Universal Declaration of Human Rights "represented secular understanding of the Judaeo-Christian tradition [that] could not be implemented by Muslims and did not accord with the system of values recognized by the Islamic Republic of Iran."[61] Most diplomatic and state spokespersons, most ideologues, and many academics prefer to say not that they reject human rights but that they accept them, merely rejecting the particular *type* of human rights that the international documents represent. They then convert debate over whether or not a country accepts and protects human rights into debates over ideological imperialism, cultural relativism, and the necessity to recognize all conceptions of social justice as human rights.

Although clearly Shari'a law as normally interpreted does not provide equality for non-Muslims or Muslim women, most spokespersons of the "Muslim conception of human rights" are unwilling to say that they reject certain human rights entirely. Ahmad Farraq, secretary-general in 1988 of the Islamic States Broadcasting Organization, is one of the few who is willing to state outright that he rejects certain of the international human rights provisions. He objects to the equal rights of men and women to marry whomever they please, regardless of religion. Under Islamic law, Farraq said, Muslim men may marry Jewish or Christian women, since the Muslims accept Moses and Jesus as divine messengers and a Muslim man, as head of the house, can protect his wife's beliefs without causing dissension in the family. But a Jewish or

Christian man may not marry a Muslim woman because he could not be sufficiently protective of her beliefs, thus causing that very dissension in the family that Islam deplores. Farraq is refreshingly frank: He stated outright, "As a Muslim I reject" the article of the Universal Declaration of Human Rights permitting marriage without any restrictions on race or religion.[62]

The normal response of Muslim traditionalists in the international debate on human rights is not to forthrightly state on record that they disagree with some human rights. Rather, it is to try to co-opt the language of human rights. Muslim traditionalists thus argue that Islamic social justice, with its distinctions of status based upon religion, caste, and gender, is in fact a system of human rights. As such, it has equal moral standing with the formal international consensus on human rights, even though it denies the most fundamental premise of equality contained in the Universal Declaration. "Reluctant to say that following Islam means denying human rights, Muslims who reject the international norms now argue for the substitution of Islamic human rights, or rights that Islamic sources have supposedly authorized. . . . The fabrication of Islamic pedigrees for modern human rights principles . . . demonstrates the extent to which ideas of identifiably Western, Christian provenance remain unacceptable in some Muslim milieus. [But it] also bears witness to the appeal and prestige that human rights ideals enjoy in the Muslim world."[63] In this quotation Ann Elizabeth Mayer brings to our attention that there is more than one aspect to the Muslim "tradition," that a full discussion of the Islamic perspective on human rights would include the views of all those Muslims who accept the values of—who indeed try to promote—"Western" egalitarian human rights. The ideas of liberal and progressive Muslims are every bit as authentic as those of traditionalist clerics.[64] As Rushdie himself said:

> If the worst, most reactionary, most medieval strain in the Muslim world is treated as the authentic culture, so that the mullahs get all the headlines while progressive, modernizing voices are treated as minor and marginal and "Westoxicated" . . . then the fundamentalists are being allowed to set the agenda.
>
> The truth is that there is a great struggle for the soul of the Muslim world, and, as the fundamentalists grow in power and ruthlessness, those courageous men and women who are willing to engage them in a battle of ideas and moral values are rapidly becoming as important for us to know about, to understand and support, as the dissident voices in the old Soviet Union used to be.
>
> In the Muslim world, secularism is now the fanatics' most important target.[65]

Today, the ideal of human rights embodied in the international documents does indeed have an international following. Intellectuals worldwide strongly believe in such ideals: If they did not, the sudden changes in ruling political philosophies that accompanied, indeed precipitated, the collapse of Communist rule in Eastern Europe and the former Soviet Union would not have occurred. In other parts of the world, hundreds and thousands of these liberal intellectuals are silenced and imprisoned. Prominent Muslims who defend the secular, egalitarian, and modern approach to human rights are often in involuntary de facto exile, if not in jail. It is difficult and dangerous for them to establish leagues for human rights in their own countries.[66] These intellectuals defend a worldview that is secular and humanist, one that values individual freedom.

Muslim traditionalists decry Western humanism. Although humanism is not characteristic of all Western systems of thought (neither communism nor fascism is humanist), all major Western political philosophies since the period of early capitalism have been secular in the sense that they have detached themselves from the authority of the church. Secularism is a system of thought antithetical to the sacred. There is no divine Law, there is no God but the private God in whom some individuals choose to believe. Public affairs, therefore, cannot be decided upon with reference to divine Law or to God.

Secular society in modern times even permits blasphemy. Like any other types of writing, the sacred texts are open to criticism, disagreement, even mockery. Indeed, mockery can be considered a public good, a means of debunking the myths that render religion the opium of the people, susceptible to the leadership of conservative priests. This is a technique that Salman Rushdie used: placing his characters in historical situations analogous to those of the Prophet. Rushdie was accused by Khomeini and other Muslims of being an apostate, someone who denies his faith. In traditional society one is what one is born to be; born into a Muslim family, Rushdie is perforce a Muslim. In secular society one can choose to be religious or irreligious. Under Muslim law, atheism is permitted as long as the atheist keeps his thoughts to himself, but a Muslim is not permitted to become an atheist or otherwise to deny his faith.[67]

Secular society is a society that is humanistic, man-centered. The law is created by man: It is not revealed by God. Thus in a secularized Islamic milieu the law of Shari'a, some elements of which have been fixed for almost a thousand years, would become amenable to change: It would no longer be considered the revealed word of Allah. In secular society truth must be sought and found by man in the natural world of empirical facts analyzed by reason, not faith. "Out of respect for the truth the humanist asks for the credentials of the revealed Truth. His faith manifests itself . . . in peoples' ability to come to their own judgment. . . . The discovery that both our ideas and our institutions are *nomos*, made by men, and not *physis*, imposed on us by nature or the gods, was of supreme importance in the development of modern history. This discovery ended in the idea of democracy and led to an interest in other cultures and the development of self-criticism."[68]

Once men (and sometimes women) are freed to seek the truth through their own perception and reason, the bonds of religion are broken. This is one of the most frightening aspects of the Westernization of traditional societies. Allied with nationalist reaction against former imperialists, Third World criticism of modern human rights deplores the loss of the sacred, immutable rules and order found in religion-bound societies. In this, the critique resembles that of conservative Christian critics of modern Western society, deploring the loosening of sex roles, family ties, and moral standards that liberal society seems inexorably to demand. Orderliness, security, community: These are challenged by liberal human rights, especially in the very process of claiming human rights before a new order and a new community based on equality and autonomy can be established.

Community and Individualism

The debate about community is a serious matter. Communities in the preindustrial European world and the contemporary underdeveloped world were and are based upon common birthplace, kinship ties, and ancestral links and generally reinforced by homogeneous religion, language, and custom. In the Western world, these communities have by and large broken down. The type of community that has risen to take its place is a rather thin substitute. Neighborhoods of unrelated, mobile people whose meetings take place by chance or choice, not by regulated or inbred customs, are not as dense, as glued together, as the village of precapitalist Europe or the contemporary Middle East.

In late October 1990, my elderly next-door neighbor died. My husband and I did not attend her funeral mass because we did not know of her death. We were not acquainted with her adult children, and we neglected to check the obituary columns of our local newspaper when we noticed unusual activity at her house. Like other neighbors on our street, we were distraught that we were not present at the mass. But such ignorance would be impossible and unthinkable in most traditional societies.

What appears to be the atomistic individualism of Western society is a matter of concern to both Western and Third World critics of the

"Western" human rights tradition. A society of seemingly high crime rates, decreasing family obligations, and unsafe and hostile neighborhoods is one decried not only by Western conservatives, but also by many liberals in North America. But it is important to remember that violence, atomization, and hostility also exist in many traditional societies. Inequality and brutality pervade relations among castes, and between former slaves and former slaveowners, in many parts of the world. Violence against women abounds and is positively sanctioned. Members of degraded groups are alienated, atomized, and condemned to live in complete social despair as much, if not more, in Lagos or Bangkok as in New York.

It is not surprising that the particular human rights provision that the Muslim commentator Farraq rejects is an aspect of equality of women. Fear of equality and autonomy for women underlies much of the traditionalist and communitarian reaction against human rights. Women are the carriers of tradition and community. They subordinate their own interests to those of their family and reproduce the members of the kin group. When they marry, they change their personal allegiances as their society requires, whatever the stress on them as individuals. As traditional societies modernize and norms of social interaction break down, as family support and economic redistribution give way to individualism, migration, and materialism—especially, and far more easily, for men—there is even more pressure on women to conform to their social roles. It is no accident, for example, that witch burning has been revived in the late twentieth century in such areas as the Venda Bantustan in South Africa and the state of Bihar in India, where in the 1980s 200 women were killed yearly by mobs in just one district.[69] As societies undergo severe stress, nonconformist women are scapegoated as the cause of discomfort. Resistance to the equality of women is a hidden theme in much of the culturally based critique of Western human rights norms.

In the case of women, to stress community over the individual, order over freedom, might well result in more dignity if less justice. In Western societies the formal ending of women's secondary status has cast many women adrift in a sea of normlessless, deprived of a secure role in the family and community. Their equal and autonomous human rights are protected in principle but not always in practice; thus many women have substituted for inegalitarian marriages the stressful "autonomy" of single parenthood. Many women in the 1980s and 1990s in North America, like many conservative German women during the period of cultural flowering and individual liberty of the Weimar Republic, seek to return to the old ways.[70] Such women claim that the true feminist ought to protect rather than challenge the institutions of marriage, motherhood, and family. Respect for women as individuals seems to imply disrespect for their fidelity to their social and familial duties.

There is certainly a need in the Western world for a new kind of community to replace the lost certainties of traditional life: "We . . . have to acknowledge that the emancipation [from the bonds of tradition] . . . meant at the same time a loss of many certainties. For some . . . a new certainty, a new norm, came instead: the subject became a citizen, a person who has to be conscious of his responsibility. . . . At the same time we have to live with a growing danger of alienation that can only be overcome in a common endeavor of world cooperation and human solidarity."[71] New communities must be built to provide that social and cultural integration that was characteristic of the old order, at least, that is, for those who were not slaves or untouchables. How to institute and protect equality, autonomy, and respect for all is the major issue of debate for the end of the twentieth century.

If one accepts the human rights worldview, these values may not be rejected in favor of a return to a mythical, romanticized past of community and solidarity. Indeed, one must be conscious that repressive societies in which religious fundamentalism or traditionalist rhetoric is used to buttress political authoritarianism also produce an alienated citizenry. "Rights and fundamental freedoms are denied to the Arab citizen under a variety of pretexts such as . . . the one-sided and self-serving interpretation of the Islamic doctrine (Shari'a). . . . The ultimate outcome of human rights violations is the complete lack of participation by the citizen in public affairs and the ensuing feeling of insecurity and isolation. The result is that the sole preoccupation of the individual is the earning and maintaining of a living. . . . Material values govern human relations at all levels."[72] Alienation and social isolation, commonly attributed to materialist Western society, are even more characteristic of Third World societies, whose elites rhetorically reject the Western value system while enthusiastically embracing materialism and consumerism at the expense of their fellow citizens. For them, defense of community is an easy means of deflecting commentary by Western liberals whose very tradition of intellectual self-criticism obliges them to consider carefully the imperialist implications of negative judgment on other cultures. But analysis of human rights and their violations must be equally rigorous regardless of the religious tradition, culture, or community being examined: Otherwise, we run the risk of excusing in some societies abuses that are inexcusable in others.

The saga of Salman Rushdie is a parable for our age. In his own person he encapsulates the Western threat to religion-encrusted, hierarchical, closed societies. Rushdie is a Muslim who renounced his faith and who, moreover, believed that it was his right to do so. In the symbolic role thrust upon him by the Ayatollah Khomeini, Rushdie became a greater threat to the reactionary clerics and authoritarian leaders of parts of the contemporary Muslim world than any decadent Westerner who holds the same views. The Westerner can simply be dismissed as an "Other," as an imperialist with no decent human values. Rushdie, like all other liberal Muslims, cannot be so easily dismissed.

The effective establishment of human rights does indeed threaten cultures, destroy tradition, upset communities. Where culture is embodied in formal religious codes, secularism is a threat to the deepest beliefs of many people, though for others it is a liberation. Secularism means not only a denial of the authority of religion, but a rationalist, empiricist questioning of all social values; in short, secularism is a denial that culture, in and of itself, is valuable and worth preserving.

Yet if this is true, it does not follow that the outcome is more socially valuable than the traditional, nonegalitarian community that a society protective of human rights would replace. The price of autonomy and freedom may well be too high. If the price is the type of society we see embodied in the most materialist and individualist sectors of the Western world, then perhaps the communitarian critics in both the Western and the non-Western worlds are right to try to change it or stop its emergence. But this is not an inevitable price. Community is possible in modern society. It is a community based on mobility, choice, and voluntary commitment to strangers rather than one based on stasis and involuntary commitment to family.

Notes

1. This section is a reconsideration of ideas I first aired in my "Dignity, Community and Human Rights," in Abdullahi Ahmed An-Na'im (ed.), *Human Rights in Cross-Cultural Perspectives: A Quest for Consensus* (Philadelphia: University of Pennsylvania Press, 1992), pp. 81–101.

2. Karl Mannheim, *Ideology and Utopia* (New York: Harcourt, Brace and World, 1936), p. 56.

3. United Nations, *Universal Declaration of Human Rights* (1948), Preamble, in Center for the Study of Human Rights, *Twenty-Four Human Rights Documents* (New York: Columbia University, 1992), p. 6, emphasis mine.

4. Orlando Patterson, *Slavery and Social Death: A Comparative Study* (Cambridge: Harvard University Press, 1982), p. 63.

5. On human rights in China in general, see James D. Seymour, "China," in Jack Donnelly and Rhoda E. Howard (eds.), *International Handbook of Human Rights* (New York: Greenwood Press, 1987), pp. 75–97. On the absence of the

value of individualism in China, see Barrington Moore Jr., *Privacy: Studies in Social and Cultural History* (Armonk, N.Y.: M. E. Sharpe, 1984), chapter 4.

6. Mathias G. Guenther, "Bushwomen: The Position of Women in San Society and Ideology," *Journal of Comparative Society and Religion*, vols. 10–11 (1983–1984), p. 18. For an idealized presentation of the Kung San, see Richard Lee and Richard Daly, "Man's Domination and Woman's Oppression: The Question of Origins," in Michael Kaufman (ed.), *Beyond Patriarchy: Essays by Men on Pleasure, Power and Change* (New York: Oxford University Press, 1987), pp. 33–37.

7. Adamantia Pollis and Peter Schwab, "Human Rights: A Western Construct with Limited Applicability," in Pollis and Schwab (eds.), *Human Rights: Cultural and Ideological Perspectives* (New York: Praeger, 1980), p. 8.

8. R. Panikkar, "Is the Notion of Human Rights a Western Concept?" *Interculture*, vol. 17, nos. 1–2 (January–June 1984), p. 36.

9. Patricia Begin, "Homelessness in Canada," *Current Issue Review* (Ottawa: Library of Parliament Research Branch), October 16, 1990, p. 2.

10. "Brown vs. Koch," *60 Minutes* (CBS Television), aired January 24 and June 12, 1988.

11. This argument is based on Rhoda E. Howard and Jack Donnelly, "Human Dignity, Human Rights, and Political Regimes," *American Political Science Review*, vol. 80, no. 3 (September 1986), pp. 801–817.

12. David L. Miller, "Justice," in David Miller (ed.), *Blackwell Encyclopedia of Political Thought* (Oxford: Basil Blackwell, 1987), p. 260.

13. Michael Walzer, *Spheres of Justice: A Defense of Pluralism and Equality* (New York: Basic Books, 1983), p. 313.

14. Susan Brownmiller, *Against Our Will: Men, Women and Rape* (New York: Bantam Books, 1975), p. 20; and Joseph Dahmus, *Dictionary of Medieval Civilization* (New York: Macmillan, 1984), p. 411, "Jus (Ius) primae noctis."

15. Michel Foucault, *Discipline and Punish: The Birth of the Prison* (New York: Vintage Books, 1979), p. 12.

16. Walzer, *Spheres of Justice*, 26. See also Susan Brownmiller, *Femininity* (New York: Fawcett Columbine, 1984), p. 86.

17. Panikkar, "Notion of Human Rights," p. 30.

18. George H. Mead, *Mind, Self and Society* (Chicago: University of Chicago Press, 1962 [1st ed. 1934]), pp. 173–178.

19. Herbert Blumer, "Symbolic Interactionism," in Randall Collins (ed.), *Three Sociological Traditions: Selected Readings* (New York: Oxford University Press, 1985), pp. 282–285.

20. Peter Berger, Brigitte Berger, and Hansfried Kellner, *The Homeless Mind: Modernization and Consciousness* (New York: Vintage Books, 1973), p. 86.

21. Khalid M. Ishaque, "Human Rights in Islamic Law," International Commission of Jurists, *The Review*, no. 12 (June 1947), p. 36; and Majid Khadduri, "Human Rights in Islam," *Annals of the American Academy of Political and Social Science*, vol. 243 (1946), p. 78.

22. Peter L. Berger, *Pyramids of Sacrifice: Political Ethics and Social Change* (New York: Anchor Books, 1976), p. 255.

23. On ordinary life in early-twentieth-century Spain, see the first volume of the autobiography of Arturo Barea, *The Forge* (London: Fontana, 1984 [1st ed. 1941]).

24. This section is a revised version of my "Group Versus Individual Identity in the African Debate on Human Rights," in Abdullahi Ahmed An-Na'im and Francis M. Deng (eds.), *Human Rights in Africa: Cross-Cultural Perspectives* (Washington, D.C.: The Brookings Institution, 1990), pp. 162–168.

25. Fasil Nahum, "African Contribution to Human Rights," paper presented at the Seminar on Law and Human Rights in Development, Gaborone, Botswana (May 24–28, 1982), p. 5.

26. Asmarom Legesse, "Human Rights in African Political Culture," in Kenneth W. Thompson (ed.), *The Moral Imperatives of Human Rights: A World Survey* (Washington, D.C.: University Press of America, 1980), p. 124.

27. Olusola Ojo, "Understanding Human Rights in Africa," in Jan Berting et al. (eds.), *Human Rights in a Pluralist World: Individuals and Collectivities* (Westport, Conn.: Meckler, 1990), p. 120.

28. Rhoda E. Howard, *Human Rights in Commonwealth Africa* (Totowa, N.J.: Rowman and Littlefield, 1986), pp. 27–33.

29. Legesse, "Human Rights," pp. 125–126.

30. Dunstan M. Wai, "Human Rights in Sub-Saharan Africa," in Adamantia Pollis and Peter Schwab (eds.), *Human Rights: Cultural and Ideological Perspec-tives* (New York: Praeger, 1980), p. 116.

31. Benoit Ngom, "Réflexions sur la Notion de Droits de l'Homme en Afrique," (Association des Jeunes Juristes Africains, 1981), pp. 5–6.

32. E.g., Nana Kusi Appea Busia Jr., "The Status of Human Rights in Pre-Colonial Africa: Implications for Contemporary Practices," in Eileen McCarthy-Arnolds, David R. Penna, and Debra Joy Cruz Sobrepena (eds.), *Africa, Human Rights, and the Global System: The Political Economy of Human Rights in a Changing World* (Westport, Conn.: Greenwood, 1994), pp. 225–250.

33. Ngom, "Réflexions," p. 8.

34. Elechi Amadi, *Ethics in Nigerian Culture* (London: Heinemann, 1982), chapters 7 and 11.

35. John Iliffe, *The African Poor: A History* (New York: Cambridge University Press, 1987), pp. 3, 7, 29, 34, 84.

36. Chris C. Mojekwu, "International Human Rights: The African Perspec-tive," in Jack. L. Nelson and Vera M. Green (eds.), *International Human Rights: Contemporary Issues* (Stanfordville, N.Y.: Human Rights Publishing Group, 1980), pp. 86, 93.

37. Terence Ranger, "The Invention of Tradition in Colonial Africa," in Eric Hobsbawm and Terence Ranger (eds.), *The Invention of Tradition* (New York: Cambridge University Press, 1983), 254.

38. World Bank, *World Development Report 1993: Investing in Health* (New York: Oxford University Press, 1993), table 31, "Urbanization," p. 298.

39. Joyce Olenja, "Gender and Agricultural Production in Samiya, Kenya," presentation to the Canadian Association of African Studies, Kingston, Ontario, May 12, 1988.

40. Abdullahi A. An-Na'im, "Religious Minorities Under Islamic Law and the Limits of Cultural Relativism," *Human Rights Quarterly*, vol. 9, no. 1 (February 1987), p. 3.

41. G. O. Olusanya, "African Charter on Human and People's Rights, History and Development," paper presented at the seminar marking the Centenary of the Legal Profession in Nigeria (Lagos: February 21, 1986), cited in Ojo, "Understanding Human Rights," p. 119.

42. Joseph Ki-Zerbo, "African Personality and the New African Society," in Wm. John Hanna (ed.), *Independent Black Africa: The Politics of Freedom* (Chicago: Rand McNally, 1964), p. 49.

43. For this argument, see also Busia, "Status of Human Rights in Pre-Colonial Africa."

44. Gerald Marzorati, "Rushdie in Hiding," *New York Times Magazine* (November 4, 1990), pp. 31–32.

45. Salman Rushdie, *The Satanic Verses* (New York: Viking Penguin, 1989).

46. Cyril Glasse, *The Concise Encyclopedia of Islam* (San Francisco: Harper and Row, 1989), p. 24.

47. Abdullahi Ahmed An-Na'im, *Toward an Islamic Reformation: Civil Liberties, Human Rights, and International Law* (Syracuse: Syracuse University Press, 1990), p. 183.

48. Ibid.

49. Patterson, *Slavery and Social Death*, pp. 227–228.

50. Quoted in Ishaque, "Human Rights in Islamic Law," p. 31.

51. Lee Holcombe, *Wives and Property: Reform of the Married Women's Property Law in Nineteenth Century England* (Toronto: University of Toronto Press, 1983), p. 229; and Dorothy Atkins, "Inheritance," in Sally Mitchell (ed.), *Victorian Britain: An Encyclopedia* (New York: Garland Publishing, 1988), pp. 396–397.

52. Khadduri, "Human Rights in Islam," p. 78.

53. Robert Hughes, *The Fatal Shore: The Epic of Australia's Founding* (New York: Alfred A. Knopf, 1987), p. 29.

54. An-Na'im, *Toward an Islamic Reformation*, p. 105.

55. Josef L. Altholz, "Roman Catholic Church," and Steven Bayme, "Jewry and Judaism," in Mitchell (ed.), *Victorian Britain*, pp. 674–676 and 411–413. See also Frank E. Huggett, "Catholic Emancipation," in his *A Dictionary of British History, 1815–1973* (Oxford: Basil Blackwell and Mott, 1974), p. 47.

56. Philippa Strum, "Women and the Politics of Religion in Israel," *Human Rights Quarterly*, vol. 11, no. 4 (November 1989), pp. 483–503.

57. Rosalind Pollack Petchesky, "Antiabortion, Antifeminism, and the Rise of the New Right," *Feminist Studies*, vol. 7, no. 2 (summer 1981), pp. 206–246.

58. There are numerous articles on this issue in *Index on Censorship*; e.g., Wadi Ismandar, "What Sort of Life Is This? [Syria]" vol. 16, no. 6 (June 1987), pp. 26–27; Moncef Marzouki, "Winning Freedom [Tunisia]," no. 1 (1989), p. 23; Sherif Hetata, "Censoring the Mind [Egypt]," no. 6 (1990), pp. 18–19; and Naheed Mousavi, "The Obscure Limits of Freedom [Iran]," no. 3 (1992), p. 18.

59. Bernard Lewis, "The Roots of Muslim Rage," *The Atlantic Monthly*, vol. 266, no. 3 (September 1990), p. 59.

60. Benjamin R. Barber, "Jihad vs. McWorld," *The Atlantic Monthly*, vol. 269, no. 3 (March 1992), pp. 53–63.

61. Quoted in Ann Elizabeth Mayer, "Current Muslim Thinking on Human Rights," in Abdullahi Ahmed An-Na'im and Francis M. Deng (eds.), *Human Rights in Africa: Cross-Cultural Perspectives* (Washington, D.C.: The Brookings Institution, 1990), p. 154.

62. Ahmad Farraq, "Human Rights and Liberties in Islam," in Berting et al. (eds.), *Human Rights in a Pluralist World*, p. 141.

63. Mayer, "Current Muslim Thinking," p. 138.

64. Ibid., p. 145.

65. Salman Rushdie, "Witch Hunt: Islam's War of Terror Against Secular Thought," *The Globe and Mail* (Toronto), July 17, 1993, p. D1.

66. Arab Organization for Human Rights, "Human Rights in the Arab World," *IFDA Dossier*, vol. 62 (November/December 1987), p. 64.

67. Farraq, "Human Rights and Liberties in Islam," p. 137.

68. Willem F. Heinemeijer, "Islam and the Ideals of the Enlightenment," in Berting et al. (eds.), *Human Rights in a Pluralist World*, pp. 146–147.

69. On Venda, see Philip van Niekerk, "New Victims of Ancient Fears," *The Globe and Mail* (Toronto), November 5, 1990, pp. A1 and A10; on Bihar, see Sherna Gandhy, "Crimes Against Women in India," *Philosophy and Social Action*, vol. 14, no. 4 (October–December 1988), p. 23.

70. Claudia Koonz, *Mothers in the Fatherland: Women, the Family, and Nazi Politics* (New York: St. Martin's Press, 1987), chapter 2.

71. Heinemeijer, "Islam and the Ideals of the Enlightenment," pp. 147–148.

72. Arab Organization for Human Rights, "Human Rights in the Arab World," p. 70.

5 The Modern Community

Two Views of Society

The primitivist nostalgia characteristic of relativist criticisms of human rights is part of a wider antimodernist nostalgia for community. This nostalgia permeates both Western and non-Western societies as well as much communitarian criticism of the selfish individualism and lack of obligation to community thought to be inherent in human rights.

Nostalgia for community is rooted in part in romantic perceptions of past societies. This romanticism ignores or disguises the many repressive and harmful effects of societies that reject individual human rights. Such nostalgic discourse pits the allegedly alienated individualism of late-twentieth-century capitalist society against the supposed security and personal rootedness of life in the collectivity. It ignores the liberating aspects of individualism and forgets that collectivities can be highly oppressive social entities.

Communitarians and individualists have radically different perspectives on the value of social life in the two types of societies. Tables 5.1 and 5.2 present these different perspectives in summary form. They are presented as ideal types, taking to their logical extreme the contradictions in the two perspectives; thus they are not meant to reflect either actual societies or any particular thinkers' views. I follow here Max Weber's practice of using ideal types to construct characteristic models of social behavior, without intending such ideal types to be seen as accurate descriptions of any living society.[1]

Table 5.1 presents the difference between communitarians and individualists from the perspective of the former, Table 5.2 from the per-

TABLE 5.1   Schematic Summary of the Communitarian View of Society

Communitarian Society	*Individualist Society*
1. Place in Society	
family/kin ties	no social ties
socially prescribed roles	normlessness/anomie
secure sex/age roles	androgyny/no respect for aged
social deviance punished	improper "lifestyle" choices
2. Belongingness	
tolerance within the group	tolerance of deviants
secure rules	confusion
rootedness in society	alienation
3. Social Stratification	
rank-based honor	disrespect of higher statuses
cooperation of all groups	anarchic competition among individuals
acceptable status distinctions	unpredictable class distinctions
social regulation	violation of status rules
4. Social Change	
cultural homogeneity	cultural heterogeneity
unchanging society	too much change
no social conflict	endemic social conflict
order	chaos

spective of the latter. Each table begins with a description of the individual's place in society; how her place is defined—or not—by set social roles. Roles can be set or flexible and influence how, or even whether, a person feels that she belongs in her society. Each perspective approaches social stratification from a different point of view, the communitarian favoring set statuses and the individualist favoring unpredictable achievement. Finally, each views social change differently: Communitarianism favors ordered, unchanging societies, whereas individualists consider change to be a sign of healthy progress.

Those who favor communitarian society value the fact that within it one's ties are prescribed by relations to family and kin. Within that network of ties, sex and age roles are carefully defined. Androgynous life choices that step over the boundaries of male and female roles are unheard of. Deviance, often even difference, is abhorred and punished. Communitarians worry that in individualist society androgyny is permitted and "lifestyle" choices, such as single motherhood or homosexuality, that offend the natural order of kinship and family are tolerated. In the communitarian perspective, individualists who reject family ties

TABLE 5.2   Schematic Summary of the Individualist View of Society

Communitarian Society	*Individualist Society*
1. Place in Society	
prescribed family/kin ties	chosen social networks
repressive traditional roles	choice of roles
set sex and age roles	liberating androgyny/no gerontocracy
deviance punished	"lifestyle" choices
2. Belongingness	
racial/ethnic exclusivism	tolerance of others
prescriptive social norms	autonomous sense of self
degradation and categorization	individual achievement
3. Social Stratification	
rank-based honor	earned respect
unhealthy social regulation	healthy competition
status-based dominance	no ascribed domination
status hierarchy	status equality
4. Social Change	
cultural compulsion	cultural choice
uniformity	diversity
repression	healthy conflict
stagnation	change/progress

have no other ones and consequently are victims of normlessness and anomie.

In the communitarian perspective, socially prescribed roles, freely fulfilled, result in rootedness in society. Such rootedness cannot exist for the alienated Western individual, who experiences the confusion of having to make autonomous choices about how to live her life. In communitarian society eccentricities and personal flaws are tolerated as long as social rules are obeyed. But individualist society exhibits a free-for-all tolerance of disruptive, anomic deviance that carries with it a disregard for the actual consequences of deviant acts. The individualist adrift in a sea of normlessness, casting about for new rules to regulate her life, is confused and alienated from society, while her communitarian counterpart is firmly rooted in her social group.

For communitarians, social stratification is a sensible allocation of roles. Although honor is based on rank, there is no shame attached to those who are slotted into lesser positions, as long as they fulfill their prescribed tasks with diligence. Status distinctions are acceptable and all status groups cooperate for the greater good of the whole community. In individualist society, by contrast, those inherently deserving of respect, such as the aged or priests or lawmakers, are frequently denied it. Ascribed status distinctions give way to unpredictable class distinctions arising from unregulated competition for wealth and prestige: The "fittest" dominate by ignoring their obligations to others. The social whole breaks down into anarchy. As such, neither respect nor economic security can be guaranteed even to those who dutifully fulfill their obligations to family, kin, and society.

In the communitarian view, the underlying glue that holds society together is its culture. The culture tends to be static and homogeneous; very little change is foreseen. One's primary identity comes from family or kin and then from larger social structures such as one's unchanging group—ethnic, religious, or national. There is no social conflict within this group; rather, everyone accepts the group's rules and roles. Implicitly, the communitarian view denigrates social deviance and the stepping outside of social roles that, for example, women's liberation and the black civil rights movement have fostered in the Western world. Instead, it is assumed that contentedness comes from fitting into the group. It is also assumed that members of such closed, corporate groups can and do live together in mutual tolerance when not rent by the selfish claims of individualistic deviants.

Thus individualism challenges the routine and valued orderliness of communitarian society. Upstarts abound, people abandon their social roles, honor disappears. Quiet community life gives way to normative and social chaos.

The individualist view of the antithesis between communitarian and individualist societies is quite different. It stresses the repressive, discriminatory features of the ideologized communitarian society. In the individualist view, prescribed family and kin ties are often repressive or, indeed, demeaning and violent, as in the case of patriarchal violence against women and children. The individual, therefore, ought to be free to choose other social networks that may be more important to her than family or kin. In individualist society no one is locked into traditional, prescribed social roles: Sex roles can be ignored and deviation from traditional ways of life is permitted. Lifestyle choices and the chance to establish an androgynous identity are liberating.

Individualists interpret the belongingness of closed social groups as encouraging racial or ethnic exclusivism, whereas a more open society encourages real tolerance of others whatever their racial, ethnic, or other ascriptive affiliations. In individualist society a person must form an autonomous sense of herself, which may or may not result in a conscious decision to obey the social norms prescribed by tradition. Individual achievement is celebrated, whereas categorization of people on the basis of nonautonomous ascriptive traits having nothing to do with personal achievement is viewed as degrading. Tolerance of others is positively valued, whereas in communitarian society intolerance of the outsider is the norm.

In the individualist world, respect must be earned: One is not entitled to it merely by virtue of one's rank. Status-based dominance is not permitted. Shame is just as much a characteristic of communitarian society as honor: Those who occupy lowly social positions suffer permanent dishonor. There are no hierarchies of status in the individualist world; indeed, there are no prescribed statuses at all. The unhealthy social regulation of traditional society is replaced by a healthy competition in which the best rise to the top solely on the basis of their own efforts. The social uniformity of communitarian society is repressive.

In individualist society culture is not homogeneous. Many different cultural strands interact as individuals choose those aspects of culture that they enjoy. There is no cultural compulsion, no set of customs and values to which one must adhere. Diversity makes society more interesting and social life more attractive, whereas uniformity stultifies the individual's capacity for achievement and self-expression.

Thus in the individualist view change is healthy. It permits the rise and fall of individuals as their capacities dictate, the choice and evolution of new communities and new ways of living, the end of all inherent status rankings. A society in flux is a society that is progressing. Communitarian societies, by contrast, stagnate.

These schematized ideal types do not represent real societies. Individualist societies contain many communitarian features. And as communitarian societies change, they approach the individualist model in culture as well as in politics and economics. Both in practice and in theory, we need to reconcile the communitarian and the individualist account of society. The communitarian account is too critical of the breakdown of community and tends to refer back to romanticized models, whereas the individualist account is too uncritical of the costs of individualism.

Modernity and Tradition

Communitarianism is frequently thought to characterize traditional societies, whereas individualism characterizes modern. Tradition and modernity, like communitarianism and individualism, tend to be overly dichotomized. Exaggerated ideal types are presented as reflections of historic or contemporary reality. In fact, tradition is constantly reinter-preted and re-created in response to social change. And modern soci-eties do contain communities.

The communitarian viewpoint interprets modern society as a grouping of unrelated individuals torn from their sense of collective identity. These individuals no longer follow traditional ways, which in-deed they frequently view as violations of their human rights. In modern society the hierarchy of age and wisdom gives way to a spurious equality of generations that disregards the value of experience. Order gives way to a hedonistic chaos that permits every individual to indulge the basest instincts of materialism and sensuality. Religions, customs, and rituals that once gave meaning to cohesive social wholes are lost in the rush for immediate sensory gratification.

In this picture of the world, the ideal of universal citizenship is a sham. The educated, aware citizen, the public person expounding her views in the democratic marketplace of ideas, is the person disconnected from valuable social groups that would give her opinions some validity. The public person in this view is also the person asserting individual hu-man rights against the community. Individual wants masquerade as hu-man rights. Society suffers so that individuals can attain not human needs, but human desires. What seems to be at stake is a human right not to have any obligations, not to have any duties to family or society as a whole. The individual in pursuit of human rights mocks the deeper values that hold all societies together. By rejecting tradition, the rights-seeking individual seeks to destroy the collectivity in her own short-term interest.

This bleak perspective on human rights misunderstands the nature of tradition and how traditions are retained, reinvented, and indeed sometimes created out of whole cloth as societies change. "Tradition" has a powerful hold on many people's psyches. It provides a sense of cul-tural identity and connection with history. When traditions do not exist or are not easily accessible, societies invent them in order to paint a pic-ture of themselves as coherent social units.

When I was a child growing up in southern Ontario in the 1950s, my mother, a nationalistic Highlander, attempted to imbue me with respect and nostalgia for Scottish folklore. I was regaled with stories of the valiant resistance of Bonnie Prince Charlie against the English in 1745. I thumped through Highland dancing classes in the basement of another Scottish immigrant's home; at one point I knew the steps to three ver-sions of the Highland fling and two of the sword-dance. My mother tried to interest me in the traditional tartans of the Highland clans and to per-suade me of my heroic origins as a wild, cattle-rustling McGregor.

Raised (unsuccessfully) on Scottish tradition, I was astounded a few years ago to learn its true origins. Scottish tradition is an invention;

more than that, it is a complete fabrication. The Scots created their tradition as a form of communal self-renewal after the English conquests. The Highland resisters against the English now so loved as exemplars of Scottish courage were in the eighteenth century considered by Scottish Lowlanders to be little short of barbarians. Only after the English conquest was a tradition of Highland Scottish culture and heroism invented, caused in part by "the romantic movement, the cult of the noble savage. . . . After 1746, when their distinct society crumbled so easily, [the Highlanders] combined the romance of a primitive people with the charm of an endangered species."[2]

To "resurrect" this concocted romantic heritage, an "indigenous" literature based on completely fabricated epic poetry was forged. The tartan kilt became a symbol of independent, robust Highland tribes uncowed by English conquest. Yet the kilt was actually a modern industrial invention. An English Quaker who had moved to Scotland to smelt iron ore designed it because his Highland workers kept catching their loose robes in his machinery. The kilt was "bestowed . . . on the Highlanders in order not to preserve their traditional way of life but to ease its transformation: to bring them out of the heather and into the factory." Even the clan tartans were an invention, this time of middle-class, anglicized Scots who wished to impress the King of England on his royal visit to Edinburgh in 1822. Each clan name was designated a tartan, and an enterprising Scottish firm was commissioned to make them up. Thus, Scotland witnessed "the reconstruction and extension, in ghostly and sartorial form, of that clan system whose reality had been destroyed after 1745."[3]

The Scottish invention of tradition is typical of the processes of creation and re-creation of community in which many societies engage. Tradition is valued as a representation of the way things were before conquest and change. Conquered societies create myths of community and of personal security and happiness and use these myths to strengthen the collective identity of their members.

It is possible to construct theoretically an ideal-type traditional society, which conforms both to the sociological perception of traditionality and to the conception championed by modern proponents of tradition. The sociologist Edward Shils suggested the typical substantive content of what is normally meant by tradition:

> The natural terrain of "genuine tradition" would appear . . . to lie in rule by hereditary chiefs and elders and in monarchy or oligarchy in contrast with liberal republics or democracies; in paganism and polytheism rather than in monotheism; in customary law rather than in legislation and systematic legal codes; in religious interpretations of the world rather than in secularized ones; in families, especially extended patriarchal families, in contrast with voluntary associations; and more gener-

ally in hierarchical authority rather than in widely dispersed authority; in refined and differentiated etiquette rather than free-and-easy treatment of persons; in inequality in contrast with equality.[4]

Within this idealized traditional society, every conforming person enjoys security and the comforts of belonging. It might be argued that most people prefer regulated, secure social roles, with their concomitant sense of belonging, to autonomy and its attendant insecurities. Liberal Western society is predicated upon individual self-reliance, insecurity, and competition. A person's innate sense of self-worth can be quickly undermined if she cannot support herself and has to turn to the collectivity for assistance.

In the twentieth-century Western world, the individual's life, with its multiplicity of unintegrated roles, is increasingly complex. The division of labor in a free-market economy is infinite; modern individuals can create new occupations and roles for themselves. In the course of a lifetime, an individual can change occupations several times, move from the status of employee to self-employed or unemployed, leave or return to the labor force. A computer operator may decide to become a home-based interior decorator, then enter teachers' college and eventually become a counsellor for troubled young people. The society the modern individual lives in is as complex as its division of labor. It is ethnically heterogeneous, stratified by class, and erosive of traditional status, age, and sex rankings.

In modern society the individual relies for social support less on her primary group and far more on secondary groups. Whereas primary groups are characterized by affective or kin ties that are presumed to be unchanging, secondary groups are characterized by commonalities of purpose that can change as individual members' views of their own self-interest change. New kinds of communities, formed by choice rather than by accident of birth, exist in modern environments. Even in the most supposedly alienating urban conglomerate, people form social networks, often based on modern characteristics such as education or profession. People choose their acquaintances from among fellow city-dwellers with whom, in traditional societies, they might never have had contact.[5] Among my family and friends, I know a Catholic who joined a Protestant choir and a Protestant teacher who became close friends with a Sikh parent. At the opera, I sit two seats down from a prominent Italian matriarch and next to an Egyptian Muslim colleague accompanied by his Coptic Christian wife. For several years, a Muslim has been a member of the board of my local Young Men's Christian Association.

Today these kinds of cross-ethnic or cross-religious associations and communities are so common in Western society that they are taken for granted. Human rights activists no longer try to persuade Westerners to be accepting of intermarriage or integrated neighborhoods; they take such acceptance for granted and focus instead on violations of the new norms of equality. Liberal Westerners who accept human rights ideals condemn expressions of antipathy toward individuals of different belief or ethnicity. But in so doing, they sometimes forget how new and modern are these societies in which marital patterns and social activities are not bounded by ethnicity and religion. As recently as the 1960s, interracial marriages in North America were rare and many people considered them shameful. Almost overnight, announcements of interracial marriages, for example between black sports stars and white women, are made without comment in the popular press. More and more children of increasingly complex and diverse heritage are being born. Many of these children are still subject to racist assaults, both verbally and physically. But only in a community with a principled commitment to equality and respect for all are they able to become citizens who can demand their rights against such assaults.

Ideal-type modern society, then, is radically different from ideal-type traditional society. And it threatens much of what traditionalists—both those who genuinely come from traditional societies and those who yearn for a return from modernity to a more traditional world—hold dear. The openness of modern society, its toleration of diverse beliefs and nonconforming social behavior, threatens many people's sense of order. "In the first half of the twentieth century animosity against modern civilization, which was a scientistic, rationalistic, individualistic, and hedonistic civilization, reached new heights; among the charges laid against bourgeois society was that it had 'uprooted' human beings from an order which gave meaning to existence. . . . Tradition was alleged to be a guarantor of order and of the quality of civilization."[6] This statement applies to the late twentieth century as well. Modern societies threaten many of the deepest and most ingrained of human values, even among people who have lived for generations away from their traditional "roots," of which they may be only vaguely aware.

Secularism is one strong threat against traditional order. In modern liberal societies religious tolerance is upheld as a key value. In Canada and the United States, no single religious doctrine is permitted in public schools; thus many parents find their children deprived of the fundamental teachings that they believe uphold the moral order. Worse, even heresy and atheism are permitted. By promoting secularism and removing religion from the schools, the state seems to have a deliberate policy of removing children from traditional values of respect for God, authority, and elders. The Muslim reaction to modernization is an outsider culture's analogue to the disturbance felt by many Christians in North

American society who witness their most fundamental moral values seemingly expelled from public discourse.

Urbanization also seems to threaten tradition, detaching people from their primary kin, clan, and village communities and removing them to heterogeneous, multi-ethnic, and culturally novel environments. Individuals frequently choose to go to the city, where there is more personal freedom than in small rural communities. But the choices urban environments offer include ones that many people perceive as entirely destructive of traditionalist values. In urban areas, subcultures of crime flourish. So do subcultures of sexual and social deviance. Homosexuals seek each other out; feminists renounce marriage and form groups that undermine family relations. For traditionalists fearful of modern social disintegration, the large city is the center of social deviance unrestrained by respect for others.

Nigerian popular culture encapsulates the traditionalist fear of the modern. In the consciousness of many Nigerians lies the following set of oppositions: "traditional/modern, rural/urban, common man/'big man,' poor/rich, uncorrupt/corrupt." Popular culture in Nigeria "sees excessive individualism as the main obstacle to national development. . . . Individual ambition is widely believed to be a legacy of colonialism and neo-colonialism, as traditional African societies stressed obligations to kin and community."[7]

Traditionalist reactions against modern society are understandable. The world of autonomous individualism is also the world of the market economy. People willing to work hard may find themselves without a job; entire communities can be destroyed at a moment's notice if one factory shuts down. When honest men cannot find work and decent women cannot provide secure homes for their families, their human rights to assert their individuality seem meaningless. There is no economic community and no way for most people buffeted by market forces to demand the economic rights formally written into international human rights codes.

Yet there is much that is good in modern society. Traditional village society is not the most secure place in which to live, as a classic study of modernization has shown.

> Anthropologists . . . anticipate that the introduction of urban-industrial institutions and patterns will lead, in most indigenous cultures, to massive social disorganization and to greatly intensified personal psychic stress. . . . [But]. . . the common assumption that more direct contact with the typical institutions of the modern world . . . [is] necessarily likely to induce psychic stress and nervous tension or other forms of personal disorientation [is debatable]. . . . This expectation rested on

one or both of two questionable assumptions: first, the belief that the village in traditional societies provides a highly secure, steady, calm, and supportive environment . . . and second, the idea that the pattern of a life in a modern setting would be inherently noxious to men coming out of a traditional setting.[8]

"No belief," stated Alex Inkeles and David Smith, "is more widespread among critics of industrialization than that it disrupts basic social ties, breaks down social controls, and therefore produces a train of personal disorientation, confusion, and uncertainty."[9] Yet in their study of 6,000 men in six developing countries (Argentina, Chile, India, Israel, Nigeria, and East Pakistan [Bangladesh]), Inkeles and Smith found just the opposite. The more modern men (defined as men in steady waged urban employment) felt more personally efficacious and less mentally distraught than their traditional rural counterparts.[10]

The supposedly secure village life can actually be a life of insecurity. Deviants are ostracized. Those who choose to disobey social norms are exiled. Marriages are contracted by parents on behalf of sometimes unwilling partners. A few elders control the lives of a great many other people. Custom and tradition provide security at the expense of individual expression of needs and desires and at the expense of individual creativity.

In the city, life can certainly be tough. Respect is not granted automatically, material conditions can be extremely poor, strangers are unconcerned about one's well-being. But the city also provides material and personal opportunities. In the Western world today, it is fashionable to deride wealth even as it is enjoyed and to concentrate on "personal growth" as a means of compensating for the impersonal isolation of parts of urban society. But such personal development is only possible in a society in which it is accepted that an individual may attempt to fulfill her own desires for community of a particular kind or for creative activities that are intrinsically satisfying. The obverse side of security is conformity; the obverse side of nonconformity is insecurity. Both are cultural characteristics of different kinds of societies.

The nonconformist, insecure society is relatively new and presents a threat not only to societies that retain traditional elements, but also to those members of modern societies who would prefer a return to the nostalgically evoked old ways. To many of those who favor retention of or return to closed traditional groups, human rights are not a laudable characteristic of democratic modernized societies but rather a pernicious cause of the breakdown of community. The order, predictability, and security of traditional society, even when mythological, seem far more attractive to many people than the disorder—the necessity to make choices and the possibility of uprootedness—of modern society.

Many people in the underdeveloped world today have experienced a very abrupt change from the peasant to the urban industrial way of life. The communal concept of dignity and social justice typifies the small-scale peasant worldview. Abrupt social change has replaced communalist, role-oriented notions of personhood with the values of secularism, personal privacy, and individualism.

The change from the peasant/traditional worldview to the urban, modern one is well recognized in sociological literature. In very broad terms it is the transition from what Durkheim called mechanically organized societies to those that are organically organized. Mechanically organized societies are based on homogeneity and a very simple division of labor, whereas organically organized ones are based on social heterogeneity and a very complex division of labor that ideally includes individual freedom of choice in occupation.[11] In mechanically organized societies everyone has a set role and knows her responsibilities, which tend to be unchanging over the generations. In organically organized societies individuals choose their roles, and the interaction of individual free choice produces a complex market of work and responsibilities that ties everyone together through economic interdependence.

Peasant society is usually viewed as a gemeinschaft, a thick or strong community. Modern society is a gesellschaft, a thinner or weaker community. In a gemeinschaft society social relations are a grid. All persons know and interact with each other over a variety of situations—market exchange, common worship, kinship, childrearing, recreational activities. In a gesellschaft society social relations are like spokes emanating from the individual in the center; the various ends of the spokes may have no connections with one another. One's relatives may never meet one's co-workers, co-worshippers, or sports teammates.

In Max Weber's terms, the change from the peasant to the modern worldview is a change from traditional to rational-legal forms of social organization; that is, from authority based on well-established social norms safeguarded by chiefs or judges, whose position is sanctioned by religious tradition, to authority based on formal rules administered by any individual, whose office (as opposed to her personal legitimacy) entitles her to do so.[12] In the vocabulary of Sir Henry Maine, the change can be summarized as a transition from a society based on status to one based on contract.[13] In a contract-based society choices can be made in all realms of social existence. You can freely contract a marriage rather than marry the partner chosen by your parents; you can contract to take a new type of job rather follow in your father's footsteps; you can contract to live somewhere that no one in your family has ever lived before. Your ascribed roles and statuses are no longer relevant in a contract-based society.

Defenders of the traditionalist ethic are concerned about the breakdown of ascribed statuses and the change to a society in which contract or choice is more prevalent. Human rights—the principle in part of individual freedom from ascribed social roles within the group—are seen as facilitating social breakdown. The very idea of choice, moreover, implies that a person has a frightening control over her destiny. She is responsible for her fate in a manner that is impossible in a closed, status-based peasant society.

Yet in this modern society of individuals who make autonomous choices of how to conduct their lives, community still exists. The basis of community, however, differs from the strong, kin-based connections of ideal-type traditional societies. Modern societies contain remnants of kin-based communities intermixed with communities based on neighborhood, work, or other kinds of secondary associations.

The Modern Community

Communitarians fear that individual human rights undermine collective obligation. This is a legitimate fear. Anomic individualism may well take hold if collective obligation to provide for the needs of all community members is not respected. In any society the principle of commitment to the community is necessary for the full realization of international human rights.

Protection of human rights does require a sense of community, but in modern society the community is an impersonal one, not one restricted to known members who have thick social connections with one another. The modern community is a community of obligation to strangers as well as friends. The citizen possessed of a sense of obligation to others does not confine that obligation to her family, kin, and clan. She joins community groups composed of people with whom she has little or no connections: She forms new associations designed to assist complete strangers. The modern citizen raises funds for victims of illnesses she may never have encountered; she builds battered women's shelters even though she may never have been battered; she helps refugees from places she has never visited find lawyers, housing, and schools. The community of private voluntary organizations that engage in activities conducive to public well-being is a strong antidote to anomie in modern democratic societies. Community life and a sense of obligation to others are a vital aspect of modern North American life, despite common misperceptions to the contrary.

Many commentators from the less-developed world decry the lack of religious commitment in North America. But in the 1980s a good 40 percent of Americans attended religious services weekly and 60 percent identified themselves as members of a religious community.[14] In 1981, 93 percent of Canadians claimed some religious affiliation, although in 1985 only about 30 percent of those with a stated religious affiliation attended religious services on a weekly basis.[15] Most North Americans turn to their religious communities for celebration of rites of passage (birth/baptism, adulthood ceremonies, marriage, and funerals) and religious holidays; many return to their religious communities when they have children or when they age. For many, commitment to the community arises from their religious belief. Churches in North America are the sites of myriad welfare activities, from day-care centers to programs to aid the elderly or indigent to overseas development organizations. Ecumenical organizations bring together members of different religious groupings to pressure governments for better social welfare programs or for more open refugee and immigration policies.

Commentators from the less-developed world also frequently decry the lack of commitment to the family that they believe characterizes North American society. There has never been a pervasive pattern of extended family living (either three-generational families or brothers and sisters living together) in North America, and this is something that traditionalist observers from other societies find strange.[16] Nevertheless most North Americans are strongly committed to the maintenance of family ties, even when families are dispersed over the continent. Relatives are endowed with "the deepest intensity and heaviest weight of all American personal relations," and surveys show that both rural and urban Americans maintain "high levels of contact with relatives living near and far."[17] A 1980 study of the town of Muncie, Indiana, showed that people tended to visit and talk with relatives who lived in the same town far more than with friends or neighbors.[18] Because the older generation lives longer, ties between grandparents and grandchildren are actually stronger than they were fifty years ago.[19] Although it is not the norm for North Americans to pool financial resources with their kin, most do consider it appropriate to offer financial aid when needed.[20]

Outside observers of North American society, as well as its internal communitarian critics, frequently confuse structural factors with social values. Infrequency of family contact in Western society is often the result of international and internal migration. Each year between 1985 and 1990, 18 percent of Canadians changed their residence. Although many of these moves were within the same community, others were to different parts of the province or country to seek more schooling or a better job (or any job at all). About 5 percent of Canadians who moved changed residence in order to be closer to their families.[21] With 16 percent of their population foreign born in 1986, many Canadians might also find themselves without any relatives at all in their own country.[22] Migration and job scarcity impel mobility, but they do not mean that Canadians value their families less than people living in societies where migration may be rarer.

Another common myth among traditionalist critics of modern Western society is that children are disregarded. In particular there is a myth that as soon as children are born, mothers abandon them to strangers in order to pursue a career in the workplace. But many North American mothers (and some fathers) are still the exclusive caretakers of preschool children. In 1981, 48 percent of preschool children in Canada were cared for exclusively by their parents in the home.[23] In 1984, 38 percent of those Canadian infants whose mothers worked full-time were cared for by relatives, whereas only 8.8 percent were in day-care centers cared for by strangers.[24] A corollary myth is that of the latch-key child, who returns with her key to an empty home after school. But in 1985 in Canada, only 2 percent of the school-aged children of mothers who worked full-time and 5 percent of the children of mothers who worked part-time were left alone at lunchtimes or after school.[25] Many of these were the children of mothers whose earnings were too low to enable them to hire alternate forms of care.

Mothers, in any case, do not abandon children to selfishly pursue their careers. Most working mothers do not have careers; they have jobs. A job does not promise individual fulfilment or the chance for promotion or social influence: It merely promises an income. Women work for pay in North America because they need the money for the basic necessities of life, just as do market women in Africa or female factory workers in Singapore. In recognition that most women are obliged to work for pay, North American society as a whole is beginning to adopt an attitude of collective responsibility for child care. Day-care centers, lunch and after-school programs for children of working parents, and inexpensive summer camps are all manifestations of the collective concern that children should be well cared for in healthy environments while their parents work.

Another misperception of North American society found among traditionalist critics is that "the aged grandparent is . . . thrown into a 'home for the aged' as in a refuse heap."[26] "Once someone's ability to work has gone . . . he is sent to an asylum or to an old folks' home to wait for death."[27] Nine percent of Canadians over the age of sixty-five resided in such homes in 1981.[28] Many of these residents were the "old old"— people over the age of eighty, mostly women. Either they were childless or their children, themselves elderly, could not care for them. In the United States, 4.6 percent of people over the age of sixty-five were in nursing homes in 1985; this included only 1.25 percent of people aged sixty-five to seventy-four but 22 percent of those eighty-five and older.[29] Most elderly people in North America either live in their own homes or are cared for by relatives.[30] The alleged disregard of the elderly in North America reflects demographic variables such as higher female workforce participation and increased longevity. Women working for wages cannot suddenly quit their jobs to care for elderly relatives who may live for ten or fifteen years after having become disabled. Nevertheless, many women do try to keep their relatives in their homes, even when also working for wages and raising children.

Nor does the comparatively high rate of divorce in North America necessarily reflect an ethic of individualist disregard for others. In part, the high divorce rate is a substitute for the earlier deaths of bygone days. In the late eighteenth century the average marriage in Europe lasted perhaps five to ten years, as one or the other spouse died.[31] Today, faced with unsatisfying marriages that can last twenty or thirty years after their children leave home, Western partners often choose divorce instead. Among younger families, women are less tolerant of abuse than previously; if they or their children are beaten, or their husbands refuse to contribute to family support, mothers may well choose divorce. Women's liberation does mean less female commitment to the family than in other societies, but it does not mean that anomic selfishness has taken over from concern for children's welfare. Indeed, women's lesser commitment to abusive husbands can be seen as evidence of greater commitment to their children.

These changes in family structures and attachments do not mean that a sense of community does not exist in the Western world. They mean rather that, detached from the kin and clan structures that characterized village life in earlier times, community seems invisible while, in fact, it is often thriving. North Americans are indeed a private people; they value both the physical defenses of family privacy, such as strictly defined property borders, and the customs that require social distance among those living close together. "'Love thy neighbor'—but don't pull down the fence" is the quintessential U.S. attitude to living among non-kin.[32] But North Americans frequently construct and maintain community through voluntary social relations with others who are neither kin nor neighbors.

In the modern world the homogeneity of closed, restricted social groups has broken down. The individual does not live, work, and worship with the same people, as she might have done in a small village a hundred years ago. "Today no two people share the same social space at all times of the day or week, and no one person is familiar with all the social spaces the other person occupies during the day."[33] Urbanism, associated in the traditionalist myth with frightening deviance and high crime rates, permits the evolution of myriad different selves, myriad individuals each with her particular identity. As Iris Young noted, "For many people deemed deviant in the closeness of the face-to-face community in which they lived, whether 'independent' women or socialists or gay men and lesbians, the city has offered a welcome anonymity and some measure of freedom." Young suggests that we use "our positive experience of city life to form a vision of the good society."[34] Rather than reject modern urban life, we should recognize not only its personally liberating aspects, but also its capacity to build community amidst social diversity.

Community in North America today is characterized, stated Constance Perin, by "a local system of family, political party, and social club."[35] To this one can add the communities of neighborhoods, schools, and professional contacts. "Kinship relations, for the majority of the population, remain important, especially within the nuclear family, but they are no longer the carriers of intensively organised social ties across time-space."[36] Social relations are no longer as dense as they once were; the individual's various kin, friends, and acquaintances cannot be expected to know one another.[37] But what is lost in density of social relations is replaced by complexity. In the urban societies much lamented by traditionalists, various subcultures are formed. In cities, you can choose your friends. You can reinforce or weaken your commitment to your church; you can visit the cousins you like but not the ones whose politics drive you crazy; or, as in Becker's classic study of urban subcultures, you can hang out with other musicians.[38]

Although in modern urban societies density of social relations is replaced by breadth and choice of relations, the implication for the individual is not necessarily personal confusion or alienation. Rather, the implication is often a blossoming of personality and the capacity for far more intellectual reflection than is possible in a traditional society with constricted social roles. The modern individual is capable of much more personal autonomy than the traditional: She can evaluate her own life and her own social relations and make changes if she sees fit. The complexity of her social relations reflects the complexity of her social roles; for example as mother, church volunteer, political organizer, teacher, old college friend, lover, and daughter.

The necessity to interact with various types of people in various social situations also permits the modern individual to think through her attitude to self, kin, and stranger. Strangers are no longer undifferentiated Others: They are varieties of people with varieties of attractive or unattractive features. Some ethno-religious strangers may exert strong pulls for friendship and connection, despite their outward difference. Fewer strangers automatically repel. The modern individual, with a heightened capacity for empathy, has learned to look beyond the obvious classificatory characteristics that mark strangers to deeper attributes of character and attitude. Social relations among modern individuals are marked by complexity of choices and affections.

The plurality of social relations that characterizes modern society is, as Coser stated, a source of enrichment, not alienation.[39] Middle-aged people in North America are reputed, for example, to be unhappy, overburdened by work and responsibilities to both their children and their aged parents. But in fact, the better-off middle aged benefit from precisely the social complexity that popular opinion frequently associates with alienation. "The middle-aged tend to be guided . . . by slowly dawning adaptive insights into the self and others."[40] The variety of their life experiences permits reflection, autonomy, and adjustment.

The modern person experiencing a variety of social roles is capable of an empathy with others that is not available to the traditional person.[41] This empathy modifies what critics often perceive as the selfish individualism of modern society. Although the prevalent social ethic in the United States among the culturally dominant white middle class is indeed individualism, this individualism takes a number of forms. In the United States, according to Robert Bellah et al., both what they name the "Biblical" and what they name the "republican" traditions are individualistic cultural strains that nevertheless stress obligation to others. The Biblical tradition draws obligation to others from Christian teachings, whereas the republican stresses the obligations of the citizen to society.[42]

Traditional conceptions of religion and morality, then, are still important motivations for community obligation even in the most advanced capitalist society. But a secular notion of citizenship, rooted in the egalitarianism of liberal society, is also a powerful impetus for modern individuals to exercise their obligation to the community as a whole. Modernity, claimed Anthony Giddens, implies "the institutionalisation of doubt."[43] But doubt does not necessarily imply insecurity and confused withdrawal from society. Doubt means reflexivity, the capacity to analyze the preconceptions given to you by your family or your school. Doubt also means the capacity to reject previous strictures on social relations and instead open yourself up to the wider community of diverse strangers.

It has frequently been noted that the United States is a nation of joiners and that many people enroll in voluntary organizations dedicated to the improvement of the welfare of their own community or of the wider public.[44] In Canada in 1986–1987, 27 percent of the population over the age of 14 engaged in formal volunteer work in more than 80,000 nonprofit organizations.[45] Such participation indicates the modern citizen's capacity for empathetic action. That participation in voluntary organizations is by choice rather than by ascriptive social role does not lessen the sense of obligation to the community that is entailed. In studying modern North America, then, we find that the "traditional" values of family, church, and community are not abandoned in the race for individualism and pursuit of happiness. Aside from participation in formal voluntary organizations, nearly half of the adult population in Canada in 1987 reported informal assistance to "someone in their own social network." Another 16 percent helped strangers. "Sixty percent of informal volunteers . . . helped seniors; 40 percent helped children and 21 percent helped disabled persons."[46]

This picture of modernity is at odds with the picture of the homeless mind, the allegedly anomic state of modern social life. In their classic statement on the homeless mind, Peter Berger, Brigitte Berger, and Hansfried Kellner painted a picture of modern man living in a fragmented, alienating social environment. With his life divided into unrelated component parts and his work and private lives completely separated, modern man is plagued by lack of wholeness. He is anonymous, trapped in a series of unrelated social interactions, and treated at work more as a component part of a machine than as a human being. In the plurality of social worlds that he inhabits he is ever marginal and unintegrated; he has lost his sense of place and belonging. Modern man suffers a permanent identity crisis.[47]

This description of the homeless mind is profoundly overdrawn. In the modern world man (and woman) is not cast into a vast competitive social void. The takeover of daily life by time schedules and the need for profit does not mean that pleasure in work relations and productive capacities entirely disappears.[48] In modern society some people do intensely dislike their work. But that is also true of many workers in so-called traditional societies. Work in traditional societies is not the holistic interaction of man with environment that many romantics dream of: Much of it is backbreaking labor, the daily drudgery of digging and fetching and carrying of water.

Modernity can, in fact, aid in the fulfilment of traditional obligations. In underdeveloped countries, wealthier urban townsmen, such as the factory workers that Inkeles and Smith studied, can send money home to support their kin, give cheerfully to their elders, and donate funds to sustain religious rituals.[49] Just as adults in capitalist North America invest their time and resources to sustain family connections and build a sense of community, so do adults in the developing world who find themselves with the new resources of cash and education. "The men who were classified by us as more modern were less rather than more prone to believe that possessions insure personal happiness; they were about as likely as the more traditional to urge that old people be treated with respect and consideration; they were as much inclined as anyone else to give support to a relative in need. . . . The more modern men were less alienated, anomic, and hostile to other groups in their society. . . . Neither individual modernity nor greater contact with modernizing institutions leads to greater maladjustment."[50]

In modern Third World societies as in modern North America, community is sustained even as traditional modes of life disappear. Individuals who seek urban opportunities and freedom do not necessarily discard their obligations at the same time: Indeed, their sense of obligation may be strengthened as they find themselves with hitherto unobtainable resources. The belief that modernity implies an inevitable anomic individualism thus is based on misperceptions of social values and customs not only in Western societies, but also in modernizing societies elsewhere.

The concept of human rights is individualistic; it does reflect the rise of secular, urban, and industrialized society. But secularism, urbanization, and industrialization do not harm all they affect; rather, they result in new conceptions of how to order society, which many individuals find deeply satisfying and liberating. Communities can be re-created and sustained in modern society, but in a way that is not as thick and strong as in traditional society. Modern communities do not offer the secure identity of the tribe or the peasant village. The individual in a modern community must make choices of how to live or with whom to associate. Physically removed from her kin, she must make a conscious effort to keep in contact with and support them. She must learn to live with strangers and to regard them as fellow human beings, worthy of as much concern and respect as the many cousins who inhabit her ancestral village. She must replace the strong bonds of blood with the weaker bonds of common citizenship.

Modern Community and the Extension of Human Rights

The difference between the traditional and the modern community is not one of commitment: It is one of membership. The modern community is a community of citizens. Anyone is permitted to be a member, regardless of gender, race, ethnicity, or place of origin. Although it might seem to a traditional observer that members of the modern community exhibit low commitment to their families, that is balanced by a high commitment to nonfamily members. The privatism of one's personal life is balanced by social commitment and interest in the wide networks of non-kin associates with whom one's own life is bound up.

Another difference between the traditional and the modern community is the value placed on individual self-expression. To be respected as a member of the modern community, professions of loyalty are not required. The deviant or the critic is as entitled to protection of her human rights as the conformist and the patriot. Although community is strongly valued in modern society as in traditional society, community needs are not permitted to supersede individual rights. The individual is permitted to claim her human rights against the society at large. The principle of human rights protects individuals against abuses by the collectivity.

The modern community is spreading as the processes of social change usually called Westernization spread. At the same time, the modern idea of the individual separate from her society is spreading. As a result, almost everywhere there are now people who think of themselves and define themselves as individuals—and who objectively are individuals. The individual is a social creation. In times and cultures past there have been societies in which to use the term "individual" would have been anachronistic, but all countries are now significantly modernized. All now contain significant populations of people who think about themselves and their social conditions in individualistic terms. These people want and demand their individual human rights.

The more abusive the process of modernization, the more relevant human rights are. There has been a revolution of moral expectations the world over. Individuals in less-developed parts of the world now expect to be not only wealthier, but also freer. There is now an international community of modern men and women who are increasingly capable, no matter how poor or oppressed they are, of recognizing when their human rights are violated. Human rights are a social fact not only in the Western world, but also internationally.

Modernization appears to be an unavoidable social phenomenon. It is difficult for any society to resist the impact of an international division of labor, of world information flows, of the social model of individuation and freedom. As the world converges into one, ideals of human rights affect the otherwise quiescent underclasses of many societies. Modernization brings openness, opportunity, the merit principle. It permits individuals to leave repressive families and closed communities, and to challenge the authority of established elders.

There are many social movements, many social groups, and indeed many states that attempt to resist modernization. Elders in underdeveloped societies whose authority younger people now resist are happy to join with established antiliberals in Western society to challenge the new social changes. Conservatism and traditionalism join in an antimodern reaction. They are helped along in this challenge by the left reaction against modernity as neocolonialism, a reaction that interprets all social change as a nefarious plot against subordinate groups of people.

The human rights movement, by contrast, accepts modernization as a social fact. The human rights of individuals are meant to protect what is good in modernized societies while ameliorating what is bad. Principles of economic, social, and cultural rights aim to restore those aspects of collective responsibility that existed in many traditional societies and are loosened in modern societies while assuring that the benefits of freedom and political participation are not erased.

Human rights do not necessarily favor one mode of life over another. Although individual human rights do presuppose the right of any person to remove herself from family or community controls and to "reject generally accepted morality," the existence of human rights in themselves does not impel such rejection.[51] The protection of human rights does not presume that everyone is merely an atomized individual, without connections to family, kin, ethnic group, or nation. Rather, human rights are designed to protect from the depredations of the state those families and groups in which individuals choose to define themselves (either unconsciously or consciously). Individuals who, alone or as part of larger entities, claim the right to protection of their family, to speak their own language, practice their own religion, or to educate their children in their own cultural milieu are claiming rights for their communities. Human rights do not imply family or group disintegration. A belief in the protection of the individual against the state makes no moral presumptions about the kind of life worth living, either individualistic or family or group-oriented.

Nevertheless, in the final analysis individual human rights do guarantee the primacy of the individual over the group, thus undermining in theory and frequently in practice the organizing principles of traditional society. However much one might value in private life the social connections and continuity provided by family and community memberships, this primacy cannot be avoided. It is a necessary primacy, if one acknowledges that social groups as well as states can oppress and degrade individuals. To many individuals, tradition and custom are oppressive. Modernity implies that individuals will break away from traditions. Although they will not necessarily abjure their social responsibilities and their attachment to religion, they will become less tolerant of authority and restriction.

In their research on men becoming modern, Inkeles and Smith found precisely the attitude change I describe.

Some of the men and women tied by the binding obligations of powerful extended kinship systems have sought to assert their rights as individuals. Some have tried to win more freedom of choice in residence, occupation, political affiliation, religious denomination, marriage partner, friend and enemy. They have sought to replace a closed world, in which their lives tread the narrowest of circles, with a more open system offering more alternatives and less predestination. . . . In place of fear of strangers and hostility to those very different from themselves, some have acquired more trust and more tolerance of human diversity. From rigidity and close-mindedness, they have moved toward flexibility and cognitive openness. They now seek to break out of passivity, fatalism, and the subordination of self to an immutable and inscrutable higher order, in order to become more active and effective, and to take charge of their individual lives and of their collective destiny.[52]

Without benefit of exposure to ideologies of democracy, without benefit of study of Enlightenment social thought, modernity provided for these men an open door to a freer and more autonomous sense of self. This self insisted on more individual decision-making and less reliance on authority. It is an easy step from such a new attitude of individual self-reliance to a belief that one's human rights ought to be protected.

The underdeveloped world is experiencing very rapid social change that is creating the new kind of man (and woman) that Inkeles and Smith studied. Especially in times of economic recession, such rapid social change can be very frightening. It often results in attempted returns to—often, in fact, newfound adoption of—conservative, closed, and circumscribed ideologies of social behavior based on membership in certain religious or ethnic groups. Religious fundamentalism, whether Hindu, Muslim, Christian, or Jewish, attracts many people confused by cultural complexity and freedom. The persecution of deviants who challenge established social norms, such as homosexuals or feminists, has the same sociological effect. These deviants, invoking their individual human rights, do threaten some traditional social relationships. Even in societies where human rights seem most entrenched, there can be strong public reactions against their actual protection.

The purpose of human rights is above all to protect people, individually or in groups, against the state. But it is also to protect people against other groups or, if necessary, against their own social group.

Individuals are and always will be products and members of their own societies. But social change in the modern world implies removal of many individuals from the restrictive social roles of the past. Mobility, freedom, and the complexity of modern life permit deviance and difference.

Yet human rights do not mean that everyone must be individualistic and self-seeking. Nor do they mean complete acceptance of all that is, or is perceived to be, "Western"; that is, individualist and antithetical to communitarian values. In this chapter we saw that the modern Western world is much more community-oriented and much less individualistic than many of its critics imagine. The social perception of a world run amok with individualism ignores the new community based on common citizenship and commitment to the well-being of comparative strangers.

At the same time, though, the modern community does not provide everyone with her rights. Western communities still do not include every individual on equal terms. Deviance, difference, and rejection of traditional roles still make many people insecure: Traditional conceptions of status honor still provide more secure guides to social life for some people than the modern rejection of all status differences. Above all, social class remains a determinant of how effectively one can exercise individual rights. The existence of community described in this chapter does not obviate the social problems described in the two that immediately follow.

Notes

1. Max Weber, *The Protestant Ethic and the Spirit of Capitalism* (New York: Charles Scribner's Sons, 1958), pp. 71, 98, 200 (n.25).

2. Hugh Trevor-Roper, "The Invention of Tradition: The Highland Tradition of Scotland," in Eric Hobsbawm and Terence Ranger (eds.), *The Invention of Tradition* (London: Cambridge University Press, 1983), p. 25.

3. Ibid., pp. 22 and 31.

4. Edward Shils, *Tradition* (Chicago: University of Chicago Press, 1981), pp. 17–18.

5. Claude S. Fischer, *To Dwell Among Friends: Personal Networks in Town and City* (Chicago: University of Chicago Press, 1982).

6. Shils, *Tradition*, p. 19.

7. Harriet D. Lyons, "Television in Contemporary Urban Life: Benin City, Nigeria," *Visual Anthropology*, vol. 3 (1990), p. 421.

8. Alex Inkeles and David H. Smith, *Becoming Modern: Individual Change in Six Developing Countries* (Cambridge: Harvard University Press, 1974), pp. 12–13.

9. Ibid., p. 261.

10. Ibid., pp. 6 and 290.

11. Emile Durkheim, *The Division of Labor in Society* (New York: The Free Press, 1933).

12. Max Weber, *The Theory of Social and Economic Organization*, Talcott Parsons (ed.) (New York: The Free Press, 1964), pp. 324–358.

13. Sir Henry Maine, "The Early History of Contract," in his *Ancient Law* (London: J. M. Dent and Sons, 1977 [1st ed. 1917]), p. 100.

14. Robert N. Bellah, Richard Madsen, William M. Sullivan, Ann Swidler, and Steven M. Tipton, *Habits of the Heart: Individualism and Commitment in American Life* (New York: Harper and Row, 1985), p. 219.

15. Craig McKie and Keith Thompson (eds.), *Canadian Social Trends* (Toronto: Thompson Educational Publishing, 1990), pp. 29 and 31.

16. Constance Perin, *Belonging in America: Reading Between the Lines* (Madison: University of Wisconsin Press, 1988), p. 38.

17. Ibid., pp. 28 and 39.

18. Ibid., p. 39. The Muncie, Indiana, study cited in Perin is reported in Theodore Caplow, Howard M. Bahr, Bruce A. Chadwick, Reuben Hill, and Margaret Holmes Williamson, *Middletown Families: Fifty Years of Change and Continuity* (Minneapolis: University of Minnesota Press, 1982).

19. Stephanie Coontz, *The Way We Never Were: American Families and the Nostalgia Trap* (New York: Basic Books, 1992), p. 15.

20. Perin, *Belonging in America*, p. 43.

21. Janet Che-Alford, "Canadians on the Move," *Canadian Social Trends* [Statistics Canada], vol. 25 (summer 1992), p. 32.

22. McKie and Thompson, *Canadian Social Trends*, p. 8.

23. Laura Johnson and Norma McCormick, *Daycare in Canada: A Background Paper* (Ottawa: Canadian Advisory Council on the Status of Women, 1984), pp. 26–27.

24. Status of Women, Canada, *Report of the Task Force on Day Care* (Ottawa: Ministry of Supply and Services, 1986), pp. 51–52.

25. Ibid., p. 56.

26. Fasil Nahum, "African Contribution to Human Rights," paper presented at the Seminar on Law and Human Rights in Development, Gaborone, Botswana (May 24–28, 1982), p. 3.

27. Isaac Nguema (Head of the African Commission on Human and Peoples' Rights, 1989–1990), "Universality and Specificity in Human Rights in Africa," *The Courier* (1989), p. 17.

28. Second Canadian Conference on Aging, October 24–27, 1983, *Fact Book on Aging in Canada* (Ottawa: Ministry of Supply and Services Canada, 1983), pp. 68–70.

29. *National Nursing Home Survey 1985: Summary for the United States* (Washington, D.C.: U.S. Department of Health and Human Services, 1989), p. 23.

30. Gordon E. Priest, "Living Arrangements of Canada's 'Older Elderly' Population," *Canadian Social Trends* [Statistics Canada], vol. 21 (autumn 1988), pp. 26–30.

31. Edward Shorter, *The Making of the Modern Family* (New York: Basic Books, 1977), p. 26.

32. Perin, *Belonging in America*, p. 26.

33. Rose Laub Coser, *In Defense of Modernity: Role Complexity and Individual Autonomy* (Stanford, Calif.: Stanford University Press, 1991), p. 17.

34. Iris Marion Young, "The Ideal of Community and the Politics of Difference," in Linda Nicholson (ed.), *Feminism/Postmodernism* (New York: Routledge, 1990). Quotations from p. 317.

35. Perin, *Belonging in America*, p. 8.

36. Anthony Giddens, *The Consequences of Modernity* (Stanford, Calif.: Stanford University Press, 1990), p. 108.

37. Fischer, *To Dwell Among Friends*, p. 258.

38. Howard S. Becker, *Outsiders: Studies in the Sociology of Deviance* (New York: The Free Press, 1963).

39. Coser, *In Defense of Modernity*, p. 21.

40. Winifred Gallagher, "Midlife Myths," *The Atlantic Monthly*, vol. 271, no. 5 (May 1993), p. 53.

41. Coser, *In Defense of Modernity*, p. 67.

42. Bellah et al., *Habits of the Heart*, pp. 333 and 335.

43. Giddens, *The Consequences of Modernity*, p. 176.

44. Bellah et al., *Habits of the Heart*, p. 167.

45. Doreen Duchesne, "Giving Freely: Volunteers in Canada," Statistics Canada, Labour Analytical Report no. 4 (August 1989), p. 11. See also James J. Rice, "Volunteering to Build a Stronger Community," *Perception* [Canadian Council on Social Development], vol. 14, no. 4 (autumn 1990), p. 11.

46. Rice, "Volunteering," p. 10.

47. Peter Berger, Brigitte Berger, and Hansfried Kellner, *The Homeless Mind: Modernization and Consciousness* (New York: Vintage Books, 1973).

48. Coser, *In Defense of Modernity*.

49. Inkeles and Smith, *Becoming Modern*, pp. 26–29.

50. Ibid., p. 296.

51. The quotation is from Olusola Ojo and Amadu Sessay, "The O.A.U. and Human Rights: Prospects for the 1980s and Beyond," *Human Rights Quarterly*, vol. 8, no. 1 (February 1986), p. 99.

52. Inkeles and Smith, *Becoming Modern*, pp. 4–5.

6 Honor and Shame

The Status Radical Critique

In Chapter 5 I argue that the modern community is a complex place that provides opportunities for all categories of people within the framework of respect for one another's rights. This picture is profoundly at odds with the critique of modern North American society offered by status radicals. They argue almost the opposite of what I contend, asserting that certain people's inferior social statuses completely determine their life chances in modern liberal society. Liberalism, they argue, is a cover for continued male and white domination. The ideal of individual autonomy, based as it is on a firm foundation of nondiscrimination, is fundamentally flawed. Even when laws protect equality of opportunity in the marketplace, the underlying mental tendencies of misogyny and racism deprive women and blacks (and other minorities) of the respect that is automatically tendered to males and to whites. Thus, status radicals believe, the entire framework of liberal individualism should be abandoned.

It is certainly true that modern liberalism does not provide equality of opportunity for all, nor does liberal society easily integrate everyone into its embrace. In modern Western society distinctions of caste have been rendered unclear and disreputable by the ideologies of equality and individual autonomy. Nevertheless, stratificatory practices based on unacknowledged notions of honor and shame persist and result in the continued partial exclusion of shameful Others. Women and blacks in North America continue to bear socially shameful characteristics, even as the formal rules—and increasingly the actual practice—of late-twen-

135

tieth-century society permit them far more opportunity for independence and social mobility than they have had before.

The status radical critique deserves serious attention. Their critique does point to a fundamental and seemingly ineradicable principle of inequality in Western liberal society: Large categories of people in North America seem to be systematically treated with disrespect. Third World critics also notice this disrespect, especially when it applies to people of color like themselves. It is particularly hard on men from the Third World who occupy high status at home to arrive on North American shores to be treated disrespectfully, as just another black taxi driver or busboy. Traditionalist critics will also notice that women are not honored in North America as they should be for their statuses as mothers, elders, or dutiful daughters or sisters; in fact, the latter two roles are given hardly a moment's thought in mainstream North American society.

In this chapter I analyze the persistent social bases of discrimination against women and blacks in North America as a form of dishonor. The formal liberal principle of achievement commands such respect in modern society that the underlying persistence of caste and status-based stratification is not acknowledged. Blacks in North America are descended from a slave caste. Their skin color endows them with an Otherness that keeps them apart from the central stream of achievement: They occupy, as it were, a parallel stream in which some achievement is permitted but that flows awkwardly into the larger river. Women also occupy a parallel achievement stream, enclosed as they are by their sexual status. Although the tendencies to lock women and blacks into caste-like statuses are lessening considerably in late-twentieth-century North America, they have certainly not disappeared.

Unlike blacks, women are sometimes honored if they fulfill their traditional roles well—although in the late twentieth century many women experience the confusion of simultaneously being honored as mothers by traditionalists and being degraded for their traditional status by some feminists. Blacks do not have an honored role: The very basis of their incorporation into North American society was as a dishonored social category originally fit only for enslavement.

In his discussion of social stratification, Max Weber focused on status as well as class. His analysis of status is central to understanding why liberal capitalist society, based as it is on ideals of nondiscrimination, universality, and achievement, continues to exclude large categories of people from equal participation. High status implies respect, prestige, and honor; low status disrespect, denigration, and dishonor. "We wish to designate as 'status situation' every typical component of the life fate of men that is determined by a specific, positive or negative, social estimation of *honor*. . . . Status honor is normally expressed by the fact that above all else a specific *style of life* can be expected. . . . Linked with this expectation are restrictions on 'social' intercourse. . . . Stratification by status goes hand in hand with a monopolization of ideal and material goods or opportunities."[1]

Stratification by status applies, particularly in modern Western societies, to groups that, in asserting their human rights, violate notions of social honor. Women's style of life is still expected by some reactionary conservatives and traditionalists to be one that is noncompetitive, confined to the private family sphere and removed from the public sphere of economic participation and political citizenship. Blacks' style of life is still expected, by some racists, to be confined to the margins of white society, to a deferential integration into modern economic and political life only upon invitation by the honored whites.

Honor, Shame, and Degradation

The psychologist Ervin Staub argued that most societies have a deep culture, a set of values that is a result of beliefs, customs, and historical conditions that may be centuries old. Such a deep culture includes "shared evaluation of their group, myths that transmit the self-concept and ideal self, goals that a people set for themselves, and shared beliefs (e.g., about other groups). It may also include or mask uncertainties, insecurities and anxieties." "Human beings," Staub believed, "have a tendency to divide the world into 'us' and 'them.'" They prefer what is familiar and respond with hostility to the unfamiliar. "The human mind works by categorization."[2]

Us-them distinctions, according to Staub, help the human race to create social groups. They also encourage a tendency to fear the Other, anyone who seems different. Cultural attitudes are reflected in individual propensities to openness to others and in propensities to assist, ignore, or indeed persecute others in distress. Thus a people's deep culture may include attitudes of superiority or inferiority to others, of hostility or openness to strangers. The deep culture will affect a society's willingness to afford social membership to perceived strangers, as well as its capacity to accept deviant or new forms of behavior in times of social change. Even in highly modernized societies the deep culture is likely to contain aspects of mistrust and suspicion of outsiders.

The notion of deep culture contradicts the cultural malleability that I argue is central to the capacity of societies to adjust to changing social conditions. It suggests that the cultural principle of egalitarianism that is characteristic of modern human rights–oriented society is but a flimsy camouflage for deeper tendencies to categorize everyone into us or them, self or Other. In times of stress the deep culture surfaces to replace the thin patina of liberal egalitarianism. Traditional societies based on caste and status are truer exemplars of human nature than the egalitarian, individualist societies that human rights require. The moral order of most societies is one that reinforces status categorization and severely punishes deviance; the communitarian vision of ordered society discussed in Chapter 5 is a more realistic reflection of how human beings conduct their lives than the individualist vision. The status radicals' pessimistic conviction that liberal society cannot overcome deeply rooted social categorizations is correct.

Staub's vision of a deep culture, bleak though it is, may be a truer reflection of the capacity of societies to integrate Others as equals than the idealism of the UN Universal Declaration of Human Rights. In many nonliberal societies (and among many members of liberal-democratic polities), there are and have been very deeply rooted notions of moral order that obviate the belief in that human equality and autonomy that I maintain are key to a society that protects human rights. In such societies religious and communal norms frequently entrench social inequalities that are considered immutable and reflective of the natural world.

The anthropologist Mary Douglas had a similar approach to what might be called deep culture. Human society, said Douglas, seeks orderly categorization as a means of easing the discomfort and danger of actual, unpredictable life. This includes the orderly categorization of human beings. Anomaly and ambiguity are generally shunned: In the marginal interstices between orderly categories danger lies. "Most of us . . . feel safer if our experience . . . [is] hard-set and fixed in form. . . . The yearning for rigidity is in us all. It is part of our human condition to long for hard lines and clear concepts."[3]

Douglas's viewpoint is confirmed by many anthropological studies of the way primitive societies order their world. The ordering of society reflects the ordering of the natural world: Social order guards against the possibility of cosmological chaos. The natural is ordered and hierarchical, not egalitarian and anarchically individualist. Men are identified with the sun, women with the moon; men with the right hand, women with the left; men with cleanliness, women with dirt.[4] In categorizing human beings in this way primitive societies attempt to imitate and control the natural world at whose mercy they survive. To impose order on the human world is, by analogy, to impose order on the unpredictable forces of nature; to guard against flood, earthquakes, eclipses, and other frightening phenomena. The status inequalities of human beings reflect notions of cosmological rectitude; violations of inequality, therefore, undermine not only the human order, but also the natural order of things.

Human order, then, requires categorization. To respect these categories, even if they imply a low status for oneself, is to respect society's moral code. The rules of social intercourse are inviolable: One's duty is to adhere to the rules peculiar to one's station. The respected person is he who calmly and willingly accepts his role, no matter how lowly it may be.[5] The person who asserts his rights against socially acknowledged superiors is dishonored. Even unwitting dishonor deserves shame and punishment. "Death before dishonor," for example, is still the prevailing view of rape in societies in which a woman's purity is her greatest symbolic attribute.

In modern society the idea of honor as a source of status and power is almost forgotten. Yet there are honor-based societies. "Timocracy" is an unfamiliar word meaning rule by those with the most honor; it was coined by Orlando Patterson to describe the world of slaveowner and slave. Patterson proposed that slave societies are based on different degrees of honor rather than different degrees of wealth or military prowess. Slaveowners accumulate slaves to increase their own following, hence their own honor: They may have no material use for them. In slave societies the owner's honor depended upon the slaves' dishonor.[6]

Patterson declared that to be a slave is to suffer three essential elements: namely, natal alienation, dishonor, and domination. "Slavery is the permanent, violent domination of natally alienated and generally dishonored persons."[7] First, slaves are persons who are removed from— alienated from—their own natal kin. Lacking family ties in societies in which kin and lineage completely define identity, they are nonpersons, nonhuman. Second, slaves are utterly without personal honor. They are not accorded the respect that other human beings are deemed to merit simply by being part of the community. The final characteristic of slavery, domination, is self-evident. Slaveowners held the right of physical chastisement, sometimes even the right to kill, over their slaves.

The condition of blacks in North America is in part a consequence of the dishonor brought upon their ancestors through enslavement. Alienated from all natal kin, not considered to be members of the master's family (even when they were the master's biological child), and subject to arbitrary physical force, slaves could not assert their human dignity. In North America, there is a tendency to connect this disrespect solely to the skin color of people formerly occupying the status of slave. Certainly skin color contributes to the dishonor, connected as "black" is to darkness, dirt, and evil. But in societies where slaves share skin color with their masters, the slaves are often made to wear distinguishing marks or clothing that will set them apart.[8] The dishonor thus precedes the distinction rather than being consequent upon it. In order to ensure that free strangers unfamiliar with the slave's status do not accidentally accord him undeserved honor, distinguishing marks are introduced.

Slave-based societies are but one example of timocracy. Aspects of timocracy permeate North American society but are submerged and unrecognized. Westerners recognize the phenomenon of *timor* (honor) in analyzing other societies such as Hindu India. They understand that in these societies status is something different from mere wealth or achievement and that people "irrationally" value status and honor even though they have no "real" (monetary) value. Yet honor is still sought and acknowledged even in radically egalitarian North America, even though the vocabulary of honor and shame has been abandoned and even though individuals do not use such terms to describe their feelings of superiority or inferiority.

Social dishonor creates social dirt. The dishonored group is considered to be dirty and polluted, whereas the honored group is pure. Dirt is the most important symbol of inferiority. As Douglas noted, "Reflection on dirt involves reflection on the relation of order to disorder, being to non-being, form to formlessness, life to death. . . . Certain moral values are upheld and certain social rules defined by beliefs in dangerous contagion."[9] "Cleanliness is next to Godliness" is a saying of the Western world. But certain groups are held to be inherently dirty, incapable of cleanliness. In contemporary North America, as in many other cultures, women are still affected by myths about their polluting natures; they are polluting by virtue of their biologies, the messiness attendant upon menstruation and childbirth. "Not only is their sexuality read as a sign of social disorder: To women's body products are attributed bizarre and mysterious powers of pollution and contamination."[10]

Both women and blacks are assigned society's dirty work because they are already polluted, yet performing dirty work further pollutes and shames them. Women perform private dirty work such as diapering children and taking care of incontinent adults. Men distance themselves from these household responsibilities and thus can maintain a greater semblance of purity. Men's domination of women, claimed Constance Perin, may well be "an epiphenomenon of their physical and social dissociation from the activities and relationships that are signs of dishonor and animalistic disgrace."[11] Like women, blacks are often designated to perform the public dirty work that whites eschew. Dirty work such as collecting garbage, cleaning toilets, or taking care of the sewage system is a problem in any society. Public dirt requires a distinct caste of people to be responsible for it. It is always seen as polluting; no matter how much those who perform the labor earn, they are still viewed as dishonorable status inferiors. Those who deal with dirt are declared degraded; those who are already degraded are assigned the dirty work.

Social degradation, then, is a phenomenon that we find in most societies, even the most egalitarian. While some are honored, others are shamed. Underneath the liberal norms of equality, autonomy, and respect are deeper norms of inequality, control, and dishonor. The status radical critique of modern liberal society focuses on this dishonor, especially as it is manifested in misogyny and racism.

In North America, being female or black is still a master status; it is the most important defining status most women or African-Americans have.[12] Whatever other statuses one may occupy, these two are always highly visible and remarked upon. To some North Americans, they are still signs of dishonor. To bear the mark of a dishonored person is to bear a constant, ineradicable stigma. Persons occupying these low statuses are expected to exhibit shame in their overall demeanor. Blacks in the United States were long expected to lower their eyes when a white person talked to them; women who give bold open glances to strange men on the street are still taken to be loose.

The easiest and clearest social distinction is between men and women. As the English and French languages reflect, the male is the standard of humanness and the female is the deviation. As Simone de Beauvoir put it in her classic feminist meditation, identity, existence, is defined by the male; the female is the antithesis who affirms the male thesis. "Man represents both the positive and the neutral, as is indicated by the common use of *man* to designate human beings in general; whereas woman represents only the negative. . . . A man is in the right in being a man; it is the woman who is in the wrong. . . . He is the Subject, he is the Absolute—she is the Other."[13]

Women are the original degraded social category, and such degradation is almost universal. In some simple hunting-gathering or agricultural societies, women's status seems to more closely approach that of men than it does in the contemporary Western world. But in most societies, including all state societies and all with monotheistic religions, women are seen as inferior to and as owing obedience to men.[14] Patriarchal control over the females of the family (mothers, wives, sisters, daughters, and female slaves) was encoded by law as one of the earliest forms of property.[15] The ideological degradation of women often extends to dislike or even hatred. Such dislike goes by the general name of misogyny. Misogyny often degenerates into outright violence against women, especially exemplified in rape.

The almost universal subordination of women as a group to men as a group is not an automatic outcome of the ease of categorizing obvious biological differences. The process of degradation coincides with the discovery of the myriad ways in which women's reproductive capacities and their capacity to work can be exploited for the material benefit of men. The ideological and material underpinnings of this subordination are thus deeply enmeshed, so that even in societies in which human rights are a politically salient social ideal, there are men who hesitate to extend rights to women. Even in contemporary North America, there are still some men whose feelings of self-worth derive to a significant extent from separating themselves from women and feeling superior to them. Until the feminist movement brought it to light, misogyny was a hidden undercurrent of modern society.

Racism is a better-known term than misogyny, reflecting an earlier process of self-analysis on the part of the white Western elite. Racism does not parallel misogyny in all its characteristics. To those whites (or Chinese, or Indians) who are racists, blacks are Others, the nonhuman or less-than-human, in a way that women cannot be. Blacks can be kept apart, but misogynists must live with the very women they despise. The close proximity of the two sexes breeds relations of personal dependency that members of different races can avoid.

Blacks in North America represent a caste category: former slaves. The general processes of categorization, dishonor, and dominance can be found in all caste societies. Caste-based societies are those in which individuals occupy fixed social ranks ascribed to them at birth. Caste is characterized by endogamy (marriage within the group) and by a distinct style of life.[16] Contact with people of a lower caste is considered to be polluting, "making for a ritualistic impurity . . . [or] a stigma."[17] Caste rankings can be both more comforting and more humiliating than the class stratification by wealth and income that characterizes contemporary Western society. On the one hand, caste is more comforting because it is not under the individual's control; it is societally fixed and one is not personally responsible for one's place in it. On the other hand, caste is more humiliating than a mobile class system because no matter what one does, one cannot escape the caste. Even when there are possibilities for individual social mobility based on achievement, as in contemporary North America, caste position is forever evident. In caste society lower-caste individuals earn respect by graciously accepting their demeaned status, not by trying to transcend its boundaries. They imply their agreement with societal rankings by their self-effacing demeanor and deference to higher-ranked categories. Some North American whites still expect this deferential behavior from blacks and are offended when they do not encounter it.

The caste nature of the subordination of North American blacks is hidden by the ideology that they are simply victims of anomalous racism in a society that decries caste in favor of class competition. Blacks are socially defined in North America as all people of full or partial African (Negroid) origin. The "partial" African origin is included because such origin, with its phenotypical characteristics, constitutes a master status. To be black is an immediately visible characteristic that defines and modifies any other characteristic a person may have. As Gunnar Myrdal put it many years ago, "The definition of the 'Negro race' is thus a social and conventional, not a biological concept. The social definition and not the biological facts actually determines the status of an individual and his place in interracial relations."[18] Blackness is a social category, an inherent master status overriding perceived differences among individuals. As former New York City mayor David Dinkins put it, "A white man with a million dollars is a millionaire, and a black man with a million dollars is a nigger with a million dollars."[19] For many middle-class blacks in the United States, their master status results in what Ellis Cose called "coping fatigue," the constant tension of conformity to white middle-class norms, of trying daily—indeed hourly—to overcome the inherent stigma of having dark skin.[20]

There is a certain similarity in the stereotypes of women and blacks, one that some people in North America still cling to. Both are dirty—blacks because of their skin color and women because of their bodily processes. Both are children, accorded the status of perpetual minors or wards, but they are children of two different types. The stereotyped woman is emotional and incapable of reason, as is the stereotyped black. But whereas the woman weeps, the black becomes dangerously angry. Both are spontaneous, the woman in a charming manner that entertains her husband after a hard day in the cold, rational world; the black in a way that renders it necessary to subject him to harsh discipline.

Both women and blacks are stereotyped as sexually insatiable. But for a woman to be sexually aggressive was, until recently, considered unnatural; a "good" white woman was insatiable yet passive. Blacks, on the other hand, are stereotyped as sexually aggressive and dangerous. Cornel West, the African-American philosopher, argued that "Americans are obsessed with sex and fearful of black sexuality. . . . [Blacks'] fearful sexual activities are deemed disgusting, dirty, or funky and considered less acceptable [than white sexuality]."[21] The punishment for black men who rape white women has always been severe, in part because of the myth that a white man will never be able to satisfy a white women who has had sexual relations with a black man. In these stereotypes the black represents the darker side of orderly moral society.

South Africa represents in extremis the cultural racism of the Western world. In the mid-1980s, American anthropologist Vincent Crapanzano lived in a small, predominantly Afrikaner village pseudonymously named Wyndal, where he studied his white neighbors. At best, blacks in Wyndal were invisible and irrelevant. At worst, Crapanzano's neighbors found them frightening and defiling. "Any situation in which bodily contact between members of different races is possible . . . ha[s] been precluded. Bodily contact is considered polluting." Blacks in Wyndal were seen as highly sexual: They "reproduce like rabbits." They were "barbarians, uncivilized, raw" as one woman told Crapanzano. In short, the village of Wyndal presented in raw form the racial stereotyping now considered impolite and backward in proper Western society. To quote Crapanzano once again: "Wyndal is riven by classification. . . . 'Race' and 'ethnicity' are not negotiable categories . . . but essential ones. . . . Such classifications . . . describe one's essential being."[22]

The deep cultural roots of white racism, then, are fear of pollution and evil. Such fears are also at the root of misogyny. Misogyny and racism have in common the attempt to inculcate in the victims a sense of the rightness of social ordering and a sense of their own disorderly and dishonorable essence. The degradation of persons occupying statuses of social dirt enhances the feelings of cleanliness and moral superiority of those who occupy superior status categories. These social phenomena still affect social order even in liberal rights-protective societies.

Shame and Self-Mutilation

The practice of dishonor is difficult to verify. It is almost completely hidden in North America.[23] The vocabulary of honor does not exist; people's everyday conversations do not refer to whether individuals act in honorable or dishonorable ways, whether lower-status people properly defer to those of higher status. Pollsters do not ask which are the most honored social groups. Yet the social ideology of status, and the belief that certain status groups deserve to be dishonored, is still a very important part of the North American heritage. One way to measure this is through people's sense of physical shame, the mortification they feel as a result of their own bodily characteristics. Women and blacks in North

American society today demonstrate a tragic discomfort with their own bodies. Their sense of shame is enforced by self-mutilatory practices that are designed to change their physical appearances.

I define "self-mutilation" as a self-imposed change in one's physical makeup or a way of adorning or clothing one's body that has detrimental health consequences. Self-mutilation is an active form of shame. Degraded social groups inflict violence upon themselves, attempting to deny their very identities by changing their physical appearances. In so doing, they act out their intense self-hatred, their belief that they actually deserve the disrespect they suffer.

Sociologist Edwin Schur seriously addressed the idea of women as deviant and stigmatized, what I call dishonored. Women, he stated, are routinely objectified and degraded: "In our society being treated as deviant has been a standard feature of life as a female. . . . Social stigmatization must be recognized as a key mechanism that backs up and 'enforces' many of the restrictions and limitations placed on women. . . . [The devaluation of women results in] induced female preoccupation with physical appearance; concern about ascribed deficiencies and continuous efforts to conform to 'appearance norms.'"[24] There is something wrong with and unclean about the physical makeup of women from the moment they are born. Ashamed of their own bodies, women have devised complicated means of effacing themselves by acknowledging their physical inadequacies. In ashamed reaction against their inferiority women physically mutilate themselves. Even though women have become more economically and politically liberated during the past three decades, they remain victims of the ideology of their own physical unworthiness. Many women in North America despise their own bodies and invest enormous amounts of time, energy, and money attempting to reshape themselves, cleanse themselves, and diminish their bodily size.[25]

Women in North America are subject to dual role pressures. They must continue to fulfill their traditional roles as wives and mothers and must also compete with men in the capitalist marketplace. Yet as they succeed in the marketplace they must simultaneously deride their own accomplishments and demonstrate continued acceptance of their dishonored social status. The soft-spoken, manipulative verbal techniques that Rosabeth Moss Kantor discovered women used in the business world in the 1970s, in order not to challenge their male colleagues, are still expected of many women in the 1990s.[26] Many women "know" that despite their new formal equality they are still inferior people. One way that they indicate this to themselves and to others is through continuous mutilatory activities that have severe health costs.

The Cinderella myth is very powerful in Western culture. In this myth a beautiful, virtuous girl marries a prince after she manages to fit her foot into a tiny glass slipper, which her wicked stepsisters could not squeeze into. The myth is believed to have originated in Asia; its earliest known version is from China.[27] Prerevolutionary Chinese practiced footbinding. The feet of infant females were very tightly bound together, toes to heels, to prevent their growth. This process was extremely painful and dangerous, causing infections, swellings, and deformed bones. But a tiny foot was a sign of high status. A woman with bound feet could not walk and could not work; her feet were thus a living and suffering embodiment of the wealth of the man whose daughter, wife, or concubine she was.

The Cinderella myth—the myth that the beautiful, good woman has small feet—is so ubiquitous and influential in North America that millions of women still routinely stuff their feet into shoes too narrow for them. Susan Brownmiller believed that tight, high-heeled shoes are a sexual fetish among many men: "The impractical shoe . . . induces helplessness and dependence . . . the smaller steps and tentative, insecure tread suggest daintiness, modesty and refinement. . . . The overall hobbling effect is suggestive of the restraining leg irons and ankle chains endured by captive animals, prisoners and slaves who were also festooned with decorative symbols of their bondage."[28] In contemporary North America, this particular form of bondage is declining as a result of both the fitness movement and the women's liberation movement. One frequently sees women walking to work in sensible running shoes. But they discard these sensible shoes for confining high heels when they arrive at the office. Symbolically then, high heels, like the short tight skirts that are part of much business apparel, continue to confine the very women whose elevated occupations are supposed to be a sign of their liberation in the modern world. Even for such high-status women, the "display" aspect of their jobs is important: Through their outward appearance they display both their femininity and their subordination to men.[29]

In North America, mothers teach their daughters the overriding importance of being slim and attractive. Enormous industries exist by which women assist each other to alter their shape or weight or looks. These include tanning clinics, clinics to remove excess hair, and weight-loss clinics patronized to a large extent by healthy, non-obese women. These self-mutilatory "clinics" are successful in their use of medicalized language because smoothing, reshaping, and reducing one's body are considered to be a health measure, essential to women's psychological well-being. Women are so convinced that their bodies are shameful, dirty, and degrading that mutilation for purposes of self-esteem is considered to be mutilation for health purposes.

Incessant cyclical dieting is a danger to health that is accepted as a normal female activity in North America. Anorexia nervosa (self-starvation) and bulimia (periodic binging on food followed by self-induced vomiting) increased dramatically in the 1980s. Dieting and anorexia are not discrete patterns; they are part of the same continuum. As Janet Polivy and Peter Herman argued, dieting is a "normal" eating pattern that some women with particular psychiatric problems take to the extremes of anorexia and bulimia. By the mid-1980s, dieting was more prevalent among young American women and adolescent girls than not dieting.[30] At that time between one in 800 and one in 100 females in the United States aged twelve to eighteen was anorexic: The mortality rate of anorexia was estimated to be between 5 and 18 percent.[31] In 1992, it was estimated that in the developed countries anorexia nervosa affected at least one in a thousand women aged thirteen to twenty-five, peaking at one in 200 among girls from fifteen to eighteen.[32] The actual death rate, however, is quite low: In 1988, there were sixty-seven deaths, in 1991, fifty-four, from anorexia nervosa in the United States.[33]

An "implicit rejection of oneself . . . is involved in the decision to diet (i.e., to seek to become someone other than who one is)."[34] Yet perhaps surprisingly, this desire coincides with a general loosening of women's social roles and a widening of their opportunities. Schur suggested that smallness is a physical symbol of women's acceptance of their lesser status in society: By contrast, men's greater physical size is "a symbol of 'social weight' (power, authority, prestige, etc.)."[35] An alternative explanation of the contemporary weight-loss obsession is that, in a world of uncertain social roles and a new multiplicity of role choices, women turn to control over their own bodies as the only certainty in their lives.

Self-mutilation, then, is a violent process imposed by women upon themselves. Women diminish themselves, both physically and psychologically, to fit the subordinate role imposed upon them, as they also undergo costly and repetitive cleansing rituals meant to control their polluting qualities. In an inversion of what dignity ought to mean in a liberal society, women's social honor demands acceptance of their subordination. Despite striking progress in achieving legal, economic, and political equality for women during the last thirty years, the timocratic stratification of the two sexes is still deeply rooted in the cultural psyche of North America. The recently implemented political and legal equality of the two sexes threatens the social honor of males and impels women to reassure men by intensifying their own symbolic acceptance of their proper, degraded social status.

Women are not the only status category to internalize their subordination so completely that they resort to self-mutilation. Other social groups also try to disguise degraded physical characteristics. Schur's comment about women applies equally to subordinated ethnic and racial groups: "The individual who has consistently been treated as inferior—and who also has been denied the opportunities to develop and demonstrate the capacities that would disprove this—may even come to see himself or herself as inferior. . . . Systematic devaluation implies a strong likelihood of impaired self-esteem."[36] This impaired self-esteem will be found in literal hatred of one's own physical characteristics.

In my first-year English class at McGill University in 1965 there was a striking young Jewish woman. After our freshman year she disappeared. During my senior year a student with the same name and personality became prominent on campus. It was the same young woman, with her hooked nose bobbed. I simply did not recognize her because she had changed her "Jewish" features so markedly to affect the prevailing pert-nosed ideal of the time. This tendency to self-denigration among Jews declined in the 1970s and 1980s. When the singer Barbra Streisand became a star in the 1960s and did not have a nose job, she undoubtedly helped liberate many Jewish women from their feelings of physical unworthiness.

Self-hatred among Jews in Europe before World War II was a consequence of the racist society in which they lived. "Self-hatred results from outsiders' acceptance of the mirage of themselves generated by their reference group—that group in society which they see as defining them—as a reality."[37] Jews accepted the image of themselves given them by Christians. They tried to change their looks in order to become like the Christians who despised them. But changing one's looks backfires, because one's very essence is the Other. "As one approaches the norms set by the reference group, the approbation of the group recedes. In one's own eyes, one becomes identical with the definition of acceptability, and yet one is still not accepted. For the ideal state is never to have been the Other, a state that cannot be achieved."[38] Changing one's looks merely indicates to the dominant group that one is trying to sneak in to its domain by disguising one's true nature of dirt and evil.

Referring to blacks, Jews, and homosexuals, Barry Adam stated that despite differences in the stereotypes of each group, "The common portrait retains the role of *foil* to ideals of health and the good."[39] Historically in European culture Jews and blacks were both animals. Both were hypersexual and connected to witchcraft. Jews raped

Christian virgins and castrated Christian boys; blacks were enormously overendowed and incapable of controlling their libidinous drive. Both were overvisible, "'loud,' pushy, aggressive, careless, extroverted." Both were ugly, "the black man as gorilla, the Jew as vulture."[40]

In the past, accepting white denigration of blackness and all its concomitant characteristics, blacks in the United States and elsewhere frequently affected whiteness. As the writer James Baldwin remembered: "One's hair was always being attacked with hard brushes and combs and Vaseline: it was shameful to have 'nappy' hair. One's legs and arms and face were always being greased, so that one would not look 'ashy' in the wintertime. One was always being mercilessly scrubbed and polished, as though in the hope that a stain could thus be washed away."[41]

Franz Fanon wrote extensively of the shame many blacks felt about their skin color. By "acting white," claimed Fanon, blacks attempted to eradicate or draw attention away from this naturally degrading physical attribute. One way was to try to actually become white. Fanon claimed, "For several years certain laboratories have been trying to produce a serum for 'denegrification' . . . that might make it possible for the miserable Negro to whiten himself." Even if Fanon's story is apocryphal, it demonstrates how defiling the "negroes" felt their skin color to be and how they desperately searched for a cure. As Fanon noted, "The Jew is disliked from the moment he is tracked down. But in my case . . . I am given no chance. . . . I am the slave . . . of my own appearance." The black has not even the possibility of hiding, of adopting an anonymous face in public intercourse.[42]

A recent biography of an African-American woman highlights the shame of dark skin. Born in 1914, Margaret Morgan Lawrence was the first African-American woman to graduate from Columbia University Medical School. Lawrence early absorbed racist stereotypes about the inferiority of her skin color. While she was growing up in Vicksburg, Mississippi, her parents were warned to be careful in public because her mother was so light-skinned that she might be taken for a white woman consorting with a black man. But it was not only the external world that judged Lawrence and her family by race. Because they had absorbed both the practical social meaning and the psychological shame of a dark skin, her family's internal relations were also much affected by differences in color. Her mother's family was very proud of its light skin and criticized her darker-skinned father. In return, when her parents quarrelled, "I would hear my father walking down the hall, talking out loud, 'Confound it, you white bitch.'"[43]

Nor is black self-hatred a thing of the past in North America, despite contemporary pride in African heritage. It is a phenomenon that still preoccupies African-American intellectuals. Feminist author bell hooks recounted the story of a little girl just beginning to be ashamed of her looks. "Her skin is dark. Her hair chemically straightened. Not only is she fundamentally convinced that straightened hair is more beautiful than curly, kinky, natural hair, she believes that lighter skin makes one more worthy, more valuable in the eyes of others."[44]

Cornel West connected black self-hatred explicitly to white denigration of black sexuality and white terrorizing of blacks: "Much of black self-hatred and self-contempt has to do with the refusal of many black Americans to love their own black bodies. . . . White supremacist ideology is based first and foremost on the degradation of black bodies in order to control them. One of the best ways to instill fear in people is to terrorize them. Yet this fear is best sustained by convincing them that their bodies are ugly, their intellect is inherently underdeveloped, their culture is less civilized."[45]

Self-mutilatory practices document the shame and stigma that dishonored people feel—even in supposedly egalitarian societies. "On the face of it," stated Zygmunt Bauman, "the liberal message sounds a death knell to stigma, as it saps the strongest of its foundations: the ascriptive nature of inferiority." Yet as strangers "go out of their way to suppress everything that makes them distinct," they discover that "the harder they try . . . the more the finishing line seems to be receding."[46] The liberal promise seems farcical in societies where life chances still depend so much on statuses connected irrevocably to biology.

When ethnic or racial minorities resort to cosmetic restructuring and recoloring of their own physiques, they are mutilating themselves in a symbolic if not in a medical manner. Like women on diets, they force their bodies to conform to externally generated standards of bodily beauty. In so doing, they humiliate themselves. They live in constant unease with, and distress about, their physical selves. Every confrontation with the physical self, whether a deliberate look in the mirror or an accidental glimpse in a store window, is a condemnation of their very essence. This unending daily humiliation reinforces the sense that they are degraded beings, unworthy of respect. If one feels unworthy of respect, then one is more likely to tolerate social terror that is aimed at reinforcing one's degraded status.

Social Terror

State terror is now a familiar concept in the literature on human rights. Terrorist states use violence not only to control their known opponents, but also as a form of warning to any other potential dissidents. States terrorize and torture wives, children, relatives, and friends of individuals they consider a threat to their rule.[47]

Social terror is also a common practice. Social terror consists of acts of violence perpetrated by members of an honored status category against members of a dishonored. Such terror not only frightens the actual victim, but also warns other members of the shamed status category to modify their behavior. Even if the state and the judiciary officially punish social terror, the acts of violence may enjoy social approval among some members of the population. Socially approved acts of violence by members of honored status categories against members of dishonored categories reinforce deeply held social norms. Social terror counteracts the formal liberalism and equality of Western democratic societies and ensures that honored groups maintain status privileges.

When formerly dishonored groups within a society challenge the status honor of those to whom they are expected to defer, the timocratic sense of social identity suffers. In order to maintain their power timocrats react with violence or coercion, just as plutocrats or aristocrats would. Not only the honored, but also members of the dishonored groups socialized to accept their society's culture may find challenges to rules of social honor a real threat to their identity. Those who obey the rules may wish as strongly as do the timocrats to punish those who disobey.

The function of punishment, as Durkheim made clear, is confirmation of social norms; thus punishment is an important part of any society's moral order.[48] The concept of humanity that declares physical punishment to be wrong is legalistic, liberal, and modern. What modern Westerners might consider cruel acts of punishment are in many societies considered socially valuable because they reaffirm group norms or rid the society of deviant individuals. The being who violates the moral universe is corrected by having his physical universe violated in turn. Submission of the body to social punishment indicates conformity of the mind; acceptance, that is, of the social order and one's place in it. In modern liberal societies some degraded individuals voluntarily submit their bodies to punishment: They embody their shame in self-mutilation. Other degraded individuals who do not accept their shame are subjected to social terror. Such direct violence reinforces the low status of degraded social groups, especially when some members step out of line and assert their rights to equality. This occurs even when the formal power, the state, officially condemns and punishes such violence.

Social terror is terror practiced by private citizens against degraded status groups. Unlike state terror, social terror is not generally acknowledged as a means of degradation and coercion. The idea that societies could be organized in such a way as to socially approve terror against distinct categories of people goes against the liberal grain. Yet women and blacks in modern North America are two groups still subject to sporadic social terror.

Violence against women has only recently become an international human rights issue and been brought to the attention of international human rights scholars and lawyers.[49] There is no mention of violence against women in the 1979 Convention on the Elimination of All Forms of Discrimination Against Women.[50] After much feminist pressure, violence against women was finally condemned by the 1993 Vienna Declaration of the UN World Conference on Human Rights.[51] By contrast, the international human rights world and Western society in general have long acknowledged the problem of violence against blacks (for example, in the UN convention against racial discrimination).[52] There is an international consensus against this form of terror. Racist violence is abhorred; yet social terror against women is still considered by many people to be merely a matter of individual criminal acts rather than a social phenomenon affecting women as a group.

Violence is the property not only of the state, but also of socially superior categories of people. In societies that overtly value status honor, judicious use of violence by timocratic elites in defense of central social norms is socially approved. In egalitarian societies, officially criminal acts perpetrated by individual rapists or lynchers serve to reinforce underlying social norms of honor and shame.

Rape, wife-beating, and wife-murder are the chief weapons of gendered social terror. These officially condemned acts serve to terrorize women into staying in the places and roles approved for them. As women become more equal to men in familial, economic, and political relations, some men are tempted to use violence to put them in their place. Officially condemned but still existent timocratic norms require female deference to males. As females increasingly decline to defer, hatred of women as a sex intensifies among some males. Violence serves to remind women of the illusory nature of their formal equality.

Rape is a form of torture used to control women; it is social but not state terror.[53] Even though rape is officially considered a crime, individual rapists serve the function of keeping women under control. Many people still consider rape a just punishment for women's transgressions against social norms; rape is "an extension and distortion of, rather than a complete departure from, the approved patterns of sexual behavior in our society."[54] Rape of some women is a warning to all women. The fear of rape makes women dependent on men, keeps them at home at night, causes them to avoid male strangers. Women who disobey these social rules frequently learn to their cost that they are considered responsible for their own misfortune. Many women who are raped accept that they brought it on themselves by their nonconforming behavior, by violating social codes of dress, deportment, and modesty.

Most rapes in North America are not by strangers in dark alleyways. Most rapes are perpetrated by acquaintances, dates, or relatives. In Canada in 1991, 80 percent of the female victims of violent crimes, including sexual assault, knew their attacker.[55] Acquaintance rape serves as an interesting focus of social norms, defining which rapes are considered "real." The social perception that women who dress, act, or speak in a sexually provocative manner "deserve" to be raped is declining significantly in North America, and there are fewer legal decisions that take this view seriously. Yet some men and women still assume that women who permit themselves to be alone with men of their acquaintance must have sexual intent, an intent that "provokes" men into raping them.

In North America, all women are reminded at one time or another of the insecurity of their freedom. In 1987, according to a national survey, an estimated 1.5 percent of Canadian wives were assaulted by their husbands: It is estimated that one in four women in Canada is assaulted sometime in her life.[56] It is important not to exaggerate the extent of such crimes and not to imply, as some radical feminists do, that all forms of verbal abuse or even angry behavior are "assaults."[57] Yet the figures cited above are frightening enough: Most North American women fear rape and take quite elaborate precautions to avoid it.

The rapist, according to the radical feminist viewpoint, is the stand-in for the more restrained, polite male who would never physically subordinate a woman. There is a grain of truth to this perspective: Rapists are deviant individuals who reinforce threatened social norms about appropriate gender-based behavior. Convicted rapists tend to be lower-status males.[58] Other males—including those who may commit rape themselves—can distance themselves from such noninstitutionalized violence, but they nevertheless benefit from violently reinforced gender privilege. Rapists convey a sign to women that they must be careful about stepping beyond restrictive boundaries that are officially considered to be retrogressive and undignified, yet unofficially continue to influence much social behavior. Timocratic norms of behavior are reinforced by individual violent fiat, even when the state supports equality of rights and opportunities for men and women.

It is unclear if the rate of actual rape has increased in North America in the last thirty years, or whether the rate of reporting has increased while the actual incidence has not. In the United States, rates of forcible rape doubled between 1970 and 1980 and then leveled off, suggesting perhaps that the reported rape rate began to reflect the actual rape rate in the 1980s.[59] In Canada, the rate of rape tripled between 1962 and 1982 and the total recorded rate of sexual assault (replacing the crime of rape) more than doubled between 1983 and 1989.[60] If rapes or sexual assaults have actually increased, the answer may be found in women's strong challenge to male status honor. "There is good reason to believe that many men, frustrated by a world they have no hope of controlling in the wake of an erosion of their advantages and the social relevance of their physical superiority, are increasingly tempted to use that strength in the one situation in which it still clearly gives them an advantage—their personal relations with women."[61] Although many men have reacted to the women's liberation movement by examining their preconceptions about gender relations and modifying their behavior, others find women's liberation a threat. Thus women are caught in a contradictory situation: While their material opportunities have greatly expanded over the last thirty years, they are also more aware of the risk of assault. Even though the legal system takes sexual assault far more seriously than it used to, some individuals are still influenced by conservative social perceptions that "liberated" women deserve punishment because they are violating deeply held rules of gender behavior. Such violations undermine the norms of social honor, deference, and shame.

Similarly, timocratic racial norms are reinforced by lynchings, quasi-lynchings, and other forms of violence against blacks—even when the state officially condemns and punishes such behavior. Just as the rapist is the stand-in for the remnants of patriarchy, the lyncher is the stand-in for the remnants of racial hatred and bigotry in the white community.

During the era of slavery in the United States, physical violence against slaves was legal; thus, it could be considered both state and social terror. Slaveowners had the right to beat, whip, mutilate, and torture slaves, in some instances even to kill them. Once slavery was abolished, social terrorism of blacks substituted for state terrorism. The state looked on with a neglect almost approvingly as whites began to lynch "uppity" blacks. Lynchings were common in the post–Civil War South. From 1882 to 1892 alone more than 1,400 people were lynched.[62] Black men and boys had to be constantly on their guard against white vigilantes, whose restrictive norms of appropriate interracial relations constantly threatened their lives. Local and state governments colluded in this individualized violence; sheriffs sometimes posed for pictures with the leaders of lynch mobs.[63]

Nor were white women innocent in some of these lynchings. A white woman accused of consorting with a black man could protect herself by claiming she was raped.[64] In an atmosphere that presumed that all black men were constant sexual threats, such claims were easily believed; since all blacks "looked alike" it was easy to find a culprit. Between 1865 and 1965, one researcher estimated, there were thousands of lynchings of black men for allegedly raping white women as well as hundreds of legal executions for the same alleged crime.[65] In 1955, Emmett Till was lynched at age 14 for whistling at a white woman.[66]

In the 1980s and 1990s, as blacks asserted their rights and some managed to move up in the social scale, a new social phenomenon appeared: northern urban quasi-lynchings. In December 1984, a white New York subway commuter, Bernard Goetz, shot four young black men whom he felt threatening. Many New Yorkers defended Goetz for finally taking action against the young (black) thugs of the subway system.[67] But no such populist defense could be seriously evoked in two later quasi-lynchings. In 1986, a group of white teenagers in New York City's Howard Beach chased a group of blacks who had inadvertently wandered into the white neighborhood in search of help after their car broke down. One escaping victim fled onto a highway, where he was struck and killed.[68] In August 1989, some white teenagers in the Bensenhurst section of Brooklyn decided to stop a local white woman from consorting with black men. Yusuf Hawkins, a sixteen-year-old boy who as it happened was not an acquaintance of the woman in question, was beaten to death.[69]

Public (white and black) outrage at these latter two crimes was severe. But the point had been well taken. As they make autonomous attempts to improve their social status, blacks are reminded by social terror of their precarious equality in civil society. Although the young men Bernard Goetz shot did have criminal records and may well have had criminal intent, many other law-abiding young black men suffer the stigma of being considered potential criminals by any white they encounter.[70] The brutal police beating of Rodney King that set off the 1992 Los Angeles riots was not considered in the black community to be an anomalous event: Rather, police beatings of blacks are considered to be routine. Even prosperous, "assimilated," middle-class blacks felt that King's beating was a reminder that they too were at risk.[71]

Many whites fear black violence: Black crime rates in the United States are disproportionately high and there are black areas that most white people would never enter. But black violence against whites does not shame its victims. It is a threat but not a reminder of inherent social inferiority. By contrast, the white-on-black racial violence of the late twentieth century serves to warn blacks of the limits of recently won freedoms. The actual terrorizers—quasi-organized lynchers or gangs or outright mobs of angry white boys—can be legally and socially rejected by the white community even as the terrorism serves its function of intimidation and humiliation. Blacks as a collectivity are frightened even when it is individuals who randomly suffer. Quasi-lynchings have a social function: to keep a degraded status group in its place even as some individual members join the white-dominated meritocracy.

Violence or its threat is the first and last weapon of social degradation. It is first because it is crude, immediate, and self-revelatory; he who employs violence cannot claim that fear and punishment are not his intent. It is last because in societies in which degradation is officially condemned by political authorities yet socially approved, coercion remains the ultimate weapon against those who otherwise might escape degrading conditions. Honored social groups benefit from the violent actions of their deviant members. These violent actions reinforce in the shamed social groups feelings of unworthiness and restrain shamed individuals who try to escape their confining self-perceptions. Social terrorism, self-hatred, and self-mutilation illuminate deep-rooted tendencies in human behavior that liberal principles of formal equality are not sufficient to eliminate.

Liberalism and Social Honor

In strong liberal societies culture forbids overt social categorization and law forbids violence. A cultural belief in human rights implies more than just protection against certain identifiable abuses. It also implies respect and concern for all citizens by all citizens. Citizens, as well as the state, must treat each other equally and refrain from harmful acts. Citizens must also exhibit concern for one another; they must feel a sense of obligation even to others who are socially, racially, or biologically different. Such respect and concern supply the cultural underpinning for a system in which all categories of people are respected and no one suffers degradation.

But that culture does not exist: It remains an ideal even in the most egalitarian societies. The entrenchment of formal legal and political rights cannot, on its own, eliminate the social viewpoint that some status groups are by definition degraded or the companion viewpoint that, should they step out of their subordinate social roles, violence should be brought to bear. The capacity of societies to degrade their dishonored members must be integrated into our perception of what constitutes a "community." The status radical critique points out the dangers of assuming that the ideal of individualist egalitarianism on its own is sufficient protection for those who choose to avoid traditional social controls. Although the political culture assumes that they are acting as rational independent citizens, the social culture often condemns them. Women and blacks in modern North America who buy into the liberal dream may find their capacity to act autonomously blocked by cultural norms of shame and dishonor.

"To understand the production and maintenance of social order necessitates focus upon the social accomplishments of inferiorization in everyday life."[72] Inferiorization, that is, degradation, is not an atypical aspect of social life. It is a regular social phenomenon that forms an intrinsic part of the way almost all societies organize themselves. Western liberalism is unusual among social philosophies in its direct attack on practices of degradation. International human rights norms reflect this direct attack and thereby "impose" liberal social philosophies on societies that wish to retain social orders based on categorization and degradation.

In the modern world all governments officially denounce racism and most also denounce caste- and gender-based discrimination. But in practice the elites of many societies still defend both. The processes of Westernization are thus viewed as cultural imperialism. Yet liberal human rights are the strongest ideological and legal weapons available in the modern world to individuals degraded because of their ascribed social status. Westernization makes available the ideal, and sometimes the legal practice, of liberal human rights. Thus it threatens traditional degradation practices and the power of traditionalists, whether those in the Third World who still persecute historically subjugated people or those in the Western world who still believe that women and blacks should know their place and stay in it.

To status radicals, individual human rights reflect the competitive capitalism that characterizes liberal society. Human rights do not protect the degraded; they merely hide degradation under the belief that everyone is responsible for his own fate. But to status radicals the solution to this problem is not a reintegration into a traditional communitarian order, where their dishonored status would be reinforced rather than eliminated. Rather, the solution for the most radical critics of white- and male-dominated society is a form of withdrawal into black-only or female-only communities, if not in a physical sense then in a social and psychological sense. Weber noted that "the sense of dignity of the negatively privileged strata naturally refers to a future lying beyond the present, whether it is of this life or of another."[73] Because the present, the concrete, is so degrading, myths of a better world—beyond or outside the current one—are developed by some status radicals. Despairing of social inclusion, separatist radicals want to withdraw from the larger society and set up their own communities.

Withdrawal is of course physically impossible: There is no room in modern North America for geographically encapsulated, isolated communities of Others. Moreover, withdrawal assumes that women or blacks are completely defined by their degraded social status and have no interest in remaining part of the larger society. Status radicals advocate collective rights granted to organized and closed groups of women or blacks. This assumes a false homogeneity within both the degraded and the honored groups.

The situation of women in the United States in the 1990s is far improved over the situation that generated the feminist movement of the late 1960s. Women have made substantial gains in the professions. For example, 18 percent of physicians and 22 percent of lawyers were women in 1989 compared to 10 and 5 percent in 1970.[74] The female-to-male income ratio is improving, especially among younger women: In the 25-to-34 age range full-time, year-round women workers made 79 percent of the incomes of male counterparts in 1990, compared to 65 percent in 1960.[75] Countless other statistics tell the same story. Although women are certainly far from equal to men in North America in the 1990s, they have made extremely rapid progress in the last 30 years in large part because formal discriminatory barriers to their progress have been eliminated. There is now a very large cadre of highly educated, professional women who are not financially dependent on men and who are fully capable of exercising all their human rights. Class distinctions among women, based on their own rather than the husband's statuses and achievements, are much more evident in the 1990s than they were 30 years earlier. Some women have far more privileges than many men.

Blacks have not progressed as well. In 1990, full-time, year-round black male workers earned about 71 percent of the income of white counterparts, an improvement of only 5 percent over the 66 percent they earned in 1960.[76] Nor have blacks had the same success in education as whites, either male or female. In 1991, 25 percent of white males and 19 percent of white females over the age of 25 had four or more years of college education: The comparable figures for blacks were 11 percent for both sexes. Even in the 25-to-34 age range only 12 percent of black males and females had four or more years of college education compared to 25 percent of white males and females.[77] In 1989, the median income of U.S. black households ($18,083) was over $12,000 less than the median income of white households ($30,406).[78]

Despite these discouraging average figures for black education and income, there is nevertheless a significant black middle and professional class in the United States today. In 1989, 37.3 percent of black households had incomes of over $25,000 and 11.5 percent had incomes of over $50,000.[79] Although the black middle class continues to be affected by racist perceptions and social violence, individual African-Americans, like individual white women, have multiple interests, identifications, and roles that link them to the wider society even as some social forces try to push them back.

Thus blacks and women in North America do not all suffer dishonor at the same rate or intensity. Like everyone else in North American society, women and blacks occupy a variety of social roles, although the range of roles open to most blacks and some women is narrower than the range open to honored white males. To contend that there are unchangeable status groups in North American society today is to deny both empirical and normative reality. The radical feminist position—that society is divided into "an undifferentiated class of victimizers (male) against an undifferentiated class of victims (female)"—is irresponsible, as Jean Bethke Elshtain has argued.[80] For status radicals who reject the liberal premise of individual opportunity and equality, "the category of 'citizen' is a matter of indifference at best: contempt at worst."[81] Yet the category of citizen is not irrelevant; indeed, it has been the fairly recent legal recognition that women and blacks ought to be full citizens that has helped facilitate three decades of progress. To discard the principle of citizenship because social practice has not kept up with legal and political rules might permit individual women and African-Americans to retreat into a safer, more closed world of interaction with others of their own status. But it would also encourage those who still hold to racist or misogynist views to reincorporate those views into the wider civil society.

Recognition of the status categorization of dishonored groups does not presuppose collectivist remedies. The great advantage of individual human rights is that they allow, even encourage, persons occupying dishonored categories to join together to collectively pressure for recognition of their human rights. But at the same time, individual human rights protect actual human individuals from being falsely incorporated into status categories that they may not in fact occupy. Status becomes irrelevant in a human rights–protective regime. Women are more than female; blacks are more than their skin color. Collectivist remedies, separatist or other, deny the complexity of modern life and the multiple needs and interests of the individual.

Societies dedicated to human rights are expected to be inclusive: Indeed, they are expected to overcome status distinctions and allow everyone an equal and respected place as a citizen. When slaves rebelled against their condition, according to Patterson, it was this inclusion that they sought. "To be dishonored—and to sense, however acutely, such dishonor—is not to lose the quintessential human urge to participate and to want a place."[82] What the slave who sought honor wanted was not the freedom to ignore society; he was not interested in the right to seek his own pleasure or self-fulfilment, liberated from obligation to family and community. Slaves did not want to free themselves as individuals from all social bonds or to go off in splendid isolation in pursuit of their own individualized pleasure. Rather, they wanted to belong, to be acknowledged members of the community. As Igor Kopytoff and Suzanne Miers put it in their classic analysis of slavery in Africa, freedom is belonging, having a respected and acknowledged role in society.[83] Slaves wanted both to form and maintain their own families and communities and to join the larger society from which they were excluded. Declared to be nonpersons, they sought social membership.

Slaves sought freedom as it was originally defined in the Western ideology of human rights. Freedom was not an individual luxury but a necessity for decent living. Slaves wanted protection from their masters and the state; they wanted freedom from execution, torture, and what we might (anachronistically) call the disappearances of their families, sold elsewhere to other slavemasters. They wanted the right to earn a decent living by their own hard work. They wanted nondiscrimination, to be judged by their contribution to the community rather than by the color of their skin. This freedom, sometimes forgotten in the individualist pleasure-seeking culture of some wealthy North Americans, is the freedom that human rights are meant to guarantee. Human rights are meant to make possible social inclusion, to overcome the social exclusion consequent either upon the status categorizations that I discuss in this chapter or upon the class categorizations to which I turn in Chapter 7.

Notes

1. Max Weber, "Class, Status, Party," in H. H. Gerth and C. Wright Mills (eds.), *From Max Weber: Essays in Sociology* (New York: Oxford University Press, 1946), pp. 186, 187, and 190; emphasis in original.

2. Ervin Staub, *The Roots of Evil: The Origins of Genocide and Other Group Violence* (New York: Cambridge University Press, 1989), quotations from pp. 104–105 and 58–59.

3. Mary Douglas, *Purity and Danger: An Analysis of the Concepts of Pollution and Taboo* (London: Routledge and Kegan Paul, 1966), p. 162.

Honor and Shame

4. On these oppositions in Africa, see, e.g., Bridget O'Laughlin, "Mediation of Contradiction: Why Mbum Women Do Not Eat Chicken," in Michelle Zimbalist Rosaldo and Louise Lamphere (eds.), *Woman, Culture and Society* (Stanford, Calif.: Stanford University Press, 1974), p. 315; and Claire Robertson, "Developing Economic Awareness: Changing Perspectives in Studies of African Women, 1976–1985," *Feminist Studies*, vol. 13, no. 1 (spring 1987), p. 112.

5. For a brilliant fictional depiction of societies in which honor is a matter of major concern, see *Leo the African*, by the Lebanese writer Amin Maalouf (New York: Quartet Books, 1988). This novel is set in Europe and North Africa at the turn of the sixteenth century.

6. Orlando Patterson, *Slavery and Social Death: A Comparative Study* (Cambridge, Mass: Harvard University Press, 1982), p. 79.

7. Ibid., p.13.

8. Ibid., pp. 58–62. See also Gerda Lerner, *The Creation of Patriarchy* (New York: Oxford University Press, 1986), pp. 135–137.

9. Douglas, *Purity and Danger*, pp. 5 and 3.

10. Constance Perin, *Belonging in America: Reading Between the Lines* (Madison: University of Wisconsin Press, 1988), p. 176.

11. Ibid., p. 222.

12. The term "master status" is originally from Everett C. Hughes's phrase, "master status-determining trait," in his "Dilemmas and Contradictions of Status," *American Journal of Sociology*, vol. 50 (March 1945), p. 357.

13. Simone de Beauvoir, *The Second Sex* (New York: The Modern Library, 1968), pp. xv–xvi; emphasis in original.

14. Peggy Reeves Sanday, *Female Power and Male Dominance: On the Origins of Sexual Inequality* (New York: Cambridge University Press, 1981).

15. Lerner, *The Creation of Patriarchy*, pp. 8–10.

16. Max Weber, "India: The Brahman and the Castes," in Gerth and Mills, *From Max Weber*, pp. 396–415.

17. Weber, "Class, Status, Party," p. 189.

18. Gunnar Myrdal (with the assistance of Richard Sterner and Arnold Rose), *An American Dilemma: The Negro Problem and Modern Democracy* (New York: Harper and Row, 1944), p. 115, quoted in Barry D. Adam, *The Survival of Domination: Inferiorization and Everyday Life* (New York: Elsevier, 1978), p. 14.

19. Ellis Cose, *The Rage of a Privileged Class* (New York: HarperCollins, 1993), p. 28.

20. Ibid., p. 63.

21. Cornel West, *Race Matters* (New York: Vintage Books, 1994), pp. 119–120.

22. Vincent Crapanzano, *Waiting: The Whites of South Africa* (New York: Vintage Books, 1986), quotations from pp. 39, 143, and 19.

23. This section is based on my "Health Costs of Social Degradation and Female Self-Mutilation in North America," in Kathleen E. Mahoney and Paul Mahoney (eds.), *Human Rights in the Twenty-First Century: A Global Challenge* (Boston: Martinus Nijhoff, 1993), pp. 503–516.

24. Edwin M. Schur, *Labeling Women Deviant: Gender, Stigma and Social Control* (Philadelphia: Temple University Press, 1983); quotations from pp. 3, 11, and 33.

25. A popular account of these practices is Naomi Wolf's *The Beauty Myth: How Images of Beauty Are Used Against Women* (New York: Doubleday, 1991).

26. Rosabeth Moss Kantor, *Men and Women of the Corporation* (New York: Basic Books, 1977), chapter 8.

27. Maria Leach (ed.), *Funk and Wagnall's Standard Dictionary of Folklore, Mythology and Legend,* volume I (New York: Funk and Wagnall, 1949), p. 233.

28. Susan Brownmiller, *Femininity* (New York: Fawcett Columbine, 1984), pp. 184–185.

29. On display jobs, see Schur, *Labeling Women Deviant,* p. 142.

30. Janet Polivy and C. Peter Herman, "Diagnosis and Treatment of Normal Eating," *Journal of Consulting and Clinical Psychology,* vol. 55, no. 5 (1987), pp. 640 and 636.

31. Figures are from American Psychiatric Association, *Diagnostic and Statistical Manual of Mental Disorders,* Third Edition—Revised (Washington, D.C.: American Psychiatric Association, 1987), p. 66.

32. Suzanne Abraham and Derek Llewellyn-Jones, *Eating Disorders: The Facts* (New York: Oxford University Press, 1992), p. 64.

33. Christina Hoff Sommers, *Who Stole Feminism? How Women Have Betrayed Women* (New York: Simon and Schuster, 1994), p. 12.

34. Polivy and Herman, "Diagnosis and Treatment," p. 641.

35. Schur, *Labeling Women Deviant,* p. 72; quotation from Erving Goffman, *Gender Advertisements* (New York: Harper Colophon Books, 1979), p. 28.

36. Schur, *Labeling Women Deviant,* pp. 38–39.

37. Sander L. Gilman, *Jewish Self-Hatred: Anti-Semitism and the Hidden Language of the Jews* (Baltimore: Johns Hopkins University Press, 1986), p. 2.

38. Ibid., p. 3.

39. Adam, *Survival of Domination,* p. 42.

40. Ibid., pp. 42–49, quotations from p. 49.

41. James Baldwin, *Nobody Knows My Name: More Notes of a Native Son* (New York: Dial, 1961), p. 80, quoted in Adam, *Survival of Domination,* pp. 100–101.

42. Frantz Fanon, *Black Skins, White Masks* (New York: Grove Press, 1967), quotations from pp. 111 and 115–116.

43. Sara Lawrence Lightfoot, *Balm in Gilead: Journey of a Healer* (New York: Addison-Wesley, 1988), pp. 39–42.

44. bell hooks, *Black Looks: Race and Representation* (Boston: South End Press, 1992), p. 3.

45. West, *Race Matters,* p. 122.

46. Zygmunt Bauman, "Strangers: The Social Construction of Universality and Particularity," *Telos,* vol. 78 (1988–1989), pp. 14–15.

47. Michael Stohl and George A. Lopez, "Introduction" to Stohl and Lopez (eds.), *The State as Terrorist: The Dynamics of Governmental Violence and Repression* (Westport, Conn.: Greenwood Press, 1984), pp. 3–10.

48. Emile Durkheim, *The Division of Labor in Society* (New York: The Free Press, 1933), book 1, chapter 2.

49. E.g., by Charlotte Bunch, "Women's Rights as Human Rights: Toward a Re-

Vision of Human Rights," *Human Rights Quarterly*, vol. 12, no. 4 (November 1990), pp. 486–498.

50. In Center for the Study of Human Rights, *Twenty-Four Human Rights Documents* (New York: Columbia University, 1992), pp. 49–57.

51. United Nations General Assembly, "Vienna Declaration and Programme of Action," 25 June 1993, article 38 (A/Conf.157/23, 12 July 1993).

52. International Convention on the Elimination of All Forms of Racial Discrimination, Articles 4)a and 5)b, in Center for the Study of Human Rights, *Twenty-Four Human Rights Documents*, p. 42.

53. Catherine A. MacKinnon, "On Torture: A Feminist Perspective on Human Rights," in Kathleen E. Mahoney and Paul Mahoney (eds.), *Human Rights in the Twenty-First Century: A Global Challenge* (Boston: Martinus Nijhoff, 1993), pp. 21–31.

54. Schur, *Labeling Women Deviant*, p. 148.

55. Shelley Trevethan and Tajeshwer Samagh, "Gender Differences Among Violent Crime Victims," *Juristat Service Bulletin* [Statistics Canada], vol. 12, no. 21 (November 1992), p. 8.

56. Holly Johnson and Peter Chisholm, "Family Homicide," in *Canadian Social Trends* [Statistics Canada], autumn 1989, p. 18; and House of Commons Canada, Standing Committee on Health and Welfare, Social Affairs, Seniors and the Status of Women, "The War Against Women: The Incidence of Violence Against Women in Canada," 3rd Session, June 1991, p. 6.

57. Sommers, *Who Stole Feminism?*, chapter 9, "Noble Lies."

58. W. L. Marshall and Sylvia Barrett, *Criminal Neglect: Why Sex Offenders Go Free* (Toronto: Doubleday, 1990), pp. 64–65; and Ronald M. Holmes, *Sex Crimes* (Newbury Park, Calif.: Sage, 1991), p. 78.

59. Cynthia Taeuber, *Statistical Handbook on Women in America* (Phoenix: Oryx Press, 1991), table D8-3, p. 347.

60. "Violent Crime in Canada," *Juristat Service Bulletin* [Statistics Canada], vol. 10, no. 15 (October 1990), p. 4.

61. Elizabeth Fox-Genovese, *Feminism Without Illusions: A Critique of Individualism* (Chapel Hill: University of North Carolina Press, 1991), p. 255.

62. Adam, *Survival of Domination*, p. 21.

63. C. Vann Woodward, "The Mississippi Horrors" (Review of Neil R. McMillen, *Dark Journey: Black Mississippians in the Age of Jim Crow*), *New York Review of Books*, vol. 36, no. 11 (June 29, 1989), p. 16.

64. Bertram Wyatt-Brown, *Southern Honor: Ethics and Behavior in the Old South* (New York: Oxford University Press, 1982), pp. 316–317.

65. Laurence Alan Baughman, *Southern Rape Complex: Hundred Year Psychosis* (Atlanta: Pendulum Books, 1966), p. 136, cited in Lawrence J. Friedman, "Rape Complex, Southern," in David C. Roller and Robert W. Twyman (eds.), *The Encyclopedia of Southern History* (Baton Rouge: Louisiana State University Press, 1979), p. 1029.

66. Henry Mayer, review of Henry Hampton and Steve Fayer with Sarah Flynn, *Voices of Freedom: An Oral History of the Civil Rights Movement* (New

York: Bantam Books, 1989), in *New York Times Book Review*, January 28, 1990, p. 12.

67. *Facts on File*, vol. 47, no. 2430, June 19, 1987, p. 447.

68. Ibid., vol. 47, no. 2457, December 25, 1987, p. 957.

69. Ibid., vol. 49, no. 2535, June 23, 1989, pp. 458–459.

70. Cose, *Rage*, pp. 70–71.

71. Ibid., pp. 180–184. See also West, *Race Matters*, pp. 8–9.

72. Adam, *The Survival of Domination*, p. 2.

73. Weber, "Class, Status, Party," p. 190.

74. Francine D. Blau and Marianne A. Ferber, *The Economics of Women, Men, and Work*, 2nd ed. (Englewood Cliffs, N.J.: Prentice-Hall, 1992), p. 124.

75. Ibid., p. 135.

76. Ibid., p. 137.

77. Claudette E. Bennett, "The Black Population in the United States: March 1991," U.S. Department of Commerce, *Current Population Reports: Population Characteristics P20-464* (Washington, D.C. : U.S. Government Printing Office, 1992), p. 42.

78. U.S. Department of Commerce, Bureau of the Census, *Statistical Abstract of the U.S., 1991*, 11th edition, table 721, "Money Income of Households," p. 449.

79. Ibid.

80. Jean Bethke Elshtain, *Democracy on Trial* (Concord, Ontario: House of Anansi, 1993); quotation from p. 22. See also Sommers, *Who Stole Feminism?*, p. 24.

81. Elshtain, *Democracy on Trial*, p. 41.

82. Patterson, *Slavery and Social Death*, p. 97.

83. Igor Kopytoff and Suzanne Miers, "African 'Slavery' as an Institution of Marginality," in Miers and Kopytoff (eds.), *Slavery in Africa: Historical and Anthropological Perspectives* (Madison: University of Wisconsin Press, 1977), p. 17.

7 Social Exclusion

Poverty and Social Exclusion

In Chapter 2 I detail what I call the Central Park thesis, the belief that the high crime rate in New York City exemplifies the breakdown of society caused by individualistic claims for human rights. I argue that this belief confuses a surfeit of civil rights with the real cause of social breakdown in the United States, namely, lack of economic rights. The United States exemplifies the radical capitalist approach to human rights, in which civil and political rights and property rights are protected but economic, social, and cultural rights are considered to be superfluous.

Critics of the "Western" perspective on human rights usually focus both on U.S. practice and what is perceived to be U.S. ideology. This focus biases the discussion, as the United States is not representative of the entire Western world. Indeed, it can be argued that the United States is an anomalous Western country. "One factor that distinguishes the American welfare state from many others," said Mary Ann Glendon, "is the absence of a *constitutional* commitment to affirmatively protect the well-being of citizens."[1] In contrast to Western European nations such as France, state provision of welfare benefits in the United States is a last resort, as Louis Henkin explained:

> Few judges . . . have been prepared to declare basic human needs—subsistence, education—to be fundamental rights. . . . Congress need not appropriate money to make it possible for the poor to enjoy their rights effectively. . . . Congress is not required to add new twentieth century kinds of welfare rights. . . . Even when some societal responsi-

bility for individual welfare was finally accepted, it was seen as secondary and supplemental. Especially in austere, conservative times, that responsibility is seen only as residual, only to help those who cannot help themselves, and only with respect to minimum necessities at poverty levels. The primary responsibility for individual welfare . . . was on the individual.[2]

The most degrading characteristic one can possess in modern North American society is to be part of the class of permanently poor people. The poor, unlike "us" (the prosperous), lack dignity; they do not deserve the respect the prosperous accord one another.[3] In capitalist society the supreme value is wealth and the supreme activity is striving for it. To justify the value put on wealth, an ideology exists that it is freely available to all those who willingly work for it. "Mainstream discourse [in the United States] about poverty, whether liberal or conservative, largely stays silent about politics, power and equality. . . . The culture of capitalism measures persons . . . by their ability to produce wealth and by their success in earning it: it therefore leads naturally to the moral condemnation of those who . . . fail to contribute or to prosper."[4] The "Protestant" ethic of work, savings, and investment is expanded to a belief that the ethic itself is sufficient to accomplish the valued social goal of wealth. Advocates of the poor, recognizing this, try to point out how hard the poor work and how few are shirkers. The ideological enterprise that goes into this endeavor to demonstrate the respectability of the poor detracts from consideration of more important structural underpinnings of poverty, such as low minimum wages, low rates of unionization, and declining numbers of unskilled jobs in heavy industry.

The poor are by definition those who have not achieved. In a society in which honor attaches to material wealth, the poor by their lack of achievement are stigmatized: They are dirty and disorderly. It is assumed that anyone who wants to achieve can do so; thus the poor must possess dishonorable personal characteristics that result in their voluntary exclusion from prosperous middle-class society. Philosophical rejection of economic human rights permits satisfied bourgeois culture to neglect the need for a social democratic welfare state that might incorporate the poor into the community. "According to bourgeois standards, those who are completely unlucky and unsuccessful are automatically barred from competition. . . . Good fortune is identified with honor, and bad luck with shame. . . . The difference between pauper and criminal disappears—both stand outside society."[5]

Outside observers, such as critics from the underdeveloped world and from developed social democracies, cannot understand why the United States rejects what other societies take for granted as elementary principles of social justice. The republic's stress on individual civil and political rights at the expense of economic rights seems to outsiders a perverse denial of what is necessary for a community to be just to its members. The United States appears to favor a system that rewards and intensifies inequality, exploitation, and individualist self-seeking. Most other prosperous Western states favor a more collectivist vision of welfare over this extremely individualist model.

The United States has not signed the United Nations Covenant on Economic, Social and Cultural Rights. Yet for most Western states, this Covenant does not constitute a new or unusual set of rules. Rather, it is merely an obvious retelling of principles that should guide any civilized society. In welfare states, provision of economic benefits is a matter of entitlement. To be a citizen is to be entitled to education, health care, and a minimum decent standard of living. It is assumed that all people need these things, which must be provided by the society as a whole for those individuals who cannot provide them for themselves. Economic security is not a matter of desert, served only to those who deserve it, as demonstrated through hard work and achievement. Need, not achievement, is a guiding principle of the redistribution of social benefits in advanced welfare societies.[6]

In comparative terms, U.S. welfare policies lag behind those of most of its Western allies, even Canada, which is usually viewed by analysts as closer to the United States than to Western Europe in its welfare programs. Of twenty OECD (Organization for Economic Cooperation and Development) countries in 1985 for which data were available, the United States ranked eighteenth in the percentage of GDP (gross domestic product) invested in social expenditure, ahead only of Japan and Spain. At 18 percent, it ranked well below the top nine countries, ranging from Belgium at 36 percent to Ireland at 26. It tied for seventeenth place out of twenty-one countries in public expenditures on health and ranked thirteenth in education.[7] In 1989, the United States ranked last of fifteen industrial countries for which data were available in percentage of central government total expenditure on social security and welfare (27 percent as compared to 52 percent spent by Sweden, the leading country). By contrast, the United States spent twice as much on defense (25 percent in 1989) as the next highest country in the list (the United Kingdom, which devoted 12 percent of its central government expenditure to defense).[8]

The comparative paucity of expenditure on social welfare in the United States has led one social critic to characterize its policies as sub-welfare. "The 'welfare state' idea is fundamentally misleading. The welfare provided is not the general well-being of the people. It is welfare, rather, in the narrow and restrictive sense of public assistance to the poor. . . . If this be the general welfare it is 'subwelfare.'"[9] The seeming lack of basic respect for its citizens by the U.S. government strikes many outsiders as extraordinarily callous.

Outsiders from Western social democratic states are particularly astounded by the U.S. attitude toward health care. In 1992, 35.4 million Americans lacked health insurance, including 8.3 million under age 18.[10] In the late 1980s, about 17 percent of American women of childbearing age had no medical insurance.[11] The U.S. infant mortality rate in 1991 was worse than that of nineteen other high-income countries.[12] Its vaccination rate for children under two was worse than that of all other countries in the Western hemisphere except Bolivia and Haiti.[13] Although in 1994 reforms were offered by the Clinton administration, Congress did not pass legislation guaranteeing universal health care.

The United States is particularly derelict in its obligation to protect mothers and children, as stated under Article 25.2 of the Universal Declaration of Human Rights: "Motherhood and childhood are entitled to special care and assistance."[14] U.S. social ideology seems to assume that childbearing and rearing are an individual choice that requires little social investment. "In the United States," as Sylvia Ann Hewlett put it, "a baby is seen as a private consumption item, a little like a winter vacation or a second car."[15] Whereas paid maternity leave is assumed to be an absolutely essential part of family policy in many Western social democratic states, in the United States some civil liberties and feminist organizations resist maternity leave, contending that it would bestow an unequal benefit to women. In 1985, the California branches of the American Civil Liberties Union and the National Organization for Women opposed a state law mandating universal maternity leave on precisely these grounds.[16]

On February 5, 1993, President Clinton signed a toothless family leave bill mandating twelve weeks' unpaid family leave (including for adoption or birth of children) with job and seniority guaranteed on return. However, employers with fewer than fifty employees are exempted; employers also have the right to deny family leave to the highest-paid 10 percent of their workforce.[17] Thus a significant proportion of the U.S. workforce is still without the right to maternity leave, which in any case is still unpaid, by contrast with the programs of other Western countries.

There is also no national system of family allowance in the United States (meaning financial assistance packages to assist families with children), although "indigent families" are assisted through the Aid to Families with Dependent Children program (AFDC). Between 1980 and 1986, U.S. child-care subsidies suffered a 21 percent cut.[18] In 1986, 3 million more American children lived in poverty than in 1980, 700,000 had been struck from the Medicaid rolls, and 200,000 had lost their day-care subsidies.[19] Cuts in welfare policies made by President Ronald Reagan in 1981 meant that the average disposable income of working families who also received AFDC dropped from 101 percent to 81 percent of the poverty line.[20] By contrast, child cash allowances in such countries as Spain, Germany, Belgium, and Switzerland can amount to as much as 5 to 10 percent of average gross wages; Great Britain, France, Sweden, and Canada spend two to three times as much as the United States on families with children.[21] In 1992, more than 20 percent of American children lived in poverty.[22] Thus the data on U.S. social policy expose the shallowness of current political posturing in the name of family values. Real families—of the poor both employed and unemployed, of mothers and children without fathers, of the struggling lower middle classes—are not protected.

Thus in the dominant U.S. social ideology, a citizen's right to be respected, to be treated with dignity, is not seen to rest on a floor of economic security. In fact, as the lack of a universal health program attests, nor are basic economic rights even a matter of need—of minimal physical care rather than of the respect that every citizen ought to enjoy. The principle that the entire society has a collective, nondebatable responsibility to care for the poor is not part of the national social ideology. The major social policy debates in the United States center around means to alleviate inequality of opportunity, not around means to provide a satisfactory floor of economic security for all citizens.

One's chances of being poor in the United States are considerably greater if one is black, Hispanic, or female than if one is white or male. In 1990, the ratio of black to white unemployed was 276:100.[23] In 1991, 32.7 percent of blacks were poor, in contrast with only 11.3 percent of whites (and 9.4 percent of non-Hispanic whites).[24] Yet in real numbers the white poor vastly exceeds the black poor. In 1991, 23,747,000 whites in the United States were poor, as opposed to 10,242,000 blacks, a ratio of 2.3:1. Of non-Hispanic whites, 17,741,000 were poor, a ratio to blacks of 1.7:1.[25] Similarly, although female-headed households are proportionately more likely than male-headed households to be poor, in a significant proportion of poor households an adult male is present. In fact, 43.7 percent of all poor families in the United States in 1987 contained a married couple.[26] Poverty is a matter of social class. Being a member of the working poor or of the chronically unemployed classes is disabling for a number of reasons, including but not limited to inequality of opportunity based on race or gender.

Thus poverty in the United States cannot be ameliorated merely by focusing on improved opportunities for nonwhites and women. To increase the numbers of wealthy women, blacks, or Hispanics is not to alleviate the structural conditions that keep poor citizens poor. Equality of opportunity fits the U.S. approach to human rights, with its stress on everyone's right to private property and to equality in the competition for material goods. Clearly, to exclude someone from the right to property ownership or from the competition for wealth because of race or gender is illegitimate. But poverty itself is not universally viewed as a condition requiring societal amelioration.

An ideology of the culture of poverty blames those on welfare for their own fate. The poor are assumed to be passive, to have disorganized families, to have rejected the middle-class work ethic.[27] The structural factors that, in any capitalist state, prevent huge numbers of people from acting efficaciously in the economic marketplace are ignored in favor of this ideology that, in effect, blames the victims of capitalism for their own fate. Thus scholars discuss the decline of the black family structure, especially the very high rates of births out of wedlock. In 1988, 56 percent of black families in the U.S. had only the mother present; for white families the figure was 18 percent (and for Hispanics of any race, 29 percent).[28] Insofar as poverty is seen as a characteristic only of nonwhite populations, reformers can institute antiracist measures, such as the unpopular busing legislation obliging white schools (frequently, as in Boston, mainly in working-class areas) to accept students from black schools.[29] The assumption behind this legislation is that equal access to education will promote equal access to employment. But judicial activism cannot go so far as to impose requirements that the poor be accorded more material security.

The complete elimination from the U.S. political scene of parties that elsewhere advocate economic redistribution and radical change of the structures of power effectively excludes the poor from political activity. When communism and social democracy were imported into the United States by European immigrants, both the left-wing activists and the ideologies they espoused were quickly suppressed. "The result is a country in which . . . politics, media and the general culture are to an extraordinary degree (in comparison with Western Europe), dominated by the upper-middle and upper classes; the problems and points of view of millions of poor Americans get little attention; and systematic critiques of flaws in the American capitalist democratic system are almost never aired in the mass media."[30] There are no parties of the poor in the United States. In their attempts to be politically efficacious, the poor are obliged to identify themselves by their ascribed characteristics. Ethnic characteristics (black or Hispanic) are the usual means of mobilizing the poor, although gender characteristics are also stressed as women become more politically astute. The inequ:ties of capitalist social relations are folded into critiques of discrimination; there is no comparable challenge to class relations.

A very large sector of the U.S. population acknowledges the need for better welfare provisions and more attention to the poor. The liberalism of human rights—even, in the case of the election of Bill Clinton, of social democratic reform—provides a strong antidote to social closure. There is a very strong modern community, of the sort that I describe in Chapter 5, that includes millions of citizens dedicated to the common good. Many status radicals and leftists in the United States also agree on the need for more attention to economic human rights in their country.

There are also, however, two ideologies of social exclusion in the United States and, perhaps less significantly, in Canada. Adherents of both ideologies subscribe to the view that they bear little if any responsibility to the poor. The first ideology, social minimalism, is dedicated to the hedonistic pursuit of wealth. The second, reactionary conservatism, is dedicated to the "responsible" pursuit of wealth. Both ideologies deny societal concern for and respect to the poor, whose behavioral deviation is assumed to have caused their privations. The rise of social minimalism and reactionary conservatism is one important reason that class relations are neglected in U.S. political debate. Immediately below I discuss these two social trends, both of which characterize significant sections of the U.S. population and foster exclusionary tendencies. These social trends are presented as ideal types, not as factual descriptions of particular political parties or identifiable philosophies.

Social Minimalism

Throughout this book I stress three core values that I believe ought to exemplify a liberal world of genuine dignity for the individual: equality, societal respect, and autonomy. If people are treated in a manner that is respectful regardless of status or class position; if they are allowed autonomy both in life choices and in social and political debate; and if they are guaranteed relatively equitable access to the society's wealth as well as formal legal and political equality, then much potential unhappiness can be avoided.

Social minimalism is a worldview that supports the principles of civil and political rights and of legal and political equality. It does not support the principle of economic equality or even of economic redistribution or reorganization, which might guarantee each citizen her basic economic needs. Social minimalism lays great stress on individual autonomy but very little on the principle of respect for others. This social minimalism derives from the political minimalism of the nightwatchman state, which protects a small, or minimal, number of human rights. These include the right to private property and only those classic civil and political rights that protect the individual against the state. The citizen of a minimalist state is assured that her property is her own and that she can, by and large, say and do what she wants without interference by the state. On the other hand, the state and the society make very little commitment to protect her economic well-being, which is perceived to be in her own hands.

Social minimalists are liberals in the classic sense that they believe in the principle of equality of legal and political condition. Social minimalists are uninterested in correct or conforming social behavior. As long as your behavior does not interfere with another's capacity to pursue her own self-interest, you are free to do as you like. Unlike conservative communitarians, minimalists do not disapprove of everyone's seeking self-fulfilment. Quite the opposite: The private realm is completely open. Any type of behavior is permitted, and everyone is encouraged to seek the maximum happiness and gratification, just as she is encouraged to seek the maximum material wealth. Social minimalists do not long for a golden age of deference to social superiors. Everyone is entitled to autonomy in pursuit of her own self-interest.

Women, blacks, and members of other previously subordinated groups are welcomed into the social world of the minimalists, who agree that all ascriptive barriers to achievement should be removed. Minimalists do not care what people do in their private lives, as long as their activities do not impinge on other people's comfort. Women are permitted to strive for their own personal satisfaction at the expense of their traditional roles as mothers; indeed, women who ask for special consideration because of their child-care responsibilities are considered to be making excessive demands on the rest of society. Homosexuality is also a permitted lifestyle; indeed, homosexuality bears the underlying advantage of reducing short-term social burdens by not producing children (although lately the epidemic of AIDS among gays has increased the social burden). Permitting individuals to behave in ways that reduce social needs increases the amount of disposable income available to others.

Social minimalism thus reflects what Michael Sandel called the unencumbered self. "For the unencumbered self, what matters above all, what is most essential to our personhood, are not the ends we choose but our capacity to choose them." The unencumbered self has no history or community prior to its own existence; it is not a member of "any community bound by moral ties antecedent to choice." Sandel worried that such abstraction from community creates a situation in which, from a moral point of view, fellow citizens become Others to whom one has no natural duties, no mutual indebtedness.[31]

Sandel's description of the unencumbered self is too strong. He found communities of choice to be morally secondary to communities of kinship bound by common history. As I argue in Chapter 5, communities of choice can be morally compelling; the individual may take her obligations to such chosen communities very seriously and devote considerable resources to them. Social minimalism does exemplify Sandel's concern, however. Social minimalists do not substitute for their communities of kin or nation communities of choice; rather, they deny community altogether.

Liberalism's pursuit of autonomy, respect, and equality is replaced in social minimalism by a single-minded pursuit of autonomy alone. For the minimalist, human dignity is expressed principally in the consequences of private action. The minimalist philosophy of rights allows, in theory, equal respect to all individuals. In practice, however, respect goes to the self-made man (and lately woman)—to those who work hard and achieve their material goals. The ideology of work, then, is conflated with the ideology of material success. Material possessions become a mark of individual worth. The individual measures himself (and increasingly herself) by the value and variety of material goods accrued. Autonomy means the capacity to spend money primarily on oneself, in whatever way one sees fit.

Personal choice of life "style" is also a requirement of autonomy in its modern North American meaning. Determination and acquisition of one's appropriate, uniquely suitable lifestyle is advocated by many pop sociologists and pop psychologists who maintain that everyone is responsible for her own happiness. The stress is on the self. The self-help books that proliferated in North America beginning in the 1970s and 1980s are the concrete manifestation of obsession with private, personal, material, and often sensual (rather than spiritual) self-satisfaction. "Self-awareness," as Edwin Schur noted in 1976, "is the new panacea."[32] By focusing entirely on the self, it implies "that somehow human beings can act and interact within a social and moral vacuum. That social structures and forms are meaningless and unnecessary. That unhappiness is due to our not realizing our true selves. . . . We cannot expect other people to solve our problems for us. By the same token, we cannot solve theirs. . . . The latent political implication seems . . . apparent: complacency for those who have succeeded, resignation or self-blame for those who have not."[33] This convenient philosophy relieves the individual of the burden not only of understanding the problems of her own life, but also of speculating on her role in the structures that cause other people's suffering. "That people might gain a large measure of self-fulfilment precisely by taking their social responsibilities seriously, never seems to occur to the current self-fulfilment experts."[34]

Social minimalists have adopted the belief that the self is necessarily the center of concern. There is no possibility, in the modern world, for the citizen to act as the public person: only the self, not society, can be changed. There is no social, political, or economic reality. Anything that happens to you is an experience, something to be worked through and conquered but not attributable to outside social conditions. "Nobody is responsible for us but ourselves. . . . And we are pretty much free to shape our lives as we ourselves see fit."[35] This belief is a way to induce the poor to accept their lot, "to quietly make the best of things. Seduced into interiorizing their problems, the poor . . . [are] diverted from the more urgent task of advancing their real collective interests."[36]

Social minimalists exemplify the narcissistic personality characteristic of contemporary North America. Social minimalism takes to its highest plane Georg Simmel's belief that the modern world creates societies of strangers. He once said that modern urban society is highly impersonal, yet simultaneously promotes "a highly personal subjectivity" characterized by a "blasé attitude" of nondiscrimination among various types of values. Yet at the same time, as the individual's meaning in society is increasingly confined to his role in the division of labor, he has to summon "the utmost in uniqueness and particularization, in order to preserve his most personal core." In 1990s North America, where the word "unique" seems to be ubiquitous, Simmel's analysis that the individual "has to exaggerate this personal element in order to remain audible even to himself" rings all too true.[37]

The evolution of recent capitalist society has contributed to the development of a "cult of privatism," in which people compensate for an inner emptiness by satisfying sensual cravings of various kinds.[38] In this new culture personality has replaced liberty: The freedom to be one's self has become more important than the freedom to be an actor in the public realm. People have become inverted, self-preoccupied, and uncaring about their fellow citizens; politics has been converted into personality. "[The] public world has come to be lost in modern urban culture, a culture replacing the expressive life and identity of the public man with a new life, more personal, more authentic, and, all things considered, emptier."[39]

The family receives short shrift in a society in which the principle "me first" receives ideological justification. Although there are many reasons for the fragility of the nuclear family in late-twentieth-century

North America, one reason is undoubtedly minimalist individualism's stress on immediate, tangible happiness. A more collectivist society might encourage a calmer adjustment, accepting of temporary or even permanent difficulties and problems, as the ideal relationship within the family. If happiness means abandoning or disregarding commitments to family or community, then to the social minimalist the price is worth paying. The result in North America has been a voluntary abandonment of familial responsibility by parents, primarily fathers. And though this has "liberated" many parents from the strictures of uncomfortable social roles and relationships, it has helped to create a generation of insecure, frightened children.[40]

Hedonism is the ideal of minimalist society. Each individual seeks to maximize her pleasure. Material wealth and self-indulgence are two sides of the same coin of pleasure. Indeed, large sectors of North American society have adopted the ideology of the youthful counterculture of the 1960s, which sidestepped work and materialism completely to go directly to the sensual gratification that sex and drugs could provide.[41] In the hedonist vision self-respect is reinterpreted as respect for one's own desires. Desire, for those who can fulfill it through their own resources, is of greater import than the needs of those who cannot support themselves. The community, indeed the family, is lost in the social minimalist quest for individual self-fulfilment.

To communitarian critics—both those within North America and those outside—social minimalism seems to exemplify the complete breakdown of essential social mores that keep a community together. Privacy seems to mean that no one has any right to comment on or censure anything you do that is not actually illegal. Sexuality seems not to be subject to censure or control by state, church, or society. How, where, and on whom you spend your money is entirely up to you. So is whether you honor your parents, care for your children, or stay faithful to your spouse. The social mores of decent society are rejected in the minimalist vision of the proper way to live.

The Central Park thesis, then, is in part an accurate perception of social behavior in the United States. When only the extremes of social minimalism are noticed, U.S. society seems far less cohesive, far less respectful of family and community obligation, than most Third World societies or than the reactionary conservative dream of how American society used to be. Critics of Central Park perceive the costs of social breakdown, though they do not accurately address its cause. The cause is not overprotection of civil and political rights but the violation of fundamental economic rights that stems from a philosophy of social irresponsibility. Social minimalism permits anyone to strive for material wealth but it does not accept any obligation to those who fail to acquire enough material security once barriers to discrimination are removed. If human rights are to mean massive social inequality, then their price seems very high.

But for many who subscribe to the Central Park thesis, the problem is not social inequality or absolute poverty. Rather, it is disorder, the breakdown of older relations of deference that prevented the poor, women, and blacks from venting their rage on the prosperous, males and whites. Conservative communitarians within North America agree with much of the critique of hedonistic minimalism put forth by Third World traditionalists. They too perceive the massive disorder of Central Park. They attribute this disorder to the general decline of the conservative social values of family and home: Thus we turn to the second dominant trend in American social ideology—the conservative reaction against excessive, but not necessarily possessive, individualism.

The Conservative Reaction

Reactionary conservatives are conservatives who have reacted against social change by looking backward to a myth of the orderly past, which they hope to restore in modern society. This type of conservatism is also reactionary in the classic sense of being backward-looking. It is permeated by nostalgia for a world that never was, yet a world that has functioned as an organizing social myth for many Americans for several decades. "Nostalgia," as Christopher Lasch explained, "appeals to the feeling that the past offered delights no longer obtainable. . . . Nostalgia freezes the past in images of timeless, childlike innocence."[42] The myth of the orderly past presents the independent white nuclear family, with fathers, mothers, and children playing appropriate roles of authority and deference, as the ideal for which all Americans ought to strive.[43] It harkens back to the nineteenth-century myth of frontier days, each family caring for itself in rugged conditions in "a virtuous republic of small farmers."[44]

Although this organizing myth of the family is in fact "an ahistorical amalgam of structures, values and behaviors that never co-existed in the same time and place," during the 1950s it described social reality for a large section of the white population in the United States.[45] Whereas in 1986 only 6 percent of the U.S. population lived in family units consisting of "a breadwinning husband, a dependent homemaking wife, and two or more children," in the 1950s *half* of all American families did.[46] Unprecedented economic prosperity made single-family homes supported by one earner a reality for many returning war veterans. The new suburban society permitted a partial return to that mythical rural life:

Families lived in detached homes on their own private plots of land, where parents could garden on the weekends and fathers and sons could join together in household repairs. During the 1950s, it seemed, life was orderly and stable. Family roles were known and approved, fathers earning money and mothers staying home to care for the children. Sunday mornings were spent in church; neighbors knew and helped each other; and public streets were safe. The image of the "elm-shaded small town" could be realized in practice.[47]

Since the 1960s, the myth of community- and family-oriented life has been severely challenged. Women insisted on returning to work; indeed, many of them had continued to work during the 1950s, even though they had been pushed out of higher-paying jobs by returning veterans.[48] Male students challenged the ideal of the white patriot who, when he was not off to war to preserve the American Way, slogged daily to the office to support wife and family. The counterculture movement rejected work and self-discipline. These challenges signaled to conservatives a threat to the way of life they valued. Hard work, self-sacrifice, and social rectitude seemed to give way to hedonism, self-indulgence, and rejection of commitment to God, family, and community.

Liberal culture, seemingly glorifying abortion, abnegation of family responsibility, and rebellion against authority and against one's country, seemed to attack the very core of what made the life of the ordinary working person worthwhile. "Here were these rich kids, rich kids who could go to college, who didn't have to fight . . . telling you your son died in vain [in Vietnam]. It makes you feel your whole life is shit, just nothing," said one in the mid-1970s.[49] And as the supply of stable blue-collar jobs shrank in the 1980s, more and more men and women found their lives suddenly torn apart. The stable working class—indeed much of the middle class as well—was at risk of falling into the ranks of the truly poor.[50] The fear of losing all to the vagaries of uncertain market forces heightened the loss of respect and deference paid to honest folk fulfilling their social roles without complaint.

"Traditional" norms of deference disappeared after the 1960s. Black political activists pointed out how impossible it was for their communities to share in the American ideal as they exposed the hypocrisy of prosperous white communities that lived cheek-by-jowl with black slums. The black civil rights movement attacked the relations of authority and subordination that simmered beneath stable community relations. With blacks no longer respecting whites (or so it seemed), rising crime rates and urban disorder appeared to be the result.

Arising out of the black civil rights movement, the women's liberation movement seemed to turn the family on its head. Wives and children no longer honored husbands; indeed, some feminists pressured women who were raising children to get out of the home. Women's autonomy undermined their roles in the community. No longer, it seemed, were they willing to keep together their families while fathers spent long hours at work; to take care of elderly relatives; or to volunteer to run churches, parents' associations, and other community concerns. Women's new sexual freedom undermined the value of virginity and the principle that a woman should "belong" to only one man.

As the women's liberation movement rejected the ideal of the subordinate wife, the gay liberation movement went so far as to assert that even the heterosexual ideal had no particular value. Gays challenged not only the family, but also fundamental aspects of the male and female identities. While battles raged about whether male homosexuality was biologically rooted or a chosen sexual orientation, some lesbians seemed to elect their sexuality as a politicized revolt against patriarchy.[51] People who might agree that women and blacks had valid claims to equal treatment did not necessarily accept the same argument for gays. Indeed, for some, to equate the gay struggle with the women's or blacks' struggles insulted the latter two groups, who clearly had no choice in sex or skin color. Republican politician Pat Buchanan, for example, objected to attempts "to put homosexual behavior . . . on the same moral plane with being female or being black."[52]

Homosexuals challenge and undermine the conforming heterosexual investment in gender roles. "Being a man is a crucial component of personal identity for males in our society. . . . Being a man requires . . . not having relationships with men that are sexual or overly intimate." Ironically, as homosexuality becomes more acceptable, so heterosexuality is more challenged, and "pressures to define . . . one's status as a heterosexual man are likely to intensify."[53] These pressures combine with disgust at homosexual erotic practice to magnify dislike of gays. Homosexuals engage in practices, especially anal intercourse, that many heterosexuals consider the epitome of filth, even though some heterosexuals also practice them.[54] The perceived glorification of "unnatural" oral and anal sexuality by homosexuals undermines the rules of intimacy even more than does feminist rebellion against set gender roles.

The conservative reaction stresses the values of family, community, and religion in an attempt to stem those changes in society that appear, since the 1960s, to have been undermining these social institutions. Increasingly, North Americans live in nonfamily units (alone, with someone of the opposite sex not one's spouse, in homosexual arrangements) and have fewer or no children. North Americans are highly mobile and often have no home community, nor do they necessarily become involved in community affairs when they adopt new residences.

Although, as I note in Chapter 5, perhaps 40 percent of Americans and 30 percent of Canadians attend religious services weekly, many other North Americans are nonreligious. Although modern society provides many opportunities for new forms of community or association, many people prefer to withdraw from the community altogether.

The conservative reaction reflects the stress imposed on individuals by the new ideology of individualism that permeates late-twentieth-century North America. Intrinsic to this ideology is the belief that individuals can control their own fate. If life is hard on them, it is their own fault. Spiritual health is one's own responsibility: Self-fulfilment is an individualized matter depending on recognition and satisfaction of one's own potential. Such a culturally individualized society results in extreme strain for many people, a strain that can be overcome by a return to the fundamental values of home, community, or church.

Reactionary conservatives, then, intensely dislike the individualism and hedonism that characterize social minimalism. They connect this individualism with the recent social movements for human rights by blacks, women, and gays. Social minimalists and reactionary conservatives disagree strongly on the value of individual autonomy. The extreme individualist American—the person who puts self over family and society—is the target of the greatest conservative concern.

Yet this conflict between social minimalists and reactionary conservatives conceals an essential agreement on core values. Although they disagree strongly on the value of individual autonomy in the social sphere, they agree on the value of autonomy in the economic sphere. They share the core values of the American work ethic and materialism. Both social minimalists and reactionary conservatives believe in hard work and individual or family economic autonomy, and both reject responsibility for nonworkers, those who by their own "fault" have not managed to acquire membership in the prosperous consumerist classes. Like social minimalists, reactionary conservatives agree with formal equality of opportunity but do not advocate amelioration of unequal economic conditions. Also like social minimalists, they deny respect to the poor. Reactionary conservatives value hard work for its own sake as a moral good; wealth should be acquired through personal effort and discipline. The wealthy person is an autonomous being who, through his own private efforts, acquires socially acceptable goods in the marketplace.

The only exception to the moral imperative to economic independence in the reactionary conservative vision is the married woman. In the minimalist vision women, like men, are expected to be economically independent and their former strong links to the family are considered demeaning; in the conservative vision married wives and mothers are exempt from the requirement of personal economic autonomy. For reactionary conservatives, strong personal commitment to the family is a moral imperative. In Sandel's terms, the self ought to be encumbered. The responsible male is encumbered with financial obligations to his family and the responsible female is encumbered with social obligations.

But like social minimalists, reactionary conservatives do not look outward to the community as a whole. Their community is the circumscribed family; the social minimalist's is the circumscribed individual. And though social minimalists accept the right of all individuals to pursue their own happiness on their own terms, reactionary conservatives believe that the only appropriate form of happiness is that based on the maintenance of communities of self-sufficient families that share a common culture and (white) identity. Thus while both value economic independence, reactionary conservatives intensely disagree with hedonistic individualism.

The materialism of individualism in itself is not the problem; conservatives favor accumulation of wealth. Hedonism—the waste on personal pleasure of money that should be saved and invested—is the culprit. Thus, for example, accumulation of real estate is a legitimate use of wealth. But spending on ephemeral pleasures of the self, such as clothing, drugs, or luxury vacations, or on expensive urban pursuits, such as restaurants and nightclubs, is a sign of degeneracy. Autonomous lifestyles should not, in the conservative view, mean playfulness, a lack of that foresight that careful harboring of resources implies. Hedonistic individualism seems to have risen from the social movements of the 1960s to deride the values of the earlier world of the work ethic. Reactionary conservatives view hedonistic individualism as the prime cause of the breakdown of the orderly community that they believe existed in North America in decades past.

Reactionary conservatives are correct in their belief that hedonistic rejection of public commitment undermines community. But the community they want preserved is not the heterogeneous community that exists and needs protection today. In the modern world citizens must choose to devote their time and effort not only to preserving communities of those who are alike, but also to creating communities among those who may differ. A collective dedication to ensure the basic economic and social rights of all members of a society is the key to preservation of community in North America today. The poor, especially, cannot be equal or respected members of society unless the community recognizes their needs and ameliorates their condition. But this is not the kind of community obligation that reactionary conservatives have in mind for the United States. In the right-wing political agenda the rich are not expected to give up their wealth for redistribution to the poor. Private economic activity and the right to accumulate unlimited wealth are the hallmark of the reactionary conservative as much as the social minimalist.

Social minimalists also contribute to the breakdown of community. They reject the conservative community that required that subordinated groups defer to people in authority yet replace it only with self-fulfilling individualism. Thus many individuals who enjoyed new opportunities and success in recent decades became social isolates as they acquired enough wealth to entertain hedonistic self-indulgence. At the other end of the social scale, those who failed, despite new and nondiscriminatory economic opportunities, are left to find comfort in sex, drugs, and crime. These discarded, rootless individuals cannot participate in the community in any meaningful way.

It is easy for liberals to mock reactionary conservatives. Their nostalgic view of the past and their fears of blacks, feminists, and gay activists suggest fundamental intolerance and racism. The upwardly mobile urban professional who gladly admits women, gays, and blacks into his circle seems more tolerant, open, and at ease with social change. Yet the politically liberal social isolate also excludes the less privileged Other from his circle of concern. In capitalist society social closure can result from both ascriptive prejudice and economic irresponsibility.

Social Closure

Human rights ought to ensure all citizens the minimum necessities for a decent life. A "decent" life implies not only a reasonably secure economic situation, but the chance to make autonomous personal choices and to participate in public decision-making. This will help create a community in which citizens exhibit concern and respect for one another, though the kind of community it creates will contain elements of individualistic hedonism that will continue to offend conservatives. Human rights do not necessitate any particular style of life, but the lack of human rights, whether of personal freedom or basic economic decency and social respect, forecloses choices and leaves individuals vulnerable to asocial, atomistic despair.

The concept of human rights is liberal. Liberalism in principle demands respect for all individuals regardless of their status, whether that status be ascribed or achieved. Thus liberalism is one of humankind's great achievements. Liberalism has freed hundreds of millions of people from the constraints that made them miserable; that subjected them to the arbitrary authority of the honored; and that rendered them unable to make personal decisions and take personal actions to ameliorate their own suffering and that of their families.

Yet in North America, liberalism has failed to incorporate those who cannot achieve a minimum level of material security on their own. Prosperity is a goal that can be realized by many individuals through hard work and dedication: Successive waves of immigrants have realized this dream. The prosperous are a very large group; by any stretch of the imagination they include the vast majority of the population. But in both Canada and the United States, there is still a proletariat of the unemployed and the working poor. A disproportionate number of the proletariat are black but many are white; their social flaw is not race but class. Both black and white members of the unemployed and poor retreat into self-hatred and self-destruction.

The prosperous classes can tolerate the self-destruction of the neglected as long as it does not touch their own lives. But as self-destruction affects the wider community—through theft, drug addiction, and the spread of infectious diseases—the prosperous retreat into self-protection. In recent years one response to social unrest and conflict in the United States has been a closing-in of white society's collective identity and an exclusion of nonwhites and other deviants who do not fit within the collective view. Both social minimalism and reactionary conservatism share this tendency to social closure. Reactionary conservatives, whose voice was most strongly articulated in the 1992 platform of the Republican Party, try to extirpate social trends such as secularism and abortion that threaten their worldview and condemn fellow citizens who indulge in them.[55] Social minimalists tolerate deviant or racially differentiated groups that do not threaten their own way of life but ignore, rather than assist, the destitute.

In 1980, Bertram Gross argued that the United States exhibits "friendly" fascist tendencies. We are in danger of not recognizing fascism, contended Gross, when it appears in a relatively friendly, nonvirulent and nonracist (at least explicitly) form. Under friendly fascism, the community of insiders is well protected; defined lines are drawn between insiders and outsiders. Degraded outsiders are permitted to live their lives in their own enclaves as long as their existence does not threaten the insiders. Indeed, although the degraded are denied bread, they are permitted circuses. Indulgence in drugs, alcohol, and sex, Gross argued, is actively encouraged by the state because it deflects attention from larger social problems.[56]

Gross's use of the word "fascist" is far too strong. Fascism is connected primarily with Nazi genocide, even though some fascist regimes of the past, such as in Spain, were not genocidal. But even nongenocidal fascist regimes are products of historical forces that might never apply to the United States. Societies with entrenched human rights provisions protected by the rule of law do not necessarily deteriorate into fascism—even under very severe economic and military pressures.

Yet it is useful to revisit the history of fascism to illuminate how liberal Western societies are susceptible to romantic, collectivist views of the world that exclude social outsiders and other deviants. Modern Westerners who adhere to romantic communitarianism as a legitimate argument against individual human rights ignore the Western world's own history. Anti-Semitism and the romanticization of the pure community are part of all Western history, even though their genocidal culmination in Nazi-controlled Europe was geographically limited.

The Nazi ideology of the Aryan *Volk* was rooted in a romantic notion of an abandoned communitarian past. Nazism glorified the collectivity over the individual and built up a myth of a pre-Christian (non-Judaic) past in which, supposedly, a community of Aryan beings lived in close communion with nature. "In the beginning, the [Nazi] 'New Order' appeared as an instant solution to the quest of the masses for social dignity and a renewed community spirit."[57] Nazism epitomized tendencies in Western culture to retreat from secularism, liberalism, and humanism into a romanticized past of order, stability, unchanging social roles, and complete social homogeneity.[58]

Fascism had its intellectual roots in the anti-Semitism of the nineteenth century, a period of great social malaise brought about by the decline of the traditional order.[59] Urbanization, secularism, and capitalism had uprooted the authority of landlord, church, and nobility that had kept the masses under control for centuries. Democracy and universal male suffrage had been instituted, religious minorities were being freed, women were being granted minimal rights. In Western Europe, the victory of the Dreyfusards over the anti-Semites in the treason trial of the French Jewish military officer, Alfred Dreyfus, roused anxieties among those who connected military and state with the Christian church.[60]

Jews in nineteenth-century Europe symbolized the social change that made many ordinary people uneasy. According to popular perception, Jews were urban and landless. They dealt in the intangibles of banking and high finance, new institutions perceived to be at the root of capitalism's social upheaval. In the service of the new centralizing kings and presidents of modern Europe, they crossed national borders with

ease. Their loyalty to their own religious community seemed to supersede any loyalty to the nation-state in which they lived.[61]

Emerging from their allocated ghettoes and discarding the distinctive clothing that warned strangers of their Otherness, the Jews nevertheless brought their foreign religion with them. Yet even those who secularized were feared, more so even than those who remained religious.
Secular Jews further defied traditional boundaries and some threatened
the sacred domain of home, church, and family by marrying Christian
daughters. Jews were marginal men, half-in and half-out of the community, suspected of observing, criticizing, and perhaps undermining entrenched social norms.[62] The Jew became, in the hardened Nazi anti-
Semitism of the 1930s, the cosmopolitan Other, scorning the mythical
lost world of closeness and sameness. By extirpating Jews from their
world, the Nazis hoped to extirpate modernity itself.[63]

The Nazis were particularly frightened by modern, open, secular society, by the erosion of social order and social categorization. They mur-
dered Jews because they regarded them as modern, cosmopolitan, rootless slime.[64] They persecuted homosexuals because gays repudiated
their prescribed sex roles and their obligations to the German family, ex-
hibiting, especially during the Weimar Republic, a free, autonomously
chosen, and deviant lifestyle.[65] They debated whether to preserve a few
Roma (Gypsies) as ethnographic museum specimens of the noble savage or to kill them all as unauthentic half-breeds; they finally chose the
latter course.[66] In the Nazi mind, Jews and homosexuals epitomized selfish commercialism and individualism; Gypsies symbolized the worst
impurities of contact between self and Other, the Aryan and the primitive.

The Nazis took to a ghastly extreme the fears that modernity, openness, and secularism inspire in many social conservatives. This does not
mean that the United States is in danger of adopting Nazism; it does
mean that social closure against threatening groups can exist even in
formally liberal societies that protect individual human rights. Those
who cross social boundaries now are those who challenge the most fundamental basis of society: the family. Thus reactionary conservatives
dislike overt homosexuals, who do not incur obligations to the next generation. They also dislike women who support or undergo abortion and
thereby also deny the inevitability of familial responsibility. The real situations of those who seem to challenge familial responsibility are not
acknowledged by reactionary conservatives. Homosexuals may have
been married, may still be married, and may have children; or they may
enjoy stable long-term relationships and have aspirations for material
security and community life similar to those of the conservatives.

Women who abort may already have children or may hope to have children in the future. But the insistence on a private life, with autonomous decision-making and the right to regulate personal relations in a manner that does not conform to traditional social norms about the family, causes great anxiety among reactionary conservatives. Thus, for example, former first couple Ronald and Nancy Reagan masked their anxiety about their own unorthodox family histories—divorce, adoption, estrangement from children—with a sentimental celebration of the myth of the white picket fence.

Although social minimalism would seem to be far more tolerant of deviance than reactionary conservatism, nondeviant individualistic hedonists can easily conform to reactionary norms. Heterosexual hedonists can adopt an outwardly conservative lifestyle that permits them to be materialistic and preoccupied with self. Achieving women who are not feminists can adopt a similar approach; as long as they concentrate on morally approved preoccupations, raising children or improving themselves, their submerged hedonism will mesh easily with social conservatism. "Investment" by career women and their husbands in the best clothes, schools, and summer camps for their children is a choice of lifestyle that meshes nicely with the conservative belief in the value of the stable white family, even if it does require the mother to hire a nanny instead of staying home all day herself to raise her children.

Society, it seems to reactionary conservatives, is disintegrating. More noxious than the actual changes are people who celebrate such changes, who actively say that the disintegration of the family is a matter for rejoicing. Like the European Jews of a century ago, homosexuals and women's liberationists in North America today challenge the established order of things. "As a 'people,' they [homosexuals] substitute for Jews in the hate literature of far-right groups—symbols of urban degeneracy, unearned pleasures, and defiance of all that is Christian and 'natural.'"[67]

Homosexuals and women's liberationists are cosmopolitan. They live in cities and frequently celebrate the urban hedonist lifestyle. They interact with others of their kind with apparent disregard for the proprieties of ethnic and religious exclusivism. They advocate internationalism, making connections with other gays and women the world over. Nevertheless they refuse to be ghettoized, to be excluded from the larger community. Overt, activist homosexuals do not accept the stigma attached to their way of life; rather, they insist on their rights to go to church, even to be ordained; to have custody of their biological children or to adopt children; to have their living arrangements recognized under laws that provide health coverage, rent-controlled apartments, and insurance benefits to partners.[68] In 1993 in Canada, gays directly challenged heterosexual definitions of family by demanding the right to marry and have all the legal benefits of marriage.[69] A bill to provide full spousal rights to homosexuals was defeated in the legislature of the province of Ontario in 1994.

Like gays, feminists also refuse to be ghettoized. Women's liberationists permeate almost all communities. They propagandize; they open up women's centers; they insist on speaking publicly about taboo topics such as incest. Formerly pliant wives announce that they have been liberated and, seemingly overnight, leave their husbands. It seems that human rights demand that the natural order of things be upset and that the security of day-to-day living be undermined by constant demands for liberation and equality. Conforming men and women are told that all of the psychic energy they have invested in adopting their appropriate gender-specific cultural behaviors was unnecessary. "Do your own thing" and "be yourself" are implicit challenges to people's sense of inner worth and the comfort they derive from knowing that, whatever the personal price, they have done what is expected of them. Thus we see the New Right's effort to restore the consequences of unbridled sexual activities by abolishing abortion and recriminalizing homosexuality.[70]

The homosexual or feminist behavioral deviation in itself is not the threat. Many deviations are tolerated by society as long as they are not overt and are not claimed to be an alternate, indeed better, way of life than the conservative social norm. Infidelity in marriage is extremely common, though not socially acknowledged. Even highly deviant sexual behaviors do not necessarily threaten social conservatives, as long as approved social roles are upheld. Thus, the short-lived fashion of wife-swapping parties in the 1960s and 1970s may have been distasteful but was not a danger. Wives were swapped by husbands; approved relations of dominance and submission were not disturbed. Incestuous relations between fathers and daughters can go on for years with the full knowledge of families and friends, unchallenged precisely because they confirm, rather than deny, the father's right to rule his family and the female's obligation to submit to the male.[71]

Homosexuals and women's liberationists invite severe public reaction because they challenge, indeed sometimes deride, cherished social norms. Margaret Atwood's novel, *The Handmaid's Tale,* refers to the Nazi *Lebensborn* ("well of life") project to hasten the creation of a master race by mating young "Aryan" women with SS officers. In Atwood's version, women of the master race are controlled by a system designating one as a (barren) wife, a "breeder," or a prostitute, leaving no woman any choice as to which subservient role she will occupy.[72] In the real world of late-twentieth-century North America, the tendency some people still have to assume that those "free" women who attend bars alone or walk unescorted on darkened streets deserve to be raped is not merely a hangover from times less enlightened about the need for gender equality. It is also a harbinger of reaction. If the most fundamental unit of society is the family, then the most fundamental social relationship of power is that of males over females. The patriarch whose rule over family is threatened may find himself reacting with violence.

As for homosexuals, it appears to a great many that an incurable plague sent by God will wipe them out and vindicate conforming heterosexuals. About a quarter of respondents to *Los Angeles Times* polls consistently agreed as late as 1988 that "'AIDS is a punishment God has given homosexuals for the way they live."[73] Moreover, 34 percent of Americans polled in 1991 and 33 percent of Canadians polled in 1990 agreed that "I sometimes think that AIDS is a punishment for the decline in moral standards," although these numbers had decreased from 43 percent of Americans in October 1987 and 35 percent of Canadians in August 1988.[74] AIDS, many people believe, is a direct consequence of promiscuous male intercourse, frequently the most polluting anal intercourse. "AIDS offers an opportunity to propagate the belief . . . that homosexuality is itself a disease and a threat to human survival. . . . AIDS has become the metaphor for the *sin* of homosexuality and . . . the *sin* of sexual pleasure."[75]

Personal mistreatment of homosexuals can reinforce the insecure heterosexual male's sense of self. Gay-bashing in the 1980s and 1990s serves much the same function as Jew-bashing in the 1930s; it is a means of asserting control over an uncertain social environment. Surveys of American gays and lesbians in the 1980s indicated an increase in the number of attacks throughout the decade, with almost a quarter of gay men reporting in one national study that at least once in their lives they had been physically attacked for being gay. Such assaults on gay men include antigay male rape.[76] Overt, activist gays are perceived as deviant and dirty. Unlike covert homosexuals, they do not make a show of public respect of social norms, thus confirming the timocratic privilege of heterosexuality. As Jews symbolized the breakdown of social order sixty years ago in Europe, so gays and feminists symbolize it in North America today.

There is a danger of social closure in combining the minimalist ethic of disregard for the community with the reactionary dislike of nonconforming social categories. As honored social groups are incorporated into the community, degraded groups are progressively excluded as un-deserving of concern. In this respect, some social behavior in late-twen-tieth-century North America resembles the social attitudes that con-tributed to fascism. Fascism is actively hostile to privacy and private life. In reaction to the perception of unabated individualism, fascism pro-claims a romantic ideology of consensus, homogeneity, and personal comfort in conforming to social roles. Human dignity is to be achieved through integration into an all-encompassing moral order, represented by the fascist state. Any challenge to this order, including deviation in personal values and beliefs, is treated as a threat to the entire social fab-ric.

Symbols of American-ness, such as the flag and the national an-them, are already used to great effect by reactionary conservatives in the United States. Attempts to reintroduce God and Christianity into public discourse also have a powerful psychological impact on conservatives. They serve notice to secularized, nonreligious people of their outsider status. George Bush's 1988 campaign strategy, which painted liberalism as a taboo almost as strong as communism during the McCarthy era, is a frightening sign. If liberalism becomes a dirty word, as was the case in some circles during the late 1980s, then the sullying of human rights will not be far behind.[77] Bill Clinton's 1992 election did not remove this threat to liberal society.

Although homosexuals and feminists are the most visible targets of reactionary conservatives, poor blacks are the neglected victims. They are no longer necessary as workers in the U.S. economy, not even in the reserve army of labor, they are truly Marx's lumpenproletariat. They are too poor to provide a market; except for ephemeral consumer products. They are perceived as a drain on social resources, on policing capacity, on schools. Hedonistic social minimalists have no interest in supporting the black poor, and reactionary conservatives consider them immoral people who do not deserve support because they have brought their suf-ferings on themselves.

These social trends of minimalism and reaction undermine the lib-eralism of the U.S. political and legal systems. Officially the United States is a secular society; one's adherence to or rejection of religious be-lief does not affect one's relations with the state or its institutions. Many matters of personal life in the United States are officially matters of pub-lic indifference. But the realm of personal autonomy in thought, reli-gion, and choice of lifestyle is now under increasing attack. Public social scapegoating of deviant people can satisfy the need for confirmation of their identities that the reactionary conservatives seem to have. Meantime, minimalists acknowledge no obligation to protect the scapegoated as long as they, and their agenda of personal development and personal wealth, are not threatened.

North American culture in the late twentieth century is undergoing enormous upheaval. Groups of people who previously bore their degradation in silence are now not only denying it, but implying in their public rhetoric that previously honored categories are in fact dishonorable and no longer—if they ever were—worthy of respect. Established racial, gender, and family relations are under severe attack. Timocracy, the last psychological weapon of the dominant in situations of rapid social change, is itself disappearing. Social closure is a defensive reaction by the previously honored against this challenge to their ideals and way of life.

Social closure is, however, not inevitable. In Chapter 6 I argue that despite the persistence of timocratic behaviors, women and blacks are not entirely excluded from the opportunities provided by liberal society. Indeed, their inclusion has been proceeding apace even as shame and social terror continue to undermine their gains. Homosexuals have only recently been included in the discourse of human rights, yet they too have already had many of their rights affirmed. Similarly, welfare policies can and do ameliorate some of the worst effects of poverty. But, for the socially excluded, this is not enough. Status radicals, especially, challenge the fundamental premises of liberalism. The question for liberals at the turn of the millennium is this: Will those who have been heretofore excluded from North American society be willing to wait for more openness and attention to economic human rights or will a new, antiliberal agenda for reform fracture the consensus around the need for human rights?

Notes

1. Mary Ann Glendon, *Rights Talk: The Impoverishment of Political Discourse* (New York: The Free Press, 1991), p. 99.

2. Louis Henkin, "Rights: Here and There," *Columbia Law Review,* vol. 81, no. 8 (December 1981), pp. 1588–1590.

3. Barbara Ehrenreich, *Fear of Falling: The Inner Life of the Middle Class* (New York: HarperCollins, 1989), pp. 48–56 and 183–195.

4. Michael B. Katz, *The Undeserving Poor: From the War on Poverty to the War on Welfare* (New York: Pantheon Books, 1989), p. 7, emphasis in original.

5. Hannah Arendt, *The Origins of Totalitarianism* (New York: Harcourt Brace Jovanovich, 1973), pp. 141–142.

6. Jan Berting, "Societal Development in Relation to Human Rights, Rights of Peoples, and Sociological Theory and Research" (Rotterdam: Erasmus University, 1985, unpublished), p. 19.

7. Organization for Economic Cooperation and Development, *Future of Social Protection*, OECD, Social Policy Studies No. 6 (1988), pp. 10–11.

8. International Monetary Fund, "Government Finance Statistics Yearbook," vol. 16 (1992), p. 62.

9. Bertram Gross, *Friendly Fascism: The New Face of Power in America* (Boston: South End Press, 1980), p. 44.

10. U.S. House of Representatives, Committee on Ways and Means, *Health Care Resource Book* (Washington, D.C.: U.S. Government Printing Office, February 2, 1993), p. 81.

11. Sylvia Ann Hewlett, *When the Bough Breaks: The Cost of Neglecting Our Children* (New York: HarperCollins, 1991), p. 215.

12. The World Bank, *World Development Report 1993: Investing in Health* (New York: Oxford University Press, 1993), table 28, pp. 292–293.

13. Stephanie Coontz, *The Way We Never Were: American Families and the Nostalgia Trap* (New York: Basic Books, 1992), p. 2.

14. Center for the Study of Human Rights, *Twenty-Four Human Rights Documents* (New York: Columbia University, 1992), p. 8.

15. Hewlett, *When the Bough Breaks*, p. 240. See also Glendon, *Rights Talk*, pp. 75 and 135.

16. Sylvia Ann Hewlett, *A Lesser Life: The Myth of Women's Liberation in America* (New York: Warner Books, 1986), pp. 144–146.

17. "Family Leave Law: Provisions," *Congressional Quarterly—Weekly Report*, vol. 51, no. 7 (February 13, 1993), p. 335.

18. Hewlett, *A Lesser Life*, p. 91.

19. Ibid., p. 129.

20. William Julius Wilson, *The Truly Disadvantaged: The Inner City, the Underclass, and Public Policy* (Chicago: University of Chicago Press, 1987), p. 186.

21. Hewlett, *When the Bough Breaks*, pp. 221 and 17.

22. Coontz, *The Way We Never Were*, p. 2.

23. Andrew Hacker, "The New Civil War," *New York Review of Books*, vol. 39, no. 8 (April 23, 1992), p. 30.

24. U.S. Department of Commerce, Bureau of the Census, *Poverty in the United States: 1991*, Consumer Income Series P-60, no. 181, p. x.

25. Ibid., p. x.

26. U.S. Department of Commerce, Bureau of the Census, Current Population Reports, Series P-60, no. 163, *Poverty in the United States: 1987* (Washington, D.C.: U.S. Government Printing Office, 1989), p. 3.

27. For critical discussions of this perspective, see Katz, *The Undeserving Poor*, chapter 1, and Wilson, *The Truly Disadvantaged*, pp. 13–18. For an earlier discussion, see Charles A. Valentine, *Culture and Poverty: Critique and Counter-Proposals* (Chicago: University of Chicago Press, 1968).

28. Steven W. Rawlings, "Single Parents and their Children," in U.S. Bureau of the Census, Current Population Reports, Series P-23, no. 162, *Studies in Marriage and the Family* (Washington, D.C.: U.S. Government Printing Office, 1989), table A, p. 13.

29. On the controversy over busing in Boston, see Christopher Lasch, *The True and Only Heaven: Progress and Its Critics* (New York, W. W. Norton, 1991), pp. 496–504.

30. Robert Justin Goldstein, "The United States," in Jack Donnelly and Rhoda E. Howard (eds.), *International Handbook of Human Rights* (Westport, Conn.: Greenwood, 1987), pp. 435–436. For a detailed history of the suppression of labor and radical political movements in the United States, see Goldstein, *Political Repression in Modern America: From 1870 to the Present* (Cambridge, Mass.: Schenkman, 1978).

31. Michael J. Sandel, "The Procedural Republic and the Unencumbered Self," *Political Theory*, vol. 12, no. 1 (February 1984), quotations from pp. 86 and 87.

32. Edwin Schur, *The Awareness Trap: Self-Absorption Instead of Social Change* (New York: Quadrangle, 1976), p. 1.

33. Ibid., pp. 3 and 4.

34. Ibid., p. 194.

35. Ibid., p. 52.

36. Ibid., p. 90.

37. Georg Simmel, "The Metropolis and Mental Life," In Kurt H. Wolff (ed.), *The Sociology of Georg Simmel* (New York: The Free Press, 1950), pp. 413, 414, and 422.

38. Christopher Lasch, *The Culture of Narcissism: American Life in an Age of Diminishing Expectations* (New York: W. W. Norton, 1979), p. 71.

39. Richard Sennett, *The Fall of Public Man: On the Social Psychology of Capitalism* (New York: Vintage Books, 1978), p. 109.

40. Hewlett, *When the Bough Breaks*, chapter 4, pp. 127–173. See also Barbara Dafoe Whitehead, "Dan Quayle Was Right," *The Atlantic Monthly*, vol. 271, no. 4 (April 1993), pp. 47–84.

41. Barbara Ehrenreich, *The Hearts of Men: American Dreams and the Flight from Commitment* (New York: Anchor Press, 1983), p. 113.

42. Lasch, *The True and Only Heaven*, pp. 83 and 118.

43. Coontz, *The Way We Never Were*.

44. Lasch, *The True and Only Heaven*, p. 94.

45. Quotation from Coontz, *The Way We Never Were*, p. 9.

46. Hewlett, *A Lesser Life*, p. 135.

47. Lasch, *The True and Only Heaven*, p. 100.

48. Coontz, *The Way We Never Were*, p. 31.

49. Quoted in Lasch, *The True and Only Heaven*, p. 492.

50. Lasch, *The True and Only Heaven*, pp. 479–483; Hewlett, *When the Bough Breaks*, pp. 48–51.

51. On the possible biological roots of male homosexuality, see Chandler Burr, "Homosexuality and Biology," *The Atlantic Monthly*, vol. 271, no. 3 (March 1993), pp. 47–65.

52. P. J. Buchanan, "AIDS and moral bankruptcy," *New York Post*, December 2, 1987, p. 23, cited in Gregory M. Herek and Eric K. Glunt, "An Epidemic of Stigma: Public Reactions to AIDS," *American Psychologist*, vol. 43, no. 11 (November 1988), p. 888.

53. Gregory M. Herek, "On Heterosexual Masculinity," *American Behavioral Scientist,* vol. 29, no. 5 (May/June 1986), pp. 567–568 and 571.

54. Richard Poirier, "AIDS and Traditions of Homophobia," *Social Research,* vol. 5, no. 3 (autumn 1988), p. 466.

55. Roberto Suro, "Bush Gets Full Support at Religious Gathering," *New York Times,* August 23, 1992, p. 15; and Editorial, "Mr. Bush, Crossing the Line," *New York Times,* August 26, 1992, p. A18.

56. Gross, *Friendly Fascism,* pp. 315–316.

57. Christa Kamenetsky, "Political Distortion of Philosophical Concepts: A Case History—Nazism and the Romantic Movement," *Metaphilosophy,* vol. 3, no. 3 (July 1972), p. 216.

58. Steven Lukes, *Individualism* (Oxford: Basil Blackwell, 1973), pp. 19–21.

59. Lucy S. Dawidowicz, *The War Against the Jews, 1933–1945* (New York: Bantam Books, 1975), chapter 2, pp. 29–62, and Arendt, *Origins of Totalitarianism,* part 1.

60. On the Dreyfus affair as a symbol of secularism and modernity, see Arendt, *Origins of Totalitarianism,* chapter 4, pp. 89–120, and Sennett, *The Fall of Public Man,* pp. 240–251.

61. Arendt, *Origins of Totalitarianism,* part I, "Anti-Semitism."

62. Robert Ezra Park, *Race and Culture* (Glencoe, Ill.: The Free Press, 1950), pp. 354 and 376.

63. Zygmunt Bauman, *Modernity and the Holocaust* (Ithaca, N.Y.: Cornell University Press, 1989), chapter 2.

64. Ibid., p. 39.

65. Richard Plant, *The Pink Triangle: The Nazi War Against Homosexuals* (New York: Henry Holt, 1986).

66. Donald Kenrick and Grattan Puxon, *The Destiny of Europe's Gypsies* (London: Chatto; Heinemann, 1972), p. 92.

67. Ehrenreich, *The Hearts of Men,* p. 129.

68. On nonbiological lesbian parents (adult caretakers of a partner's biological offspring) suing for custody rights, see Carlyle C. Douglas, "Lesbian Child-Custody Cases Redefine Family Law," *New York Times,* July 8, 1990, p. E9.

69. Joe Woodard, "Gay 'Families' Await the Verdict: The Supreme Court Ponders Homosexual Marriage," *Alberta Report,* vol. 19, no. 37 (August 31, 1992), pp. 23–24; and "Cases of Note: 'Family Status' Excludes 'Sexual Orientation,'" *Canadian Human Rights Reporter,* vol. 17 (May 27, 1993), pp. i–ii.

70. Ehrenreich, *The Hearts of Men,* p. 161.

71. Judith Lewis Herman, with Lisa Hirschman, *Father-Daughter Incest* (Cambridge, Mass.: Harvard University Press, 1981), chapter 4, pp. 50–63.

72. Margaret Atwood, *The Handmaid's Tale* (Toronto: McClelland and Stewart, 1985). On the *Lebensborn* program, see Helen Fein, *Accounting for Genocide: National Responses and Jewish Victimization During the Holocaust* (Chicago: University of Chicago Press, 1979), p. 27.

73. Herek and Glunt, "An Epidemic of Stigma," p. 889.

74. The Gallup Poll (U.S.), *Public Opinion 1991,* "May 15, AID" (Wilmington, Del.: Scholarly Resources Inc., 1992), p. 113; and Lorne Bozinoff and Peter MacIntosh, "Public Increasingly Fearful of AIDS Epidemic," *The Gallup Report* (Canada), August 13, 1990.

75. Poirier, "AIDS and Traditions of Homophobia," pp. 463–464, emphasis in original.

76. Gregory M. Herek, "Hate Crimes Against Lesbians and Gay Men: Issues for Research and Policy," *American Psychologist,* vol. 44, no. 6 (June 1989), pp. 949–950.

77. Ehrenreich, *Fear of Falling,* pp. 192–193.

8 Individualism and Social Obligation

Individualism and Social Obligation

Social critics in the United States have begun only recently to discuss seriously the lack of common obligation. One such critic, Amitai Etzioni, used the term "communitarian" in referring to what I call social democracy and "authoritarians" and "radical individualists" to describe what I call reactionary conservatives and social minimalists. Although our differing terminology is potentially confusing, we share the same concern to increasing social obligation in capitalist North American society.[1] We agree that there is a need to modify social individualism with concern for the collectivity; we also agree that this can be done without eroding individual human rights.

In another very influential volume, Mary Ann Glendon makes the same point. Without denying or wishing to undermine human rights, Glendon is concerned by excessively individualistic "rights talk." "In its silence concerning responsibilities, it [rights talk] seems to condone acceptance of the benefits of living in a democratic social welfare state, without accepting the corresponding personal and civic obligations. In its relentless individualism, it fosters a climate that is inhospitable to society's losers, and that systematically disadvantages caretakers and dependents, young and old. In its neglect of civil society, it undermines the principal seedbeds of civic and personal virtue."[2]

Both Etzioni and Glendon acknowledge the deep social structural inequities of the contemporary United States: Unlike conservative social critics, neither attempts to gloss over racism, sexism, or class inequalities. The remedy for the problem of lack of common obligation lies in socially concerned adjustment to the realities of modern life, not in backward-looking mythologizing. The idealized "traditional" community in North America never did exist. Inside the two-story shingled home surrounded by a white picket fence often lurked patriarchy and, sometimes, physical violence or incest. On the other side of the tracks from those orderly white fences lived the poor and the blacks, while miles and states away, out of sight, lived North America's indigenous peoples. The socially constructed myth of the white picket fence exerts a powerful hold on the collective psyche of people who find the crass materialism, individual self-centeredness, and competitiveness that characterize much of modern North American culture highly objectionable. But it is a myth.

Rather than focus on the past, I focus on the present. I defend those aspects of individualism that ensure that every citizen is treated equally and with respect, and that permit economic, social, political, and intellectual autonomy. This type of individualism is possible in modern society. The complexity of role-sets and the individual's capacity for autonomous thought about his society allow social activities of a kind unknown in premodern society. Tens of millions of North American citizens join in projects whose object is to ameliorate the social and economic suffering of their compatriots. These citizens frequently display a capacity to empathize with the Other that is unknown in societies in which the community consists of in-groups and in which outsiders are unworthy of concern or respect.

The individualism I advocate is ethical rather than materialist. This is an ideal, perhaps as idealist as the myth of the lost American community. But it is an ideal that does not close its eyes to past social injustices and to the degradation that large categories of people still suffer in most Western societies. It is an ideal that requires the society and polity to recognize their obligations to all citizens and that expects the ethical individual to act on his obligation to the community. For such an individual, it is the intricate and freely maintained network of multifarious connections to others that constitutes community. Some of these connections, such as those to family of origin, will be determined at birth; others will result from changing life circumstances or active choice.

A human rights–based political regime can incorporate concern for the community via a serious effort to protect economic rights as well as civil and political rights. Many people, without work and without decent living conditions, are too poor and alienated to take part in the collective activities of the society as a whole. Poverty undermines community. The capacity to lead an intrinsically satisfying life enmeshed in a variety of social relations depends to a considerable extent on one's educational level and income.[3] Even the capacity to help others varies: The more highly educated and wealthy one is, the more likely he is to engage in voluntary activities dedicated to helping others.[4] "Poverty and power-lessness . . . offer a bad foundation for the development of individual autonomy, intellectual flexibility, and creativity," precisely the characteristics that lend texture, depth, and meaning to life in the modern world.[5]

People whose basic material needs are satisfied and whose personal dignity is upheld by respect for their autonomous choices—whether those be religious commitment or atheism, heterosexuality or homosexuality, ethnic belongingness or cosmopolitan heterogeneity—will feel free to select their own communities and to donate their own time, energy, and financial resources to improve them. In North America at its best, a network of small communities makes up the core of larger community life: Charities join with lobbying groups to pressure for greater public welfare commitment; different religious and ethnic groups get together for ecumenical or multinational celebrations; coalitions of previous "out-groups" make common cause to pressure for greater political inclusion.

The modern individual has a wide variety of statuses, interests, and memberships that do not overlap as they once did in closed, homogeneous village societies. He may suffer inequalities or indignities in one status yet be equal to everyone else in another. Michael Walzer suggested that in modern democratic societies, the key to equality is to avoid the piling up of inequalities, for example, piling up racial, income, educational, and political inequalities so that one group suffers them all.[6] Given the inevitability of inequality (some people will be more beautiful than others, learn more easily, or have more supportive family connections), this is a useful way of defining the aim of equality in complex societies. If certain kinds of inequalities such as discrimination in politics or education can be completely eliminated, if others such as unemployment can be distributed in a random fashion, and if still others such as poverty can be ameliorated, then the un-piling of inequality can produce a society in which citizens wield relatively equal amounts of influence and command relatively equal amounts of respect.

Inequalities are frequently also indignities. In past societies the piling up of indignities meant that some individuals might be completely excluded from the community. Thus the disobedient son might be cast out not only from his family, but also from church and village life, even if he had valid reasons for refusing to submit to his father. The multiple social memberships of modern society render this type of social exclusion less probable. The man or woman who deviates from the social norms of one community can join another, as do many religious converts and eccentric individuals. For most people in modern North America, indignities cannot be piled up in such a way as to result in multiple exclusions from the various aspects of society.

For some people, though, multiple indignities can result in multiple exclusions. This is particularly so for blacks and aboriginal North Americans, whose role-sets are still considerably circumscribed by their racial origins. It is much more difficult for a black or aboriginal person to ignore his shamed social status than for a woman to do so. Women are far more randomly dispersed in the class structure than are blacks and aboriginals and have far more variety in the roles they occupy.

In the minds of many privileged whites, the circumscribed world of the black or aboriginal must be justified. As Erwin Staub noted in his psychological analysis of genocide, most people prefer to believe in a just world.

> People tend to assume that victims have earned their suffering by their actions or character. . . . People believe in a just world with different degrees of conviction. Those whose belief is strong derogate poor people, underprivileged groups, or minorities. Strong belief in a just world is associated with rigid application of social rules and belief in the importance of convention. . . . Devaluation [of the victim] is especially likely if the victims' continued suffering is expected. To feel empathy results in empathic distress. To avoid that, people distance themselves from victims.[7]

This psychological discussion helps to explain the attractiveness of social closure, of rejecting any obligation to those whose situation, in modern North America, seems almost hopeless. So that they can believe in a just world, privileged people ascribe qualities of undeservingness to those who suffer piled-up inequalities.

Thus the modern community is not one that encompasses all citizens. Community of choice, of social obligation to selected strangers, is a reality for many upper- and middle-class individuals in North American society, who participate actively in voluntary groups and subcultural activities unconnected with their family lives, their ethnicity, or their religion. This is also the reality for some less prosperous people who form voluntary and political organizations that give them the capacity to withstand institutional and social degradation. It is not the reality for those people upon whom indignities have been piled up to such an extent that the only escape is anomie—family violence, addictions of various sorts, and crime. It is not the reality for those poverty-stricken citizens for whom community can only mean submission to authority, whether of employers, welfare officials, or the police.

The victims of piled-up indignities are those whom liberal society has failed. To remedy their indignities, the state and society must guarantee not only civil and political rights to formal equality, but also those economic rights that show, in practice, equal respect for all citizens and that allow all citizens a degree of personal and political autonomy in their everyday lives. Such a system requires social democracy.

Social Democracy

In the international human rights debate between the liberal "Western" position and the various communitarian critiques, the social democratic perspective has had very little airing. The United States, with its feeble approach to economic rights, is taken as representative of Western human rights practice, and U.S. practice is seen as the only possible variety of liberalism. Yet social democracy is a distinct variety of liberalism that bridges the gap between individual and community. It is committed politically to providing and protecting the entire range of human rights.

Social democracy is a variant of liberalism that views the social provision of economic security as an inherent part of respect for the individual. This is somewhat different from a standard definition of social democracy as "an ethos and a way of life characterized by a general levelling of status differences."[8] Social democracy does not require the radical leveling of economic differences: Leveling discourages the initiative necessary for economic progress both on the collective and the individual plain. Leveling can result in an overall lowering of a society's standard of living, as in many of the former Communist societies of Eastern Europe.

Rather, economic security can be provided by ensuring that there is a reasonable floor for the poorest in every society. Social democrats do try to reduce the differences between rich and poor, but not in a manner that reduces the total amount of wealth in a society in order to eliminate a class of wealthy people. The purpose of social democracy is to provide a welfare net that ensures all the basic needs of citizens will be met. Economic rights are a matter of entitlement, not a matter of desert. Basic needs are socially defined. They are not merely biological but encompass what is necessary to function as a citizen in society. Thus, for example, in the Nordic social democracies state-provided child care and generous parental leave policies are socially defined necessities designed to enable women to participate in the labor force and as citizens equally with men.[9]

Social democracy does not mean abolishing capitalism; it does mean ameliorating radical capitalism. Social democracy requires a mixed economy in which the social provision of economic security is one of the chief aims of society and the state. But this does not imply public ownership of the entire economy or even of most of it. Social democracy retains the basic principles of liberal society. An economic system that is substantially separate from the political system helps to ensure that power is dispersed. So do the key characteristics of liberal democracy: namely, competing political parties that have the right to assume office, an independent judiciary, a free and critical press, and a plethora of interest groups. This dispersal of power provides a variety of means for citizens to protect themselves against the state's tendency to ignore (at best) and violate (at worst) human rights. Thus social democracy demands all those aspects of civil and political rights that both right and left communitarians disregard as socially divisive and inherently individualistic.

An important aspect of contemporary social democracy is social feminism, which includes especially the protection of mothers and children.[10] In North America, reactionary conservatives are far more concerned with the protection of motherhood than are social minimalists, but their solution to the problem of the disintegrating family disregards the social evolution of women's economic roles. Reactionary conservatives want women to give up their jobs and return to the home to be dependent on the male breadwinner. Thus in the United States, the price of family stability frequently is severe economic insecurity for mothers and children, who must rely on one man for their support. By contrast, Western European social democracies try to enable mothers to stay home with their children without endangering their economic well-being.

Social feminism and social democracy seek to preserve the family and the community by recognizing how these fundamental social institutions have been affected by changing structural conditions—such as the large-scale entry of women into the paid labor force. Rather than try to turn the clock back on these changes, social democracy provides state-mandated institutional supports that ameliorate the trend to economic individualism and family breakdown. Social democracy recognizes the common responsibility of all members of society to ensure that children are properly raised.[11] It does not penalize women for exercising their individual rights to work; it accepts the individual, female as well as male, as the basic social unit of modern society. Social democrats seek to create in the modern world a community of individuals who freely choose to live together and follow common social goals, permitting choice while preserving the sense of belonging.

Amy Gutmann argues that rather than focus on a false antithesis between individualism and communitarianism, one should realize the "constructive potential" of the communitarian critique to modify excessively individualist politics. "Communitarianism has the potential for helping us discover a politics that combines community with a commitment to basic liberal values. . . . Communitarian values . . . are properly viewed as supplementing rather than supplanting basic liberal values. . . . The potential of communitarianism lies . . . in indicating the ways in which we can strive to realize not only justice but community through the many social unions of which the liberal state is the super social union."[12] This is also the key focus of Amitai Etzioni's call for a return to communitarian values in the United States: "A paradox highlights a major aspect of contemporary American civic culture: a strong sense of entitlement—that is, a demand that the community provide more services and strongly uphold rights—coupled with a rather weak sense of obligation. . . . [But] Americans . . . can now act without fear. We can act without fear that attempts to shore up our values, responsibilities, institutions and communities will cause us to charge into a dark tunnel of moralism and authoritarianism that leads to a church-dominated state or a right-wing world."[13]

The fear of authoritarianism can be relieved if community obligation always rests on a strong foundation of individual civil and political rights and a strong belief in the necessity for equality. Social democracy conserves these two principles. It is not incompatible with claims presented by groups on behalf of their individual members nor with preservation of those aspects of traditional cultures that, voluntarily chosen, can and do enhance the quality of life. But it recognizes that group values, norms, and customs are not permitted to override the rights of any individual, whether inside or outside the group. The focus on the individual in social democratic societies is not incompatible with community.

An ideal social democratic society will, via democracy, protect its citizens from abuse by the state and, via collective commitment to the common economic welfare, provide its citizens with a standard of living that grants them life with dignity. It will guarantee the civil equality of all its citizens and provide a floor of economic security that will protect them from social degradation. But at the same time a social democratic society will allow plenty of scope for community and for collectivist concerns, voluntarily chosen. Personal identifications with status groups will be a matter of individual choice; deviant or outsider individuals will be permitted to join insider organizations or create their own as they see fit. Group life and cultural life will be matters of private individual choice that, nevertheless, will provide a sense of membership and community to each individual precisely because those matters are freely chosen.

In a social democratic society concern for others' individual rights will often be realized, as it already is to some extent in classically capitalist societies, through community-based associations. Thus in a social democratic society social welfare will not be a matter entirely in the hands of the state. Intermediate associations that are the underpinnings of political democracy will not disappear; they will mediate between citizen and state, providing a mode of civic organization through which individuals can band together to achieve collective goals. Associations can be based on individual choices of preoccupations, anything from hobbies such as chess or gardening to social concerns such as abortion rights or preservation of the family. Associations can also be based on communitarian concerns, on membership in traditional communities defined by religion, language, culture, or kin. Culture and belongingness in social democratic society are matters not of static categorization or genetic kinship but of choice and individual decision-making. Community is valued as an association of individuals.

The reintegration of community into the minimalist framework of liberal human rights is an urgent necessity. With its essential focus on economic as well as civil and political rights, only such a reintegration can answer the communitarian charge that human rights are symptomatic of overly individualist and materialistic societies. The reintroduction of community is a requirement for a real democracy, in which not only individual human rights but also collective social obligation are taken seriously. A democracy in which individual citizens do not feel responsible for other citizens is one in which competition for advantage will undermine the provision of economic human rights.

For a society to function as a true democracy, all individuals must be treated as if they are of equal moral worth. One must be able to assume "that the individuals of whom the society is composed see themselves, or are capable of seeing themselves, as equal in some respect more fundamental than all the respects in which they are unequal."[14] This fundamental equality is not measurable in quantitative terms, nor is it merely a matter of legal status or political rights. It must be an equality of societal concern and respect. Each individual must be able to depend on others' respect for him and concern for his well-being, so that when he cannot rely on his own resources, he can at least trust society to make sure that he falls neither into destitution nor into despair.

Social trust, a sense of real community in which no category of individuals is considered to be the Other/outsider and in which everyone is considered the responsibility of the citizenry as a whole, is a fundamental underpinning of democracy. Constance Perin noted:

> Tensions between how we bring people in and keep them out, how we trust and distrust, how we honor and disparage are never very far from the surfaces of American life. When ordinary social trust is missing, so is the foundation of democracy. "The role of social trust and cooperativeness as a component of the civic culture cannot be overemphasized. It is, in a sense, a generalized resource that keeps a democratic policy operating. . . . Social trust facilitates political cooperation . . . without it, [formal] institutions may mean little." Belonging depends on trust: the less there is of any kind, the less there is of every kind.[15]

A political regime protective of human rights, then, demands first of all the elimination of social degradation and implied insider-outsider social statuses. But such formal civil equality is not enough. A community of trust is also required to ensure not only the substantive protection of civil and political rights, but also the substantive protection of economic rights. The state in and of itself cannot protect the latter. A minimal standard of economic well-being is only possible in a community of obligation. In modernized societies social democracy is the best political expression of this community of obligation. That is why, among all the political forms of the twentieth century, social democracy is the rarest and most difficult to attain. Even formally social democratic societies tend to exclude those who are radically different from the majority, although they are more inclusive of the poor and of social deviants than either minimalist radical capitalist or traditional communitarian social systems.

Social democratic societies are the best guarantors of the full range of human rights (economic, civil, political) that allow a person to live the good life as he sees fit. Yet in the United States, social democracy is not even a viable political option. If the richest country in the world excludes social democracy from its political agenda, then this is a telling indictment of the "Western" approach to human rights. But the United States is not the only Western country that fails to live up to its human rights obligations.

Continued Inequities in a Social Democracy: Canada

It would be unfair to indict the United States alone for the excesses of hedonistic materialism and discrimination against outsiders. I am privileged to live in a wealthy country, Canada, that has mild social democratic and welfarist leanings. Yet in Canada as in the United States, social

outsiders, especially the indigenous peoples but also blacks, suffer de-
privations of their human rights. And in Canada as in the United States,
poor citizens, though formally inside the system of social obligation,
nevertheless find themselves living on the margins of society.

Canada lies between the United States and Western Europe in the
extent of its commitment to social democracy. Many Canadians pride
themselves on the differences between their society and U.S. society.
One of the most noticeable differences is Canada's greater commitment
to social welfare. Unlike the United States, Canada has a universal system of health insurance for all citizens and landed immigrants. Canada
also has a universal system of maternity leave for a minimum period of
seventeen weeks, which pays mothers unemployment insurance benefits for fifteen weeks and protects job and seniority upon return to the
workplace.[16] Although there is some concern about the cost of the health
system (at 9.1 percent of the GDP in 1990, Canada's system is still
cheaper than the nonuniversal system in the United States, which
stands at 12.7 percent),[17] the principle of universality is still an important
aspect of Canadians' attitude toward social welfare. The provision of basic needs such as health care is seen as a matter of citizen entitlement
rather than a matter of desert.

Thus in Canada, there appears to be a stronger sense of obligation
toward fellow citizens than in the United States. This sense of obligation
is reflected in a recent government proposal for a "social charter" to sup-
plement the formal Charter of Rights and Freedoms. In the Constitutional Accord defeated by national referendum in October 1992, a
new provision entitled "The Social and Economic Union" was included.
The policy objectives of this Union included maintenance of Canada's
universal health care system and provision of "adequate social services
and benefits to ensure that all individuals resident in Canada have reasonable access to housing, food and other basic necessities."[18] Such an
amendment would not, however, have entrenched economic human
rights as justiciable under the Charter of Rights and Freedoms. There is,
for example, no legal right to food in Canada.[19]

The Canadian sense of community is also reflected in the country's
official policy of multiculturalism.[20] It acknowledges the diverse origins
and cultures of the people who make up Canadian society and recognizes in principle that the diversity of cultural practices enhances everyone's culture. Thus, multiculturalism is seen as a tool to bridge the gap
between native-born white Canadians and the "other" nonwhites, or
visible minorities as they are called, who have been immigrating to
Canada in large numbers since racially exclusive immigration criteria

were abandoned in the 1960s. Multicultural programs, however, absorb only a minuscule part of the federal budget (0.047 percent in 1992).[21]

Despite Canada's commitment to general social welfare and cultural pluralism, several groups of Canadians still suffer serious discrimination and disadvantage. These groups are, in particular, indigenous peoples, blacks, and the poor.

There are about 950,000 people of aboriginal ancestry in Canada in a total population of just over 27 million.[22] Aboriginal Canadians are severely disadvantaged compared to Canadians of other origins. In 1981, male aboriginal Canadians still had a life expectancy (62) that was ten years shorter than that of all male Canadians. The aboriginal infant mortality rate (15 per 1,000) was twice as high as that of all Canadians.[23] Indigenous Canadians are at the absolute bottom of the income scale in Canada and experience the highest level of unemployment.[24] In 1986, the average income for indigenous Canadians in the labor force was $9,000, whereas the average for all Canadians was almost $20,000.[25] Although they constitute perhaps 3.5 percent of the Canadian population, in 1989–1990, 18 percent of those in provincial prisons and 11 percent of those in federal prisons were indigenous people.[26] Social violence is a dominating aspect of aboriginal life, with high suicide, accident, and incarceration rates reflecting the disintegration of aboriginal cultures.

The continued suffering of Canadian aboriginal peoples stems in part from the fact that until the 1960s they were legally deemed second-class citizens who did not enjoy the full range of civil and political rights. Indigenous Canadians who lived on reserves were not permitted the right to vote in federal elections until 1960 and they could not vote in all the provinces until 1969.[27] Prior to that time only natives who "enfranchised," that is, who became nonstatus Indians by leaving the reserve and integrating into the dominant culture, were permitted the vote. Status (reserve) Indians were also denied freedom of movement: From 1885 until the late 1930s, they were required by the RCMP (Royal Canadian Mounted Police) to carry passes in order to travel.[28] When native Canadians started to organize in the 1920s to oblige the government to respect their treaty rights, the government retaliated by restricting their freedom of association. A provision of the Indian Act of 1927 "made it an offence punishable by law to raise funds for the purpose of pursuing any claim to aboriginal title."[29] Attempts during the last two decades to remedy the situation of native peoples have resulted in some improvements, most notably the emergence of an educated and articulate cadre of indigenous leaders. But the legacy of discrimination, social violence, and economic misery is so strong that many indigenous Canadians now reject the ideals of liberal society and look instead to an independent, reconstituted native culture as the solution to their subordinated status.[30]

Until very recently, many Canadians of European descent, ignoring their treatment of aboriginal peoples, prided themselves on their openness to people of other races. Unlike people in the United States, they believed, they had never practiced racial segregation. This is untrue. Until 1967, there were very few blacks in Canada. Small pockets of descendants of American slaves were found in Nova Scotia (where they had been brought by their masters or emigrated on their own after the U.S. War of Independence), in southwest Ontario (where the Underground Railroad ended), and elsewhere. In Ontario, schools in areas with relatively large concentrations of blacks were segregated until 1965, when they seem to have been discretely desegregated as a reaction to the U.S. civil rights movements.[31] In Nova Scotia, as late as the 1970s blacks lived in effectively segregated communities lacking the basic social services provided by the state to the white community.[32]

Although there is now officially no segregation in Canada, racism still exists. Some blacks view their treatment by police as social terror. From 1978 to 1992, fourteen blacks were victims of police shootings in the city of Toronto alone; four died.[33] In the absence of statistics on the races of all victims of police shootings in Toronto, it is difficult to determine whether blacks are more likely than others to be shot. In 1989, a task force established by the province of Ontario to investigate police use of force said merely that "improperly used force . . . may have a disproportionate impact on visible minorities."[34]

During the past two decades Canadians have used the philosophy of human rights to try to ameliorate some of the discriminatory practices that minority groups such as blacks still suffer.[35] But as in the United States, the classic human rights liberalism of Western democracy is not sufficient to create an ethic of community in modern Canadian society. Canada's culture of human rights is limited by its very liberalism, stressing, as in the United States, equality of opportunity among status groups rather than amelioration of the indignities individuals suffer in class society. Human rights legislation in Canada concentrates on ensuring equality of opportunity and focuses on ascriptively based differences. The laws that govern Canadians forbid discrimination on the basis of a number of perceivable differences rooted either in biology or culture. Thus discrimination on grounds of race, gender, and age is prohibited, as is discrimination on grounds of language, religion, and ethnicity.

If a group can persuade Canadian society at large that the group is a status category, then it can demand human rights in order to eliminate any discrimination it might suffer. Even homosexuals can make this claim, in part by declaring that homosexuality is a matter of innate (biological) predisposition rather than a matter of choice. After a federal court in fall 1992 struck down rules barring homosexuals from military service, the government introduced legislation into the House of Commons banning all discrimination on grounds of sexual orientation.[36] (As of January 1995, after a change of government in 1993, the legislation was still pending.)

Women have benefited considerably from the egalitarian human rights orientation that has evolved in Canada during the last two decades. Upper- and middle-class women no longer find themselves confronted with the institutional barriers to success that once blocked their occupational mobility. Elite university programs are now fully open to women, and women are making substantial headway in the worlds of politics and business. Tax deductions for child care (in 1993, $5,000 per year per child under 7) in fact favor mothers in the paid labor force over women caring for their own children at home, who do not receive equivalent tax relief. Except for residual social behaviors such as the "glass ceiling" confronting high-achieving women, the ascriptively based barriers to the social mobility of upper- and middle-class women have been almost fully removed.

Working-class and unemployed women fare far less well than their more fortunate counterparts. For women as well as for men, the most deep-seated inequities in Canada remain those of social class, and the most debilitating social condition one can experience is poverty. Poverty is not an innate biological condition. People not born into poverty may descend into it during certain points in their lives, as do many older unemployed workers. Other people born into poverty may later transcend it. It is not easy to categorize the poor as a group suffering discrimination, as membership of the poor is flexible and the individual can in principle remove himself from poverty by acquiring a new job, or perhaps, for women, a new spouse.

Poverty in Canada, as in the United States, varies with social status, especially with gender, ethnicity, and age. As in the United States, poverty in Canada has become increasingly feminized. Women over the age of 65 are much more likely to be poor than men; in 1987, 22 percent of elderly women as opposed to 11 percent of elderly men were poor.[37] Many women and their children are one man away from poverty; dependent as they are on male breadwinners, they can easily fall into destitution in the event of desertion, separation, or divorce. Vastly increased labor force participation rates for women (52.6 percent of women in 1988 as opposed to 23.5 percent in 1951)[38] partially compensate for the loss of male support as divorce rates rise, but on average Canadian women in 1987 still earned only 66 percent of the income of Canadian men.[39] The difference between male and female incomes, however, is not a consequence of active discrimination as much as of different life choices rooted in social perceptions of appropriate sex roles. Married women still withdraw from the labor force when their children are small; if forced to reenter the workforce as sole supports of their families they lack the education and work experience of males the same age.[40]

Poverty also correlates with race in Canada, although the data on poverty for racial groups other than aboriginal Canadians are difficult to interpret. Some nonwhite groups fare better than some white groups in educational and income rankings: For example, in 1981, black males ranked higher than the males of at least seven European ethnic groups in education; Indo-Pakistanis outranked at least six European groups in income.[41] When Canadian immigration policy opened to nonwhites in the 1960s, the new regulations contained requirements for high education, professional training, or entrepreneurial skill. Thus nonwhite immigrants tend to be highly trained. The status of immigrants' children, however, is problematic. In 1981, Indochinese, Filipino, Japanese, and Korean Canadians exhibited high intergenerational upward social mobility, whereas black and Chinese Canadians exhibited none and Indo-Pakistanis exhibited high downward mobility.[42] These patterns cannot be interpreted without detailed information on the educational and occupational choices of second-generation children, many of whom may be less educated than their parents.

Despite these caveats, the wildcard of racism as a factor in income cannot be ignored. A study conducted in 1984 suggested that black Canadians had significantly fewer employment opportunities than whites with equivalent education; for every job offer that blacks in this study received, whites received three.[43] In 1986 in Toronto, members of visible minorities were more highly educated than whites, yet their rate of unemployment was higher (7.0 percent as compared with 5.2 percent).[44] However, this rate might have been a consequence of recent immigration (one in nine residents of Toronto was an immigrant member of a visible minority) or of foreign educational qualifications not recognized in Canada.[45] Other research suggests that in 1986 black males born in Canada suffered a 10 percent disadvantage in earnings, even when all other variables such as education were controlled.[46]

This suggests that certain types of Canadians are more likely to fall into the ranks of the poor than others. Eliminating active employment discrimination against them might ameliorate their fate. Thus the liberal agenda of equality of opportunity is an important step in remedying severe inequality of condition. But active discrimination in the 1990s is not a strong explanatory factor for the poverty of recognizable social groups. The poverty of aboriginal Canadians is explained by their long history of exploitation and consequent massive social disorganization. Discrimination against aboriginal peoples compounds these earlier and far more serious abuses of their human rights. Similarly, women experience poverty for reasons other than discrimination. Their life choices and dependence on males for income are matters of social roles and gender expectations rather than of active discrimination in the workforce. Blacks are the most obvious victims of discrimination. Canadian-born black males have life histories and life plans similar to those of white males, yet they find that skin color precludes their equal involvement in the labor market.

Even if Canada, in some utopian future, was able to eliminate all racial- and gender-based discrimination, there would still be poverty. In Canada in 1986, just over one million children under 16, about one in six of all children, lived in poverty.[47] Many lived in single-parent female-headed households but many more lived in male-headed households. Although Canada's single-parent female-headed households are more likely to live in poverty than male-headed households, the latter outnumbered the former by about 85 percent (about 253,600 households; in 1986 there were 552,300 male-headed families living in poverty as opposed to 298,700 female-headed families).[48] And since one certainly cannot assume, based on income and mobility rankings, that the majority of Canada's immigrant nonwhites are poor, it is safe to infer that the numerical majority of the nonaboriginal poor in Canada is white.

The human rights discussions in the 1970s and 1980s in Canada largely ignored the issue of social class. The dominant ideology in this discussion was the liberal one of equality of opportunity. Nevertheless, this ideology was partially extended by the social democratic belief that economic security should also be a goal of civilized modern society. Some Canadians, perhaps proportionately more people than would hold similar beliefs in the United States, believe that there is a social obligation of all to all in Canada, even to those who, because of bad luck, incapacity, or indolence, cannot "make it" on their own in a competitive society.

One might argue that Canada has a partial cultural basis to build a new community in which even the poor are not excluded from social membership. A fairly strong belief in social democracy is demonstrated by periodic elections of New Democratic Party governments in some provinces; the New Democratic Party is a party of the left. Through the mid-1980s, an average 17 percent of voters voted for the New Democratic Party in federal elections.[49] Canada also has a labor movement considerably larger than that in the United States (in 1991, 36.5 percent of nonagricultural Canadian workers were unionized as opposed to 16.1 percent of all employed wage and salary workers in the United States).[50] Some commentators also contend that Canada has a Red Tory tradition of social obligation of the rich to the poor, a kind of noblesse oblige that recognizes that the poor are always with us and must be cared for (other commentators dispute this interpretation of Canadian society).[51] It is possible that the Catholic corporatist tradition has also influenced Canadians to be more oriented to the collective social welfare than their southern neighbors, not only in Quebec but also in other heavily Catholic parts of the country.

Canadians often contrast themselves with Americans by noting the difference between the Canadian maxim of "peace, order, and good government" and the American maxim of "life, liberty, and the pursuit of happiness." Peace, order, and good government require that the poor be safely contained so that their disorder and unhappiness do not spill over into orderly prosperous society. Part of this peace and order requires provision of minimal social welfare benefits that, so far, seem to assure that the rich in Canada are not overly threatened by the poor.

Canadians tend to be smug when comparing themselves to Americans. Like much of the rest of the world, they are horrified by the violence of U.S. society. Canadian streets are relatively secure, urban downtowns are lively and livable, and there are no racially differentiated slums where whites are utterly unsafe. The Canadian homicide rate is one-fourth of the U.S. rate, another source of Canadian pride. The most significant reason that Canada is more peaceable is its smaller, more isolated pockets of endemic poverty, largely because blacks were excluded from Canada until very recently and because aboriginal peoples live in isolated reserves. The homicide rate among Canada's native peoples is well above that of nonnative Canadians. In 1986, the ratio of the homicide rate of nonaboriginal Canadians to that of nonblack, non-Hispanic Americans was 1:1.8, demonstrating that violence in both Canada and the United States is a consequence of the degrading living conditions of racial minorities.[52]

Despite Canada's apparently more social democratic ethos, Canadian income-distribution figures are only slightly more egalitarian than those of the United States. The lowest quintile of Canadians held only 5.7 percent of national household income in 1987 while the highest held 40.2 percent; U.S. figures in 1985 were 4.7 and 41.9 percent (indicating a ratio in Canada of 7:1 and 9:1 for its neighbor).[53] One consequence of this inequitable distribution of income is that the right to food is not adequately protected in Canada. Poor Canadians frequently eat nutritionally inadequate meals. A study of seven major cities in 1988 found that a couple with two children on social assistance would have to pay between 51 and 65 percent of its income on rent alone, barely leaving enough for food, let alone other necessities.[54] This suggests that Bertram Gross's "subwelfare" concept is as applicable to Canada as it is to the United States.[55] A 1990 study of poor children in Montreal showed that a quarter of them suffered from iron-deficiency anemia, which slows intellectual and physical development.[56] Throughout the late 1980s and early 1990s, food banks became conspicuous in Canadian cities, with 2.3 million Canadians expected to visit them in 1993.[57]

Poverty in Canada is a real poverty, not merely a relative poverty. Canadians do not starve to death and they do not live en masse in huddled, unserviced slums. But there are malnourished Canadians; there are some Canadians without homes; there are children whose capacity to read and write is subverted by lack of food. Children from low-income families in Canada are roughly twice as likely as other children to have a psychiatric disorder, to perform poorly in school, and to develop behavior problems.[58] If not a definite physical poverty, in the sense of being life-threatening, Canadian poverty is one of the intellect and spirit. Isolated from the larger society and often from each other by cramped housing, by the inability to pay for public transport, by unemployment, and by social despair, the poor find it difficult to be part of the community. Their opportunities to take part in collective decision-making and participate in the political process are severely limited. The poor do not have the discretionary income that other Canadians use to improve their quality of life and to enhance their capacities to act as members of the larger society.

Thus, although Canada is a better protector of economic human rights than the United States, it too fails to provide the full range of rights to which all citizens ought to be entitled. As the ethnic similarity of its rich and its poor protects Canada from the types of racial violence to which its neighbor has become accustomed, prosperous upper- and middle-class eyes can be closed to the abusive realities of a capitalist system. Meantime, however, those status categories most at risk of poverty and other human rights abuses have begun to organize politically.

In part, the recent organization of aboriginal people, blacks, and women in Canada can be seen as a triumph of liberal society: The most marginalized people today demand inclusion in the human rights bargain and demand that liberal society confront and remedy status-based abuses routinely accepted in the past. However, the new mobilizations also challenge the entire basis of liberal society. Status radicals make new political demands on the grounds of group rights that specifically undermine the individualism at the heart of liberal social philosophy. They reject even social democratic reforms that include economic human rights as important aspects of the organization of society. The fact that status radicals, in Canada as in the United States, reject the liberal human rights philosophy is an indication of its failure to incorporate all social groups in North America's heterogeneous environment.

New Communitarian Threats
Against Liberalism

Status radicals are social actors who define their identities completely by their social statuses. They accept the stigmatized master status by which others define them as their only politically and socially relevant identity. Status radicals reject the liberal paradigm of individual rights and individual mobility; they believe that only group mobility as a consequence of group challenges against the dominant status group (white, male, heterosexual) is possible. Feminists, African-Americans, African-Canadians, and aboriginal activists who reject liberalism are status radicals; so are gays and lesbians who retreat socially into their own communities.

Status radicals share with left collectivists a vision of human rights based on group claims rather than individual claims against society and the state. Left collectivists argue for group rights rather than individual rights in the context of the abuses of capitalist society. In the international arena, group rights are the rights of states or societies, especially those making claims for compensation against the former imperial powers or against the world economic system.[59] This demand for collective rights resonates strongly among many subordinated groups in Western society. Ethno-religious minorities claim rights on the basis of group minority status rather than as mere aggregates of individual claims. Other status groups who have been treated inequitably by liberal society, especially women and blacks, also favor types of group rights (affirmative action programs are an example). Claims to dignity and justice that are based on group norms are now considered legitimate in some human rights circles.[60] Those who accept group rights do so on grounds of the excessive individualism of a narrowly liberal conception of human rights and of the historic fact that the Western world colonized many of the peoples now claiming group rights.[61]

Like left collectivists, many status radicals view the liberal world as inherently exploitative of all but the dominant caste. Imperialism is viewed as both an international and an internal phenomenon: Capitalism by necessity impoverishes all but a very few. Imperialism and capitalism are also seen as impoverishing social life: Traditional cultures and communitarian visions of the good life are undermined by competitive liberal individualism. Universality is a farce in Western liberal societies in which Others, however assimilated in their behavior, are always considered strangers. Individual human rights are one culturally relative concept of justice: Group rights better suit other cultures.

Left collectivism denies the inherent value of the individual. In its categorizing of groups by imperial, racial, or gender status, it deems some status categories to be oppressors and others to be victims. Thus left collectivism is attractive to status radicals. Rather than reject their status categorization, these radicals embrace it. They accept as irremediable the categorization of all individuals into superordinate or subordinate statuses and argue for compensatory privileges afforded to the latter. Those who previously enjoyed unfair privilege have no claim now to equitable treatment. Just as communism excluded entire social categories from its definition of humanity on the basis of their real or assumed ownership of the means of production, so status radicalism denies equal treatment to those—males, whites—it considers oppressors.

Attempting to create self-respecting cultures that compensate for the social exclusion they experience in the North American mainstream, status radicals find the concept of cultural absolutism attractive. Cultural absolutism permits a closing in of the beleaguered gender or racially based community against outsiders. Cultures provide a social bond among people occupying similar degraded status positions. Status radicals retreat into cultural relativity because "Relativity is now the great equalizer: it . . . [is] through peculiarity that one escapes the stigma of difference."[62] Thus, the ideal of a women's culture, separate from men's, or a black or gay culture separate from the cultures of whites or heterosexuals.

Status radicals and left collectivists share their antiliberal critique with traditionalists and reactionary conservatives. All four groups deny the premises of liberal society. Conservative communitarians do not grant concern and respect to all individual members of society, regardless of status. They are willing to neglect nonwhite outsiders and those who appear to reject familistic social values. Traditionalists present a vision of a pre-imperial utopia, a society to which, they believe, the Third World can return if individualist values are discarded. Left collectivists agree with traditionalists that the West must be rejected but desire to discard capitalism as well as individualism. Status radicals argue that liberalism has failed. It has not incorporated the degraded and the deviant into mainstream society; with its minimalist stress on property and on empty legal and political equality, it has in fact further marginalized them.

Reactionary conservatives and status radicals both use communitarian myths to argue their case for reordering the present. For reactionary conservatives, the reference point is the disappeared paradise of the dominant, honored caste. The past was the time of collective responsibility, ordered society, and social deference. There was only one community of insiders: Outsiders did not exist in any social sense and therefore did not pose a threat. For status radicals, the situation is somewhat more complex. African-American and African-Canadian status radicals look to the past, but it is an African past. Myths of the idyllic, consensual, and redistributive African society are constructed in order to generate a sense of pride in being of African origin. Similarly, myths of the healing, collective power of Islam have a value to African-Americans who feel betrayed by white Christian civilization. Other status radicals, namely, women and gays, have to look to a myth of the future in order to construct a communitarian identity. Women use the myth of the essentially nurturing, cooperative, and pacific female who differs from the essential male in her aversion to competition, individualism, and violence.[63] The traditionalist vision of the unspoiled Third World paradise appeals to both women and blacks, presenting as it does a myth of a society in which everyone succors everyone else, each person lives for others, and the alienating individualism that characterizes complex capitalist society is unknown.

The extremist varieties of communitarianism—right and left—threaten the liberal basis of North American society. As the space for liberalism shrinks, North American society may very well be poised between reactionary conservatives and status radicals. In this new opposition the opportunity for dialogue will be closed. Neither group will recognize common humanity: Individualism, with all its liberating potential, will be lost in the collective retreat into safer communal grounds. Social exclusion will become increasingly attractive to reactionary conservatives as more members of degraded social categories reject liberalism completely. Meanwhile, status radicals will continue to reject the modern community, arguing that status categories cannot understand one another, that divisions among collective groups are insurmountable. Thus they will advocate a society in which permanently divided status groups live in a state of uneasy hostility, with no possibility for understanding or for alliances and communities that cross status lines.

The current North American debate about political correctness reflects the status radical claim that it is impossible to communicate across status barriers. The radicals contend that there is no longer any common language of communication: The multivocality of modern society precludes any kind of cross-status consensus. The very possibility of debate is resented.[64] Indeed, debate, the idea that people holding initially opposing views can persuade each other of their position through logic and reason, is rejected as a malestream, empiricist, and anti-intuitive form of thought typical of rationalist and competitive capitalist society. In this new world of nonunderstanding, a good liberal conscious of past and present exploitation of degraded status groups can only hope to adopt whatever language such groups present to him as correct. In this radical vision North America is a society of continually competitive groups with no common ground among them. Males and whites are possessed of an intrinsic, unchanging essence that makes it impossible for them to accept women and blacks as equals.

Status radicals assume that coalitions cannot be formed and that individual members of different status groups cannot join together on bases other than their status memberships. Group rights are the key to justice in societies in which the liberating possibilities of individualism are confined to the dominant race, gender, and sexual orientation. By choosing the group-rights approach, stated Nathan Glazer, "we say that the differences between some groups are so great that they cannot achieve satisfaction on the basis of individual rights." These claims for group rights undermine not only the basic principles of law in North America, but also the way we think of ourselves. "For every movement in the direction of group rights, the individual's claim to be considered only as an individual . . . would be reduced."[65] Individuals will be confined in the tight embrace of their particular status groups, alienated from the wider society and from the multiplicity of roles, interests, and contacts available to them.

The debate over the university canon exemplifies the extremes of status radicalism. Those who object to the canon as currently constituted reject the idea of knowledge that is common and valuable to all members of mankind, regardless of their origins or particular social status. Some feminists now take this approach, arguing, as Fox-Genovese put it in her critique of their position, that "women have been—and remain—fundamentally alienated from a culture that casts them as objects and with which they cannot identify." For such feminists, the Western canon of "Dead White European Males" has no meaning. In this perspective, classical scholarship represents "an oppressive and outmoded 'binary thinking'" that delineates difference and therefore hierarchy, placing men over women.[66] This essentialist position assumes that women, as women, cannot have commonalities of interest with men; they are fundamentally and irretrievably different, even in complex modern societies. Thus, as Dinesh D'Souza pointed out, intelligence and knowledge are reduced to "race and gender categories"; the end result of such reduction is that truth is reduced to gender and race-inspired bias, knowledge to ideology.[67]

There is every reason to expand the canon to include not only the great works of the Western tradition, but also the great works of others. Nor can we possibly continue to teach about the expansion of Western civilization without considering its costs not only to the colonized, but also to those inside the very core of Western culture and society. A multiculturalism in Canada and the United States that teaches all students—not only those from particular minority ethno-cultural groups—about the diversity of origins and experiences of their fellow-citizens would enrich us all. But a multiculturalism that suggests that there are "many separate Americas—a black nation, a Hispanic hemisphere, a Native American country, and so on, without overarching bonds or values" will undermine liberal universality and substitute intolerant particularities.[68]

Such a separatist perspective will also deny the commonalities of contemporary North American life—of education, mass culture, work organization, and overall democratic and secular values—that influence all citizens and bind them together. These commonalities of life experience tie together people of disparate origins and social statuses. They reflect problems of social life that anyone can encounter. Thus insofar as the great works of Western and world culture—whether by male or female novelists, white or black philosophers—address these common problems, they overcome all differences in social status in those who confront them.

The status radical denial of the possibility of rational discourse among disparate social groups undermines liberal democracy. Yet it is precisely liberalism that has permitted status radicals to evolve as a forceful social group in modern North American society. Liberalism is premised upon freedom of speech, press, and assembly; thus it permits the silenced to gain a social voice. Liberalism is also individualistic and opposed to constricting status-based categorizations of human beings; thus it permits members of degraded social groups to protest their treatment. People from honored status groups who accept the liberal paradigm must question their own preconceptions and, if they are true to their philosophy, must adjust their social behavior accordingly. The government and the courts must, in the final analysis, take cognizance of the status radical critique of liberal society as ridden with nonliberal status-based categories of honored and shamed social groups. Thus adjustments, such as programs to ensure fairness in employment, must be made.

But without the capacity to change social behavior, the government and courts are limited to changing the rules, to permit more equitable treatment in the economic and political marketplaces of individuals from degraded social groups. This is an insufficient remedy for status radicals because it does not address the social bases of their dishonor. The government and the courts can prohibit, and sometimes punish, social terror. But they cannot control or prohibit those day-to-day rejections and insults that members of degraded status groups experience in the social world. The social world is still dominated by the cultural norm of the successful white heterosexual male, at home in and comforted by bourgeois Western culture. Women's culture, gay culture, black culture are reactions against this dominant social norm, wishful attempts to create equally valid and respected cultures within, but apart from, the wider individualist, capitalist society.

Yet despite the dominant social norm of the white heterosexual male bourgeois, modern society is characterized by great cultural variety. Role complexity, physical mobility, urbanism, and secularism permit the individual to choose the set of cultural habits and organizations that best reflect his personal behavioral preferences. Just like members of superordinate groups, members of subordinated status groups exhibit diversity in their choices of roles, cultural values, and social norms. In modern North America, for example, there is not and cannot be any real "women's culture." Women, like men, cross racial, ethnic, and class lines and, moreover, differ radically among themselves in social values. Some women are parents, some are not; some women believe in sexual fidelity, some do not; some celebrate lesbianism, some abhor it. Blacks also cross class lines and exhibit a diversity of values. Some blacks are conservatives, others cultural radicals; some are devout Christians, others Muslim converts. Even when a person is a member of a status category that has suffered, or today suffers, subordination, he also has other roles and interests that define his identity. These roles and interests can lead him to behave in a highly individualistic manner not predicted by any observable or measurable status memberships. Every North American has a different set of identifications and interests that only he can express directly.

Modernized society is inhabited by individuals. As individuals, they sometimes identify themselves as members of groups or collectivities but not necessarily in a predictable or static manner. The liberal stress on individual rights therefore remains the appropriate basis for the entire conception of human rights.

The Necessity to Preserve
Individual Rights

Both right and left communitarians envision groups of people whose privileges they want to retain or whose status they want to advance. Yet the association of groups with ethnic, linguistic, or religious minorities or, indeed, with race, gender, or sexual orientation, implies a static notion of collectivity. This static notion does not reflect the reality of modern social life. Groups are changeable and permeable; membership can be asserted or denied; identities can alter. Since group membership is so malleable and so adaptive to personal desire and circumstance, no individual can be assumed to be a permanent and exclusive member of a certain closed group or even set of groups. Indeed, individuals may actually need protection against political groupings that claim to represent their particular status categories but, in fact, squeeze them into collective identities that they reject. One must be as free to leave as to join any social group, even one with which one has ascriptive affiliations.

In liberal human rights practice culture is a matter of individual choice. Minority cultures are protected by the civil and political rights to freedom of association, press, and speech and by the rights to speak one's own language and to worship one's own god. Culture, then, is a private matter: Each individual can make a private choice of what cultural practices are meaningful to him. If a woman wishes to identify with a new type of culture, such as the new culture of women's groups or lesbian groups, she is free to do so. But no one can constrain her to identify herself as Christian, or as a Chinese-Canadian, or as a woman, or as a lesbian.

The private nature of cultural practice in modern complex societies does not mean that communities are not socially valuable. Collectivities defined by cultural variables such as common (presumed or real) ancestry, common language, common religion, distinctive norms and customs, or historic ties to a certain geographical area—in a word, by common ethnicity—deserve protection. Human beings are not isolated individuals; they are also members of groups. Although some individuals would prefer to make their way on their own in a world of universal citizenship, others desire and need protection of their collective affiliations. Communal or group rights, then, are deeply attractive to the modern individual who values the collectivities to which he belongs.

Liberal capitalist societies do contain deeply disintegrative social aspects. Notwithstanding the existence of a modern community, individual alienation from the larger society is frequent. A sense of isolation plagues many men and women who no longer belong to established, easily identifiable social groups (other than the nation itself). To such alienated people the cultural integrity of the group is frequently more appealing than individualism. The cultural group provides customs and norms of behavior that are familiar and comforting for insiders; it is also symbolic of the distinctiveness of its members. To cultivate an individual identity in modern society is a more demanding task than to cling to group membership. Individualized identity, by virtue of its lack of connection to a particular group of others, is grounded more in intellect and in contemplation of the meaning of life, in a society without fixed norms or authoritative spiritual leadership. It is difficult to sustain individual integrity in societies in constant normative flux.

The pull of community is a strong one. Although in modern liberal societies many people disregard their ethnic memberships as irrelevant to their personal interests, many others return to, reinforce, or re-create their ethnicity. Reasserted ethnicity helps individuals to find a place in society that is warmer, closer, and denser than their dispersed social networks of workplace, recreational, or other associations. Religion serves the same function. Especially in times of economic, political, or social crisis, the ancestral cultural community looms large in the psychological identities of many people. Such communities provide the comforts of ritual, the possibility of respect based on membership in the group rather than on achievement in the wider social realm, and the security of group-based obligations to share resources. For individuals who do not have a strong religious or ethnic affiliation, or who have rejected their particular memberships, the desire to create a new community can be very strong. Such individuals try to use ascriptive markers such as gender, race, and sexual orientation as the basis for new community.

Both members of established groups based on religion or ethnicity and members of new groups based on ascriptive social markers have asserted the claim for group rights. Yet individual human rights and group human rights are fundamentally incompatible. Conceptions of human dignity rooted in the view that nation, people, community, or family must take precedence over the individual are radically at odds with the principle of individual human rights. Group rights cannot provide the protections that individuals need not only against the abuses of the modern state, but also against those very groups that might wish forcibly to exclude or include them. It might have been possible in the past to categorize all individuals according to their group memberships and then to accord equal respect and protection to each group. But that is no longer possible. In modern Western societies that ostensibly protect human rights, the right not to be a member of any social group is basic. Individual nonconformity and nonmembership in traditional social groups is protected. One is permitted to be an atheist, not to have a family, not to assert affiliation with any ethnic group.

Beneath the entire discussion of the relevance of group rights, another discussion is largely ignored in the international human rights debate. That is, the discussion of the nature of capitalist society and its capacity to stratify people of similar racial, gender, ethno-religious, or cultural backgrounds into radically unequal economic groups. Status radicals do radical capitalists the favor of deflecting attention from the systematic abuse of economic human rights inherent in capitalist society. They pigeonhole individuals into visible status categories while ignoring class stratification. Yet in modern Western societies, to be a materially prosperous person is to have much better life chances, including a much better chance of having one's human rights protected, than a materially poor person. This advantage accrues whatever one's race, gender, or sexual orientation.

This class division extends into the international arena. All Third World societies are internally stratified between rich and poor; the elite spokespersons of Third World societies do not necessarily represent the human rights needs of the poor in their own countries. Assertions of cultural relativism and of locally rooted conceptions of human rights mask economic exploitation and the naked exercise of power in the interests of the ruling classes. This does not mean that issues of international inequality should be ignored, nor that the West's responsibility for colonial and imperial exploitation should be forgotten. But it does mean that one should look with a somewhat skeptical eye at Third World governmental assertions that international criticism of human rights records demonstrates a lack of understanding of indigenous social norms and is, in fact, a form of cultural imperialism.[69]

A community cannot exist if its less prosperous members are living in such degraded circumstances that they cannot absorb its social norms and cannot participate in it. This applies as much to the urban black underclass in the United States as to the tens of thousands of homeless street urchins in Rio de Janeiro or Nairobi. To protect themselves against the complete breakdown of community and civility, then, the prosperous majority must come to terms with the overwhelming exclusion felt by the bitterly poor. To protect the rights of the poor and to integrate them into an efficacious and meaningful civil society, social democracy is an absolute requirement.

Whether social democracy is capable of extending the bounds of respect and concern to those normally excluded from them, even in liberal society, is another matter. Canada has a welfare tradition considerably more social democratic than that of the United States. But Canada has consistently failed its aboriginal population and its pockets of native-born blacks. Its poor remain on the margins of society, susceptible to lengthy unemployment and dependent on a form of subwelfare that keeps them alive but impedes their capacity to act upon their citizenship.

Those countries in Europe that are the most social democratic, where the entire range of human rights is most respected for the entire society, are also socially homogeneous. This suggests that in heterogeneous societies the ideal of social commitment of all to all is far more difficult to realize than in homogeneous ones. Social obligation and social trust do not seem to extend easily outside the boundaries of one's own ethnic or racial group. Many social changes in Canada and the United States since World War II suggest greater social inclusiveness. Yet some social ideologies and some political platforms demonstrate extreme distaste for racial minorities (and for feminists and gays) as well as a continued unwillingness to confront problems of poverty.

In heterogeneous North America, realization of a society in which everyone is assured economic security and social respect is still far from certain. Although the status radicals' calls for a different kind of society may undermine liberalism, the social conditions that engender those claims must be ameliorated. As Etzioni noted in the debates over freedom of speech on campus, even as we protect the right to abhorrent "hateful" speech we must close ranks with its victims, sympathize with them, and cast social opprobrium upon the hatemongers.[70] Liberals must take very seriously the complaints of status radicals at the same time as they reject status radicals' undermining of fundamental liberal principles.

And liberals must extend their concern from equality of opportunity to security of condition. Equality of condition, frequently posed as the socialist antithesis to equality of opportunity, is not possible and its price is in any case too high. Equality of condition can only be attained by the radical and downward leveling of social wealth. But security of condition is within the grasp of the modern industrialized nation-state. Basic economic rights can be provided for all, and a welfare floor can be put in place for those unable to fulfil their own needs.

Neither the romantic search for the mythic community of the past by traditionalists and reactionary conservatives, nor the assertion of new communitarian interests by left collectivists and status radicals, should permit us to neglect the primacy of economic human rights as a path to social justice in the modern world. The romance of the communitarian past excludes both concern for the poor and respect for the Other. The romance of the collectivized future, however, excludes recognition of the social complexity of those who are the poor or Other. In North America and elsewhere, the chronically unemployed are in many respects the new discarded people, regardless of whether they are black or white, female or male.[71]

Race, gender, and ethnicity are not accurate predictors of one's entire socio-economic status, nor are they accurate predictors of one's political interest. A wealthy woman may well decide that she prefers not to pay taxes that will support the poor. Even a previously poor woman may decide that since her own efforts lifted her from poverty, those women who remain poor should lift themselves from poverty. Social minimalism—the denial of substantive economic rights—is a philosophy attractive to successful individuals of every color, ethnicity, gender, or sexual orientation.

Because we cannot predict the ascriptive status memberships of the poor, their economic human rights must be individual rights. And they must be supplemented by the civil and political rights that have already freed hundreds of millions of people in the Western world from serfdom and slavery. These civil and political rights are premised on individual privacy, secularism, and social mobility in the modern capitalist world.

It is possible in a world of human rights to reduce the extent of alienation in modern society, indeed to create social beings whose complex and multifarious experiences give them a capacity for reflection unparalleled in human history. When citizens are possessed of all their human rights, they can act to better not only their own lives, but also the lives of others. As Robert Bellah et al. pointed out, the phrase "private citizen" is an oxymoron.[72] To be a citizen is to act in the community, in the public realm. Community life requires that all citizens can exert their human rights. This in turn requires that poverty not exclude the citizen from education, access to the press, political activism, or the chance to better the lives of fellow citizens.

"Conditions of modernity, in many circumstances, provoke activism rather than privatism, because of modernity's inherent reflexivity and because there are many opportunities for collective organisation within the polyarchic systems of modern nation-states."[73] The activist liberal citizen, translating private reflection about the common good into public action, protects his own and other people's human rights. In so doing, he simultaneously contributes to his community and protects his own integrity as an individuated human being. Protection of his human rights is protection of everyone's rights. Protection of everyone's human rights permits retention and formation of humane, socially satisfying communities.

Notes

1. Amitai Etzioni, *The Spirit of Community: Rights, Responsibilities and the Communitarian Agenda* (New York: Crown, 1993).

2. Mary Ann Glendon, *Rights Talk: The Impoverishment of Political Discourse* (New York: The Free Press, 1991), p. 14.

3. Claude S. Fischer, *To Dwell Among Friends: Personal Networks in Town and City* (Chicago: University of Chicago Press, 1982), pp. 251–253.

4. Doreen Duchesne, "Giving Freely: Volunteers in Canada," Statistics Canada, Labour Analytical Report no. 4 (August 1989), pp. 22 and 24.

5. Rose Laub Coser, *In Defense of Modernity: Role Complexity and Individual Autonomy* (Stanford, Calif.: Stanford University Press, 1991), p. 168.

6. Michael Walzer, *Spheres of Justice: A Defense of Pluralism and Equality* (New York: Basic Books, 1983), pp. 13–20.

7. Ervin Staub, *The Roots of Evil: The Origins of Genocide and Other Group Violence* (New York: Cambridge University Press, 1989), pp. 79–80.

8. Giovanni Sartori, "Democracy," in David L. Sills (ed.), *International Encyclopedia of the Social Sciences*, vol. 4 (New York: Macmillan and The Free Press, 1968), 113.

9. Sylvia Ann Hewlett, *When the Bough Breaks: The Cost of Neglecting Our Children* (New York: HarperCollins, 1991), p. 225; and Julia S. O'Connor, "Citizenship, Class, Gender and Labour Market Participation in Canada and Australia," in S. Shaver (ed.), *Gender, Citizenship and the Labour Market: The Australian and Canadian Welfare States* (Sydney, Australia: Social Policy Research Centre, 1993), p. 15.

10. Sylvia Ann Hewlett, *A Lesser Life: The Myth of Women's Liberation in America* (New York: Warner Books, 1986), pp. 167–174.

11. Ibid., pp. 127–129.

12. Amy Gutmann, "Communitarian Critics of Liberalism," *Philosophy and Public Affairs*, vol. 14, no. 3 (summer 1985), p. 320.

13. Etzioni, *The Spirit of Community*, pp. 3 and 2.

14. C. B. MacPherson, *The Political Theory of Possessive Individualism: Hobbes to Locke* (New York: Oxford University Press, 1962), p. 272.

15. Constance Perin, *Belonging in America: Reading Between the Lines* (Madison: University of Wisconsin Press, 1988), p. 229; quotation from Gabriel Almond and Sidney Verba, *The Civic Culture: Political Attitudes and Democracy in Five Nations* (Princeton: Princeton University Press, 1963), pp. 356–357, bracketed addition Perin's.

16. Canada, Ministry of Labour, *Employment Standards Legislation in Canada*, 1993–1994 Edition (Ottawa: Ministry of Supply and Services 1993), pp. 79–80.

17. The World Bank, *World Development Report 1993: Investing in Health* (New York: Oxford University Press, 1993), table A.9, p. 211.

18. Canada, *Consensus Report on the Constitution: Final Text* (Charlottetown, Prince Edward Island: August 28, 1992), p. 2, section B.4.

19. Robert E. Robertson, "The Right to Food—Canada's Broken Covenant," *Canadian Human Rights Yearbook, 1989–1990* (Ottawa: University of Ottawa Press, 1991), pp. 185–216.

20. Bill C-93, July 12 1988, "The Canadian Multiculturalism Act," in Multiculturalism and Citizenship Canada, *Operation of the Canadian Multiculturalism Act: Annual Report 1988/89* (Ottawa: Minister of Supply and Services Canada, n.d. [1989?]), pp. 1–7.

21. Receiver General of Canada, *Public Accounts of Canada 1992*, Volume II, part 1 (Ottawa: Ministry of Supply and Services Canada, 1992).

22. This estimate is from Geoffrey York, *The Dispossessed: Life and Death in Native Canada* (Toronto: Lester and Orpen Dennys, 1989), pp. xiii–xiv.

23. James S. Frideres, *Native Peoples in Canada: Contemporary Conflicts*, 3rd ed. (Scarborough: Prentice-Hall, 1988), p. 163.

24. Conrad Winn, "The Socio-Economic Attainment of Visible Minorities: Facts and Policy Implications," in James Curtis, Edward Grabb, Neil Guppy, and Sid Gilbert (eds.), *Social Inequality in Canada: Patterns, Problems, Policies* (Scarborough: Prentice-Hall, 1988), p. 209.

25. James S. Frideres, *Native Peoples in Canada: Contemporary Conflicts*, 4th ed. (Scarborough: Prentice-Hall, 1993), p. 160.

26. Ibid., p. 213.

27. Thomas R. Berger, *Fragile Freedoms: Human Rights and Dissent in Canada* (Toronto: Clarke, Irwin, 1982), p. 229, and York, *The Dispossessed*, p. 59.

28. York, *The Dispossessed*, p. 248.

29. Berger, *Fragile Freedoms*, p. 235.

30. E.g., Mary Ellen Turpel, "Aboriginal People and the Canadian Charter: Interpretive Monopolies, Cultural Differences," *Canadian Human Rights Yearbook, 1989–1990* (Ottawa: University of Ottawa Press, 1991), pp. 3–45.

31. Robin W. Winks, *The Blacks in Canada: A History* (Montreal: McGill-Queen's Press, 1971), p. 386.

32. Frances Henry, *Forgotten Canadians: The Blacks of Nova Scotia* (Don Mills, Ontario: Longman, 1973).

33. "Black and Angry," *Maclean's*, May 18, 1992, p. 24.

34. Ontario, *The Report of the Race Relations and Policing Task Force* (Toronto, 1989), pp. 127–128.

35. Robert Allan McChesney, "Canada," in Jack Donnelly and Rhoda E. Howard (eds.), *International Handbook of Human Rights* (Westport, Conn.: Greenwood, 1987), pp. 29–47.

36. Graham Fraser, "Bill Protects Gay and Lesbian Rights," *The Globe and Mail* (Toronto), December 11, 1992, p. A4, and "Douglas v. the Queen," in Bruce Dunlop (ed.), *Dominion Law Reports*, 4th Series, vol. 98 (Aurora, Ontario: Canada Law Books, 1993), pp. 129–140.

37. National Council of Welfare, *Women and Poverty Revisited* (Ottawa: Minister of Supply and Services Canada, 1990), p. 2.

38. Alfred A. Hunter, *Class Tells: On Social Inequality in Canada*, 2nd ed. (Toronto: Butterworth, 1986), p. 125 (1951 figure), and Craig McKie and Keith Thompson, *Canadian Social Trends* (Toronto: Thompson Educational Publishing, 1990), p. 102 (1988 figure).

39. McKie and Thompson, *Canadian Social Trends*, p. 103.

40. Liviana Calzavara, "Trends and Policy in Employment Opportunities for Women," in James Curtis, Edward Grabb, Neil Guppy, and Sid Gilbert (eds.), *Social Inequality in Canada: Patterns, Problems, Policies* (Scarborough: Prentice-Hall, 1988), p. 295.

41. Winn, "Socio-Economic Attainment," pp. 201 and 197.

42. Ibid., p. 199.

43. Frances Henry and Effie Ginzberg, "Racial Discrimination in Employment," in James Curtis, Edward Grabb, Neil Guppy, and Sid Gilbert (eds.), *Social Inequality in Canada: Patterns, Problems, Policies* (Scarborough: Prentice-Hall, 1988), pp. 214–220.

44. Joanne Moreau, "Changing Faces: Visible Minorities in Toronto," *Canadian Social Trends* [Statistics Canada], no. 23 (winter 1991), pp. 26–28.

45. On percentage immigrants, see Moreau, "Changing Faces," p. 26.

46. Jeffrey G. Reitz, "Statistics on Racial Discrimination in Canada," *Policy Options*, vol. 14, no. 2 (March 1993), p. 35.

47. Ken Battle, *Poverty Profile 1988: A Report by the National Council of Welfare* (Ottawa: Minister of Supply and Services Canada, 1988), p. 2.

48. Ibid., p. 19.

49. Alan Whitehorn, "New Democratic Party," in *The Canadian Encyclopedia*, vol. II (Edmonton: Hurtig, 1985), p. 1238.

50. Canada. Labour Canada, *Union Membership in Canada 1991* (Ottawa: Bureau of Labour Information, n.d. [1992?]), p. 1; and U.S. Department of Labor, Bureau of Labor Statistics, "Union Membership 1991," in *Compensation and Working Conditions*, vol. 44, no. 2 (February 1992), p. 76.

51. For a debate on this issue see Doug Baer, Edward Grabb, and William A. Johnston, "The Values of Canadians and Americans: A Critical Analysis and Reassessment," *Social Forces*, vol. 68, no. 3 (March 1990), pp. 693–713; and Seymour Martin Lipset, "The Values of Canadians and Americans: A Reply," and Doug Baer, Edward Grabb, and William Johnston, "The Values of Canadians and Americans: A Rejoinder," both in *Social Forces*, vol. 69, no. 1 (September 1990), pp. 267–272 and 273–277.

52. Data on homicide rates from Rhonda L. Lenton, "Homicide in Canada and the U.S.A.: A Critique of the Hagan Thesis," *Canadian Journal of Sociology*, vol. 14, no. 2 (1989), p. 171.

53. World Bank, *World Development Report 1993*, p. 297.

54. "The Forgotten: The Rise of Homelessness in Canada," *Calgary Herald*, September 16, 1990, p. F2.

55. Bertram Gross, *Friendly Fascism: The New Face of Power in America* (Boston: South End Press, 1980), p. 44.

56. Alanna Mitchell, "Iron-Poor Milk Puts Many Infants in Danger of Permanent Damage," *The Globe and Mail* (Toronto), August 6, 1991, p. A1.

57. "2 Million Users Expected by '93," *Vancouver Sun*, September 26, 1992, p. A7.

58. "The Forgotten," p. F2.

59. Issa G. Shivji, *The Concept of Human Rights in Africa* (London: CODESRIA Books Series, 1989); and Richard Falk, "The Algiers Declaration of the Rights of Peoples and the Struggle for Human Rights," in Antonio Cassese (ed.), *UN Law/Fundamental Rights: Two Topics in International Law* (Alphen aan den Rijn: Sijthoff and Noordhoff, 1979), pp. 225–235.

60. On group rights, see, e.g., Vernon Van Dyke, "Human Rights and the Rights of Groups," *Midwest Journal of Political Science*, vol. 18 (1974), pp. 725–741;

Nathan Glazer, "Individual Rights Against Group Rights," in Eugene Kamenka and Alice Erh-Soon Tay, *Human Rights* (New York: St. Martin's, 1985), pp. 87–103; and Michael McDonald, "Should Communities Have Rights? Reflections on Liberal Individualism," in Abdullahi Ahmed An-Na'im (ed.), *Human Rights in Cross-Cultural Perspectives: A Quest for Consensus* (Philadelphia: University of Pennsylvania Press, 1992), pp. 133–161.

61. On peoples' rights, see e.g., Alexandre Kiss, "The Peoples' Right to Self-Determination"; Jean-Bernard Marie, "Relations Between Peoples' Rights and Human Rights: Semantic and Methodological Distinctions"; and Karl Josef Partsch, "Recent Developments in the Field of Peoples' Rights"; all in *Human Rights Law Journal*, vol. 7, nos. 2–4 (1986), pp. 165–175, 195–204, and 175–182 respectively.

62. Zygmunt Bauman, "Strangers: The Social Construction of Universality and Particularity," *Telos*, vol. 78 (1988–1989), p. 39.

63. For discussion of this perspective, see Will Kymlicka, *Contemporary Political Philosophy: An Introduction* (Oxford: Clarendon Press, 1990), chapter 7, pp. 238–292.

64. Marc Angenot, "Les Idéologies du Ressentiment" (Montreal: McGill University, unpublished, April 1993), p. 21.

65. Glazer, "Individual Rights Against Group Rights," p. 102.

66. Elizabeth Fox-Genovese, *Feminism Without Illusions: A Critique of Individualism* (Chapel Hill: University of North Carolina Press, 1991), p. 4.

67. Dinesh D'Souza, "Illiberal Education," *The Atlantic Monthly*, vol. 267, no. 3 (March 1991), pp. 51–79; quotation from p. 76.

68. Quotation from Etzioni, *The Spirit of Community*, p. 156.

69. Frank Ching, "Asian View of Human Rights Is Beginning to Take Shape," *Far Eastern Economic Review* (April 29, 1993), p. 27. See also "Final Declaration of the Regional Meeting for Asia of the World Conference on Human Rights [1993]," United Nations Document A/CONF.157/ASRM/8; A/CONF.157/PC/59.

70. Etzioni, *The Spirit of Community*, p. 202.

71. The phrase is from Cosmas Desmond, *The Discarded People: An Account of African Resettlement in South Africa* (Harmondsworth, U.K.: Penguin, 1971).

72. Robert N. Bellah, Richard Madsen, William M. Sullivan, Ann Swidler, and Steven M. Tipton, *Habits of the Heart: Individualism and Commitment in American Life* (New York: Harper and Row, 1985), p. 271.

73. Anthony Giddens, *The Consequences of Modernity* (Stanford, Calif.: Stanford University Press, 1990) p. 149.

Bibliography

Abella, Irving, and Harold Troper. 1983. *None Is Too Many: Canada and the Jews of Europe 1933–1948*. Toronto: Lester and Orpen Dennys.

Abraham, Suzanne, and Derek Llewellyn-Jones. 1992. *Eating Disorders: The Facts*. New York: Oxford University Press.

Adachi, Ken. 1979. *The Enemy That Never Was*. Toronto: McClelland and Stewart.

Adam, Barry D. 1978. *The Survival of Domination: Inferiorization and Everyday Life*. New York: Elsevier.

Altholz, Josef L. 1988. "Roman Catholic Church," in Sally Mitchell, ed. *Victorian Britain*. New York: Garland Publishing, pp. 674–676.

Amadi, Elechi. 1982. *Ethics in Nigerian Culture*. London: Heinemann.

American Psychiatric Association. 1987. *Diagnostic and Statistical Manual of Mental Disorders*. 3rd ed. (rev.). Washington, D.C.: American Psychiatric Association.

Amnesty International. 1989. "Human Rights Now! Concert Tour 1988," *Bulletin* (Canadian Section), vol. 16, no. 1 (December 1988/January 1989): 18–21.

Angenot, Marc. 1993. "Les Idéologies du Ressentiment." Montreal: McGill University (unpublished), April.

Angus Reid Group. 1993. "The National Angus Reid Poll: Tolerance and the Canadian Ethnocultural Mosaic," April 10, 1993.

An-Na'im, Abdullahi Ahmed. 1987. "Religious Minorities Under Islamic Law and the Limits of Cultural Relativism." *Human Rights Quarterly*, vol. 9, no. 1 (February): 1–18.

An-Na'im, Abdullahi Ahmed. 1992. "Toward a Cross-Cultural Approach to Defining International Standards of Human Rights: The Meaning of Cruel, Inhuman, or Degrading Treatment or Punishment," in An-Na'im, ed. *Human Rights in Cross-Cultural Perspectives: A Quest for Consensus*. Philadelphia: University of Pennsylvania Press, pp. 19–43.

An-Na'im, Abdullahi Ahmed. 1990. *Toward an Islamic Reformation: Civil Liberties, Human Rights, and International Law*. Syracuse: Syracuse University Press.

Anonymous (Brazilian anthropologists). 1975. "The Politics of Genocide Against the Indians of Brazil." (Pamphlet). Toronto, Brazilian Studies.

Arab Organization for Human Rights. 1987. "Human Rights in the Arab World." *IFDA Dossier,* 62 (November/December): 63–72.

Arendt, Hannah. 1973. *The Origins of Totalitarianism.* New York: Harcourt Brace Jovanovich.

Aries, Philippe. 1962. *Centuries of Childhood: A Social History of Family Life.* New York: Vintage Books.

Atkins, Dorothy. 1988. "Inheritance," in Sally Mitchell, ed. *Victorian Britain: An Encyclopedia.* New York: Garland Publishing, pp. 396–397.

Atwood, Margaret. 1985. *The Handmaid's Tale.* Toronto: McClelland and Stewart.

Baar, Ellen. 1978."Issei, Nisei, and Sansei," in Daniel Glenday, Hubert Guidon, and Allan Turowetz, eds. *Modernization and the Canadian State.* Toronto: Macmillan, pp. 335–355.

Baer, Doug, Edward Grabb, and William A. Johnston. 1990. "The Values of Canadians and Americans: A Critical Analysis and Reassessment." *Social Forces,* vol. 68, no. 3 (March): 693–713.

Baer, Doug, Edward Grabb, and William A. Johnston. 1990. "The Values of Canadians and Americans: A Rejoinder." *Social Forces,* vol. 69, no. 1 (September): 273–277.

Barber, Benjamin R. 1992. "Jihad vs. McWorld." *The Atlantic Monthly,* vol. 269, no. 3 (March): 53–63.

Barea, Arturo. 1984 [1st. ed. 1941]. *The Forge.* London: Fontana.

Battle, Ken. 1988. *Poverty Profile 1988: A Report by the National Council of Welfare.* Ottawa: Minister of Supply and Services Canada.

Bauman, Zygmunt. 1989. *Modernity and the Holocaust.* Ithaca, N.Y.: Cornell University Press.

Bauman, Zygmunt. 1988–1989. "Strangers: The Social Construction of Universality and Particularity." *Telos,* num. 78, vol. 21, no. 4: 7–42.

Bay, Christian. 1982. "Self-Respect as a Human Right: Thoughts on the Dialectics of Wants and Needs in the Struggle for Human Community." *Human Rights Quarterly,* vol. 4, no. 1 (winter): 53–75.

Bayme, Steven. 1988. "Jewry and Judaism," in Sally Mitchell, ed. *Victorian Britain.* New York: Garland Publishing, pp. 411–413.

Becker, Howard S. 1963. *Outsiders: Studies in the Sociology of Deviance.* New York: The Free Press.

Beer, Lawrence W. 1987. "Japan," in Jack Donnelly and Rhoda E. Howard, eds. *International Handbook of Human Rights.* Westport, Conn.: Greenwood, pp. 209–226.

Begin, Patricia. 1990. "Homelessness in Canada." *Current Issue Review.* Ottawa: Library of Parliament Research Branch, October 16.

Bellah, Robert N., Richard Madsen, William M. Sullivan, Ann Swidler, and Steven M. Tipton. 1985. *Habits of the Heart: Individualism and Commitment in American Life.* New York: Harper and Row.

Bennett, Claudette E. 1992. *The Black Population in the United States: March 1991.* U.S. Department of Commerce, Current Population Reports, Population Characteristics P20-464. Washington, D.C.: U.S. Government Printing Office.

Berger, Peter L. 1976. *Pyramids of Sacrifice: Political Ethics and Social Change.* New York: Anchor Books.

Berger, Peter L. 1969. *The Sacred Canopy: Elements of a Sociological Theory of Religion.* Garden City, N.Y.: Anchor Books.

Berger, Peter, Brigitte Berger, and Hansfried Kellner. 1973. *The Homeless Mind: Modernization and Consciousness.* New York: Vintage Books.

Berger, Thomas R. 1982. *Fragile Freedoms: Human Rights and Dissent in Canada.* Toronto: Clarke, Irwin.

Berlin, Isaiah. 1970. "Two Concepts of Liberty," in Berlin, *Four Essays on Liberty.* New York: Oxford University Press, pp. 118–172.

Berting, Jan. 1985. "Societal Development in Relation to Human Rights, Rights of Peoples, and Sociological Theory and Research." Rotterdam: Erasmus University, unpublished.

Bidney, David. 1968. "Cultural Relativism," in David L. Sills, ed. *International Encyclopedia of the Social Sciences,* vol. 3. New York: Crowell Collier and Macmillan.

1992. "Black and Angry." *Maclean's* (May 18): 24–32.

Blau, Francine D., and Marianne A. Ferber. 1992. *The Economics of Women, Men and Work.* 2nd ed. Englewood Cliffs, N.J.: Prentice-Hall.

Bloch, Marc. 1976. *Feudal Society, Volume 2: Social Classes and Political Organization.* Chicago: University of Chicago Press.

Blumer, Herbert. 1985. "Symbolic Interactionism," in Randall Collins, ed. *Three Sociological Traditions: Selected Readings.* New York: Oxford University Press, pp. 282–299.

Bodley, John H. 1990. *Victims of Progress.* 3rd ed. Mountain View, Calif.: Mayfield Publishing.

Bozinoff, Lorne, and Peter MacIntosh. 1990. "Public Increasingly Fearful of AIDS Epidemic." The Gallup Report (Canada), August 13.

"Brown vs. Koch." *60 Minutes* (CBS Television), aired January 24 and June 12, 1988.

Brownmiller, Susan. 1975. *Against Our Will: Men, Women and Rape.* New York: Bantam Books.

Brownmiller, Susan. 1984. *Femininity.* New York: Fawcett Columbine.

Brotz, Howard. 1980. "Multiculturalism in Canada: A Muddle." *Canadian Public Policy,* vol. 6, no. 1 (winter): 41–46.

Bunch, Charlotte. 1990. "Women's Rights as Human Rights: Toward a Re-Vision of Human Rights." *Human Rights Quarterly,* vol. 12, no. 4 (November): 486–498.

Burr, Chandler. 1993. "Homosexuality and Biology." *The Atlantic Monthly,* vol. 271, no. 3 (March): 47–65.

Busia, Nana Kusia Appea Jr. 1994. "The Status of Human Rights in Pre-Colonial Africa: Implications for Contemporary Practices," in Eileen McCarthy-Arnolds, David R. Penna, and Debra Joy Cruz Sobrepena, eds. *Africa, Human Rights, and the Global System: The Political Economic of Human Rights in a Changing World.* Westport, Conn.: Greenwood Press.

Calzavara, Liviana. 1988. "Trends and Policy in Employment Opportunities for Women," in James Curtis, Edward Grabb, Neil Guppy, and Sid Gilbert, eds. *Social Inequality in Canada: Patterns, Problems, Policies.* Scarborough: Prentice-Hall.

Canada. 1992. *Consensus Report on the Constitution: Final Text.* Charlottetown, Prince Edward Island, August 28.

Canada. House of Commons. 1991. Standing Committee on Health and Welfare, Social Affairs, Seniors and the Status of Women. "The War Against Women: The Incidence of Violence Against Women in Canada." Third Session, June.

Canada. Labour Canada. n.d. (1992?). *Union Membership in Canada 1991.* Ottawa: Bureau of Labour Information.

Canada. Ministry of Labour. 1993. *Employment Standards Legislation in Canada,* 1993–1994 edition. Ottawa: Ministry of Supply and Services.

Canada. Multiculturalism and Citizenship Canada. n.d. (1989?). *Operation of the Canadian Multiculturalism Act: Annual Report 1988/89.* Ottawa: Ministry of Supply and Services Canada.

Canada. Receiver General. 1992. *Public Accounts of Canada,* vol. II, part i. Ottawa: Ministry of Supply and Services.

Canada. Statistics Canada, 1991 Census of Canada. 1993. *Ethnic Origin.* Ottawa: Industry, Science and Technology Canada.

Canada. Statistics Canada. 1992. *1991 Census Dictionary.* Ottawa: Supply and Services Canada.

Canada. Status of Women, Canada. 1986. *Report of the Task Force on Day Care.* Ottawa: Minister of Supply and Services.

1993. "Cases of Note: 'Family Status' Excludes 'Sexual Orientation.'" *Canadian Human Rights Reporter,* vol. 17 (May 27): i–ii.

Center for the Study of Human Rights. 1992. *Twenty-Four Human Rights Documents.* New York: Columbia University.

Che-Alford, Janet. 1992. "Canadians on the Move." *Canadian Social Trends* [Statistics Canada], no. 25 (summer): 32–34.

Ching, Frank. 1993. "Asian View of Human Rights Is Beginning to Take Shape." *Far Eastern Economic Review* (April 29): 27.

Clifford, James. 1988. *The Predicament of Culture: Twentieth Century Ethnography, Literature and Art.* Cambridge, Mass.: Harvard University Press.

Conquest, Robert. 1986. *The Harvest of Sorrow: Soviet Collectivization and the Terror-Famine.* Edmonton: University of Alberta Press.

Cook, Rebecca J. 1990. "Reservations to the Convention on the Elimination of All Forms of Discrimination Against Women." *Virginia Journal of International Law,* vol. 30, no. 3 (spring): 643–716.

Coontz, Stephanie. 1992. *The Way We Never Were: American Families and the Nostalgia Trap.* New York: Basic Books.

Cose, Ellis. 1993. *The Rage of a Privileged Class.* New York: HarperCollins.

Coser, Rose Laub. 1991. *In Defense of Modernity: Role Complexity and Individual Autonomy.* Stanford, Calif.: Stanford University Press.

Cranston, Maurice. 1983. "Are There Any Human Rights?" *Daedalus,* vol. 112, no. 4: (fall): 1–17.

Crapanzano, Vincent. 1986. *Waiting: The Whites of South Africa.* New York: Vintage Books.

D'Souza, Dinesh. 1991. "Illiberal Education." *The Atlantic Monthly,* vol. 267, no. 3 (March): 51–79.

Dahmus, Joseph. 1984. *Dictionary of Medieval Civilization.* New York: Macmillan.

Dawidowicz, Lucy S. 1975. *The War Against the Jews, 1933–1945.* New York: Bantam Books.

de Beauvoir, Simone. 1968. *The Second Sex.* New York: The Modern Library.

Desmond, Cosmas. 1971. *The Discarded People: An Account of African Resettlement in South Africa.* Harmondsworth, U.K.: Penguin.

Dinesen, Isak. *Out of Africa.* 1972 [1st ed. 1937]. New York: Vintage Books.

Donnelly, Jack. 1985. *The Concept of Human Rights.* London: Croom Helm.

Donnelly, Jack. 1989. *Universal Human Rights in Theory and Practice.* Ithaca, N.Y.: Cornell University Press.

Douglas, Carlyle C. 1990. "Lesbian Child-Custody Cases Redefine Family Law." *New York Times,* July 8, p. E9.

Douglas, Mary. 1966. *Purity and Danger: An Analysis of the Concepts of Pollution and Taboo.* London: Routledge and Kegan Paul.

1993. "Douglas v. the Queen," in Bruce Dunlop, ed. *Dominion Law Reports—4th Series,* vol. 98. Aurora, Ontario: Canada Law Books, pp. 129–140.

Duchesne, Doreen. 1989. "Giving Freely: Volunteers in Canada." Statistics Canada, Labour Analytical Report no. 4, August.

Durkheim, Emile. 1933. *The Division of Labor in Society.* New York: The Free Press.

Durkheim, Emile. 1968 [1st ed 1915]. *The Elementary Forms of the Religious Life.* London: George Allen and Unwin.

Durkheim, Emile. 1938. *The Rules of Sociological Method.* New York: The Free Press.

Durkheim, Emile. 1951. *Suicide: A Study in Sociology.* New York: The Free Press.

Dworkin, Ronald. 1985. *A Matter of Principle.* Cambridge, Mass.: Harvard University Press.

Dworkin, Ronald. 1978. *Taking Rights Seriously.* Cambridge, Mass.: Harvard University Press.

Eberstadt, Nick. 1990. *The Poverty of Communism.* New Brunswick, N.J.: Transaction Publishers.

Editorial. 1992. "Mr. Bush, Crossing the Line." *New York Times,* August 26, p. A18.

Ehrenreich, Barbara. 1989. *Fear of Falling: The Inner Life of the Middle Class.* New York: HarperCollins.

Ehrenreich, Barbara. 1983. *The Hearts of Men: American Dreams and the Flight from Commitment.* New York: Anchor Press.

Elias, Norbert. 1978 [1st (German) ed. 1939]. *The History of Manners: The Civilizing Process,* vol. I. New York: Pantheon Books.

Elshtain, Jean Bethke. 1993. *Democracy on Trial.* Concord, Ontario: House of Anansi.

Engels, Frederick. 1972. *The Condition of the Working Class in England.* London: Panther.

Engels, Frederick. 1972. *The Origin of the Family, Private Property and the State.* New York: Pathfinder Books.

Erikson, Kai. 1986. "On Work and Alienation." *American Sociological Review,* vol. 51, no. 1 (February): 1–8.

Etzioni, Amitai. 1993. *The Spirit of Community: Rights, Responsibilities, and the Communitarian Agenda.* New York: Crown.

Facts on File. Vol. 47, no. 2430, June 19, 1987; vol. 47, no. 2457, December 25, 1987; and vol. 49, no. 2535, June 23, 1989.

Falk, Richard, 1979. "The Algiers Declaration of the Rights of Peoples and the Struggle for Human Rights," in Antonio Cassese, ed. *UN Law/Fundamental Rights: Two Topics in International Law.* Alphen aan den Rijn: Sijthoff and Noordhoff, pp. 225–235.

"Family Leave Law: Provisions." 1993. *Congressional Quarterly–Weekly Report,* vol. 51, no. 7 (February 13).

Fanon, Frantz. 1967. *Black Skins, White Masks.* New York: Grove Press.

Farraq, Ahmad. 1990. "Human Rights and Liberties in Islam," in Jan Berting et al., eds. *Human Rights in a Pluralist World: Individuals and Collectivities.* Westport, Conn.: Meckler, pp. 133–143.

Fein, Helen. 1979. *Accounting for Genocide: National Responses and Jewish Victimization During the Holocaust.* Chicago: University of Chicago Press.

"Final Declaration of the Regional Meeeting for Asia of the World Conference on Human Rights." 1993. United Nations Document A/Conf.157/ASRM/8; A/CONF.157/PC/59.

Fischer, Claude S. 1982. *To Dwell Among Friends: Personal Networks in Town and City.* Chicago: University of Chicago Press.

1990. "The Forgotten: The Rise of Homelessness in Canada." *Calgary Herald,* September 16: F2.

Foucault, Michel. 1979. *Discipline and Punish: The Birth of the Prison.* New York: Vintage Books.

Fox-Genovese, Elizabeth. 1991. *Feminism Without Illusions: A Critique of Individualism.* Chapel Hill: University of North Carolina Press.

Fraser, Graham. 1992. "Bill Protects Gay and Lesbian Rights." *The Globe and Mail,* December 11, p. A4.

Freeman, James M. 1979. *Untouchable: An Indian Life History.* Stanford, Calif.: Stanford University Press.

Frideres, James S. 1988 and 1983. *Native Peoples in Canada: Contemporary Conflicts.* 3rd and 4th eds. Scarborough: Prentice-Hall.

Friedman, Lawrence J. 1979. "Rape Complex, Southern," in David C. Roller and Robert W. Twyman, eds. *The Encyclopedia of Southern History.* Baton Rouge: Louisiana State University Press.

Gallagher, Winifred. 1993. "Midlife Myths." *The Atlantic Monthly,* vol. 271, no. 5 (May): 51–68.

The Gallup Poll (U.S.). 1992. *Public Opinion 1991,* "May 15, AIDS." Wilmington, Del.: Scholarly Resources Inc., pp. 113–115.

Gandhy, Sherna. 1988. "Crimes Against Women in India." *Philosophy and Social Action,* vol. 14, no. 4 (October–December): 22–30.

Gerth, H. H., and C. Wright Mills, eds. 1946. *From Max Weber: Essays in Sociology.* New York: Oxford University Press.

Giddens, Anthony. 1990. *The Consequences of Modernity.* Stanford, Calif.: Stanford University Press.

Gilman, Sander L. 1986. *Jewish Self-Hatred: Anti-Semitism and the Hidden Language of the Jews.* Baltimore: Johns Hopkins University Press.

Glasse, Cyril. 1989. *The Concise Encyclopedia of Islam.* San Francisco: Harper and Row.

Glazer, Nathan. 1985. "Individual Rights Against Group Rights," in Eugene Kamenka and Alice Erh-Soon Tay, eds. *Human Rights.* New York: St. Martin's, pp. 87–103.

Glendon, Mary Ann. 1991. *Rights Talk: The Impoverishment of Political Discourse.* New York: The Free Press.

Goldstein, Robert Justin. 1978. *Political Repression in Modern America: From 1870 to the Present.* Cambridge, Mass.: Schenkman.

Goldstein, Robert Justin. 1987. "The United States," in Jack Donnelly and Rhoda E. Howard, eds. *International Handbook of Human Rights.* Westport, Conn.: Greenwood, pp. 429–456.

Gross, Bertram. 1980. *Friendly Fascism: The New Face of Power in America.* Boston: South End Press.

Guenther, Mathias G. 1983–1984. "Bushwomen: The Position of Women in San Society and Ideology." *Journal of Comparative Sociology and Religion,* vol. 10–11: 12–31.

Gutmann, Amy. 1985. "Communitarian Critics of Liberalism." *Philosophy and Public Affairs,* vol. 14, no. 3 (summer): 308–322.

Haarscher, Guy. 1990. "European Culture, Individual Rights, Collective Rights," in Jan Berting et al., eds. *Human Rights in a Pluralist World: Individuals and Collectivities.* Westport, Conn.: Meckler.

Hacker, Andrew. 1992. "The New Civil War," *New York Review of Books,* vol. 39, no. 8 (April 23): 30–33.

Haig-Brown, Celia. 1989. *Resistance and Renewal: Surviving the Indian Residential School.* Vancouver: Tillacum Library.

Heinemeijer, Willem F. 1990. "Islam and the Ideals of the Enlightenment," in Jan Berting et al., eds. *Human Rights in a Pluralist World: Individuals and Collectivities.* Westport, Conn.: Meckler, pp. 145–148.

Henkin, Louis. 1981. "Rights: Here and There." *Columbia Law Review,* vol. 81, no. 8 (December): 1582–1610.

Henry, Frances. 1973. *Forgotten Canadians: The Blacks of Nova Scotia.* Don Mills, Ontario: Longman.

Henry, Frances, and Effie Ginzberg. 1988. "Racial Discrimination in Employment," in James Curtis, Edward Grabb, Neil Guppy, and Sid Gilbert, eds. *Social Inequality in Canada: Patterns, Problems, Policies.* Scarborough: Prentice-Hall, pp. 214–220.

Herek, Gregory M. 1989. "Hate Crimes Against Lesbians and Gay Men: Issues for Research and Policy." *American Psychologist,* vol. 44, no. 6 (June): 948–955.

Herek, Gregory M. 1986. "On Heterosexual Masculinity." *American Behavioral Scientist,* vol. 29, no. 5 (May/June): 563–577.

Herek, Gregory M., and Eric K. Glunt. 1988. "An Epidemic of Stigma: Public Reactions to AIDS." *American Psychologist,* vol. 43, no. 11 (November): 886–891.

Herman, Judith Lewis, with Lisa Hirschman. 1981. *Father-Daughter Incest.* Cambridge, Mass.: Harvard University Press.

Hetata, Sherif. 1990. "Censoring the Mind." *Index on Censorship,* no. 6: 18–19.

Hewlett, Sylvia Ann. 1986. *A Lesser Life: The Myth of Women's Liberation in America.* New York: Warner Books.

Hewlett, Sylvia Ann. 1991. *When the Bough Breaks: The Cost of Neglecting Our Children.* New York: HarperCollins.

Holcombe, Lee. 1983. *Wives and Property: Reform of the Married Women's Property Law in Nineteenth Century England.* Toronto: University of Toronto Press.

Holmes, Ronald M. 1991. *Sex Crimes.* Newbury Park, Calif.: Sage.

hooks, bell. 1992. *Black Looks: Race and Representation.* Boston: South End Press.

Howard, Rhoda E. 1992. "Dignity, Community, and Human Rights," in Abdullahi Ahmed An-Na'im, ed. *Human Rights in Cross-Cultural Perspectives: A Quest for Consensus.* Philadelphia: University of Pennsylvania Press, pp. 81–102.

Howard, Rhoda E. 1993. "The Full-Belly Thesis: Should Economic Rights Take Priority over Civil and Political Rights? Evidence from Sub-Saharan Africa," *Human Rights Quarterly,* vol. 5, no. 4 (November): 467–490.

Howard, Rhoda E. 1990. "Group Versus Individual Identity in the African Debate on Human Rights," in Abdullahi Ahmed An-Na'im and Francis M. Deng, eds. *Human Rights in Africa: Cross-Cultural Perspectives.* Washington, D.C.: The Brookings Institution, pp. 159–183.

Howard, Rhoda E. 1993. "Health Costs of Social Degradation and Female Self-Mutilation in North America," in Kathleen E. Mahoney and Paul Mahoney, eds. *Human Rights in the Twenty-First Century: A Global Challenge.* Boston: Martinus Nijhoff, pp. 503–516.

Howard, Rhoda E. 1986. *Human Rights in Commonwealth Africa.* Totowa, N.J.: Rowman and Littlefield.

Howard, Rhoda E. 1992. "Practical Problems of Monitoring Human Rights Violations," in Alex P. Schmid and Albert J. Jongman, eds. *Monitoring Human Rights Violations.* Publication no. 43, Center for the Study of Social Conflicts, Faculty of Social Sciences, Leiden University, pp. 73–83.

Howard, Rhoda E., and Jack Donnelly. 1986. "Human Dignity, Human Rights, and Political Regimes: *American Political Science Review,* vol. 80, no. 3 (September): 801–817.

Howard, Rhoda E, and Jack Donnelly. 1987. "Introduction," in Jack Donnelly and Rhoda E. Howard, eds. *International Handbook of Human Rights.* Westport, Conn.: Greenwood, pp. 1–28.

Huggett, Frank E. 1974. *A Dictionary of British History, 1815–1973.* Oxford: Basil Blackwell and Mott.

Hughes, Everett C. 1945. "Dilemmas and Contradictions of Status." *American Journal of Sociology,* vol. 50 (March): 353–359.

Hughes, Robert. 1987. *The Fatal Shore: The Epic of Australia's Founding.* New York: Alfred A. Knopf.

Hunter, Alfred A. 1986. *Class Tells: On Social Inequality in Canada.* 2nd ed. Toronto: Butterworth.

Ihonvbere, Julius O. 1990. "Underdevelopment and Human Rights Violations in Africa," in George W. Shepherd Jr. and Mark O. C. Anikpo, eds. *Emerging Human Rights: The African Political Economy Context.* New York: Greenwood Press, pp. 55–68.

Iliffe, John. 1987. *The African Poor: A History.* New York: Cambridge University Press.

Inkeles, Alex, and David H. Smith. 1974. *Becoming Modern: Individual Change in Six Developing Countries.* Cambridge, Mass.: Harvard University Press.

International Monetary Fund. 1992. *Government Finance Statistics Yearbook,* vol. 16.

Ishaque, Khalid M. 1947. "Human Rights in Islamic Law," in International Commission of Jurists, *The Review,* no. 12 (June): 30–39.

Ismandar, Wadi. 1987. "What Sort of Life Is This?" *Index on Censorship,* vol.16, no. 6: 26–27.

Johnson, Holly, and Peter Chisholm. 1989. "Family Homicide," in *Canadian Social Trends* [Statistics Canada] no. 14 (autumn): 17–18.

Johnson, Laura, and Norma McCormick. 1984. *Daycare in Canada: A Background Paper.* Ottawa: Canadian Advisory Council on the Status of Women.

Johnston, Hugh. 1985. "Komagata Maru," in *The Canadian Encyclopedia,* vol. 2. Edmonton: Hurtig.

Joshi, Barbara R. 1990. "Human Rights as Dynamic Process: The Case of India's Untouchables," in Claude E. Welch Jr. and Virginia Leary, eds. *Asian Perspectives on Human Rights.* Boulder, Colo.: Westview, pp. 162–185.

Kamenetsky, Christa. 1972. "Political Distortion of Philosophical Concepts: A Case History—Nazism and the Romantic Movement." *Metaphilosophy,* vol. 3, no. 3 (July): 198–218.

Kantor, Rosabeth Moss. 1977. *Men and Women of the Corporation.* New York: Basic Books.

Kashmeri, Zuhair. 1990. "Segregation Deeply Embedded in India." *The Globe and Mail* (Toronto), October 13, p. D3.

Katz, Michael B. 1989. *The Undeserving Poor: From the War on Poverty to the War on Welfare.* New York: Pantheon Books.

Kenrick, Donald, and Grattan Puxon. 1972. *The Destiny of Europe's Gypsies.* London: Chatto; Heinemann.

Khadduri, Majid. 1946. "Human Rights in Islam." *Annals of the American Academy of Political and Social Science,* vol. 243 (January): 77–81.

Kiss, Alexandre. 1986. "The Peoples' Right to Self-Determination." *Human Rights Law Journal,* vol. 7, nos. 2–4: 165–175.

Ki-Zerbo, Joseph. 1964. "African Personality and the New African Society," in Wm. John Hanna, ed. *Independent Black Africa: The Politics of Freedom.* Chicago: Rand McNally, pp. 46–59.

Koonz, Claudia. 1987. *Mothers in the Fatherland.* New York: St. Martin's Press.

Kopytoff, Igor, and Suzanne Miers. 1977. "African 'Slavery' as an Institution of Marginality," in Suzanne Miers and Igor Kopytoff, eds. *Slavery in Africa: Historical and Anthropological Perspectives.* Madison: University of Wisconsin Press, pp. 3–81.

Kymlicka, Will. 1990. *Contemporary Political Philosophy: An Introduction.* Oxford: Clarendon Press.

Lasch, Christopher. 1979. *The Culture of Narcissism: American Life in an Age of Diminishing Expectations.* New York: W. W. Norton.

Lasch, Christopher. 1991. *The True and Only Heaven: Progress and Its Critics.* New York: W. W. Norton.

Laslett, Peter. 1983. *The World We Have Lost—Further Explored.* London: Methuen.

Leach, Maria, ed. 1949. *Funk and Wagnall's Standard Dictionary of Folklore, Mythology and Legend,* vol. 1. New York: Funk and Wagnall.

Lee, Richard, and Richard Daly. 1987. "Man's Domination and Woman's Oppression: The Question of Origins," in Michael Kaufman, ed. *Beyond Patriarchy: Essays by Men on Pleasure, Power and Change.* New York: Oxford University Press, pp. 30–44.

Legesse, Asmaron. 1980. "Human Rights in African Political Culture," in Kenneth W. Thompson, ed. *The Moral Imperatives of Human Rights: A World Survey.* Washington, D.C.: University Press of America, pp. 123–137.

Lenton, Rhonda L. 1989. "Homicide in Canada and the U.S.A.: A Critique of the Hagan Thesis." *Canadian Journal of Sociology,* vol. 14, no. 2: 163–178.

Lerner, Gerda. 1986. *The Creation of Patriarchy.* New York: Oxford University Press.

Letters to the Editor. 1990. *The Spectator* (Hamilton, Ontario), March 28.

Lewis, Bernard. 1990. "The Roots of Muslim Rage." *The Atlantic Monthly,* vol. 266, no. 3 (September): 47–60.

Lightfoot, Sara Lawrence. 1988. *Balm in Gilead: Journey of a Healer.* New York: Addison-Wesley.

Lipset, Seymour Martin. 1990. "The Values of Canadians and Americans: A Reply." *Social Forces,* vol. 69, no. 1 (September): 267–272.

Littman, Sol. 1980. "'W5 Generation' Changing Chinese." *Toronto Star,* April 19, p. B4.

Locke, John. 1989. "Second Treatise of Government" [1690], excerpted in Walter Laqueur and Barry Rubin, eds. *The Human Rights Reader.* New York: New American Library, pp. 62–67.

Lord, Carnes. 1984. "Human Rights Policy in a Nonliberal World," in Marc F. Plattner, ed. *Human Rights in Our Time: Essays in Memory of Victor Baras.* Boulder, Colo.: Westview, pp. 125–139.

Lukes, Steven. 1985. "Conclusion," in Michael Carrithers, Steven Collins, and Steven Lukes, eds. *The Category of the Person: Anthropology, Philosophy, History.* New York: Cambridge University Press, pp. 282–301.

Lukes, Steven. 1973. *Individualism.* Oxford: Basil Blackwell.

Lyons, Harriet D. 1990. "Television in Contemporary Urban Life: Benin City, Nigeria." *Visual Anthropology,* vol. 3: 411–428.

Maalouf, Amin. 1988. *Leo the African.* New York: Quartet Books.

MacKinnon, Catherine A. 1993. "On Torture: A Feminist Perspective on Human Rights," in Kathleen E. Mahoney and Paul Mahoney, eds. *Human Rights in the Twenty-First Century: A Global Challenge.* Boston: Martinus Nijhoff.

MacPherson, C. B. 1962. *The Political Theory of Possessive Individualism: Hobbes to Locke.* New York: Oxford University Press.

Maine, Sir Henry. 1977 [1st ed. 1917]. *Ancient Law.* London: J. M. Dent and Sons.

Mannheim, Karl. 1936. *Ideology and Utopia.* New York: Harcourt, Brace and World.

Marie, Jean-Bernard. 1986. "Relations Between Peoples' Rights and Human Rights: Semantic and Methodological Distinctions." *Human Rights Law Journal,* vol. 7, nos. 2–4: 195–204.

Marrus, Michael R. 1985. *The Unwanted: European Refugees in the Twentieth Century.* New York: Oxford University Press.

Marshall, W. L., and Sylvia Barrett. 1990. *Criminal Neglect: Why Sex Offenders Go Free.* Toronto: Doubleday.

Marx, Karl. 1967. *Capital, Volume I: A Critical Analysis of Capitalist Production.* New York: International Publishers.

Marx, Karl. 1970. *Critique of Hegel's Philosophy of Right,* ed. Joseph O'Malley. Cambridge, Mass.: Cambridge University Press.

Marx, Karl. 1959. "Critique of the Gotha Program," in Lewis S. Feuer, ed. *Karl Marx and Friedrich Engels: Basic Writings on Politics and Philosophy.* Garden City, N.Y.: Anchor Books.

Marx, Karl. 1964. "The Meaning of Human Requirements," in Marx, *The Economic and Philosophic Manuscripts of 1844.* New York: International Publishers, pp. 147–164.

Marx, Karl. 1965. *Pre-Capitalist Economic Formations.* Eric J. Hobsbawm, ed. New York: International Publishers.

Marzorati, Gerald. 1990. "Rushdie in Hiding." *The New York Times Magazine* (November 4): 31–33, 68, 78, 84–85.

Marzouki, Moncef. 1989. "Winning Freedom." *Index on Censorship,* no. 1: 23.

Matas, Robert. 1992. "Native Ritual Ruled Subject to Law." *The Globe and Mail* (Toronto), February 8, p. A6.

Matthews, Robert, and Cranford Pratt. 1985. "Human Rights and Foreign Policy: Principles and Canadian Practice." *Human Rights Quarterly,* vol. 7, no. 2: 159–188.

Mayer, Ann Elizabeth. 1990. "Current Muslim Thinking on Human Rights," in Abdullahi Ahmed An-Na'im and Francis M. Deng, eds. *Human Rights in Africa: Cross-Cultural Perspectives:* Washington D.C.: The Brookings Institution, pp. 133–156.

Mayer, Henry. 1990. Review of Henry Hampton and Steve Fayer with Sarah Flynn, *Voices of Freedom: An Oral History of the Civil Rights Movement.* New York: Bantam Books, 1989, in *New York Times Book Review,* January 28.

McChesney, Robert Allan. 1987. "Canada," in Jack Donnelly and Rhoda E. Howard, eds. *International Handbook of Human Rights.* New York: Greenwood, pp. 29–47.

McDonald, Michael. 1992. "Should Communities Have Rights? Reflections on Liberal Individualism," in Abdullahi Ahmed An-Na'im, ed. *Human Rights in Cross-Cultural Perspectives: A Quest for Consensus.* Philadelphia: University of Pennsylvania Press, pp. 133–161.

McKie, Craig, and Keith Thompson, eds. 1990. *Canadian Social Trends.* Toronto: Thompson Educational Publishing.

Mead, George H. 1962 [1st ed. 1934]. *Mind, Self and Society.* Chicago: University of Chicago Press.

Miller, David L. 1987. "Justice," in David Miller, ed. *Blackwell Encyclopedia of Political Thought.* Oxford: Basil Blackwell.

Mills, C. Wright. 1959. *The Sociological Imagination.* New York: Oxford University Press.

Mitchell, Alanna. 1991. "Iron-Poor Milk Puts Many Infants in Danger of Permanent Damage." *The Globe and Mail* (Toronto), August 6, pp. A1 and A5.

Mitchell, Neil, Rhoda E. Howard, and Jack Donnelly. 1987. "Liberalism, Human Rights, and Human Dignity" [a debate]. *American Political Science Review,* vol. 81, no. 3 (September): 921–927.

Mojekwu, Chris C. 1980. "International Human Rights: The African Perspective," in Jack L. Nelson and Vera M. Green, eds. *International Human Rights: Contemporary Issues.* Stanfordville, N.Y.: Human Rights Publishing Group, pp. 85–95.

Moore, Barrington Jr. 1978. *Injustice: The Social Bases of Obedience and Revolt.* White Plains, N.Y.: M. E. Sharpe.

Moore, Barrington Jr. 1984. *Privacy: Studies in Social and Cultural History.* Armonk, N.Y.: M. E. Sharpe.

Moreau, Joanne. 1991. "Changing Faces: Visible Minorities in Toronto." *Canadian Social Trends* [Statistics Canada], no. 23 (winter): 26–28.

Morgan, Prys. 1983. "From a Death to a View: The Hunt for the Welsh Past in the Romantic Period," in Eric Hobsbawm and Terence Ranger, eds. *The Invention of Tradition.* London: Cambridge University Press, pp. 43–100.

Mousavi, Naheed. 1992. "The Obscure Limits of Freedom." *Index on Censorship,* no. 3: 18.

Nahum, Fasil. 1982. "African Contribution to Human Rights." Paper presented at the Seminar on Law and Human Rights in Development, Gaborone, Botswana, May 24–28.

National Council of Welfare. 1990. *Women and Poverty Revisited.* Ottawa: Minister of Supply and Services Canada.

Native Women's Association of Canada. 1992. "Aboriginal Women and the Constitutional Debates: Continuing Discrimination." *Canadian Woman Studies,* vol. 12, no. 3 (spring): 14–17.

Ngom, Benoit. 1981. "Réflexions sur la Notion de Droits de l'Homme en Afrique." Association des Jeunes Juristes Africains.

Nguema, Isaac. 1989. "Universality and Specificity in Human Rights in Africa." *The Courier,* pp. 16–17.

Ngugi wa Thiong'o. 1981. *Detained: A Writer's Prison Diary.* London: Heinemann.

Nordahl, Richard. 1992. "A Marxian Approach to Human Rights," in Abdullahi Ahmed An-Na'im, ed. *Human Rights in Cross-Cultural Perspectives: A Quest for Consensus.* Philadelphia: University of Philadelphia Press, pp. 162–187.

O'Connor, Julia S. 1993. "Citizenship, Class, Gender and Labour Market Participation in Canada and Australia," in Sheila Shaver, ed. *Gender, Citizenship and the Labour Market: The Australian and Canadian Welfare States.* Sydney: Social Policy Research Centre, pp. 4–37.

Ojo, Olusola. 1990. "Understanding Human Rights in Africa," in Jan Berting et al., eds. *Human Rights in a Pluralist World: Individuals and Collectivities.* Westport, Conn.: Meckler, pp. 115–123.

Ojo, Olusola, and Amadu Sessay. 1986. "The O.A.U. and Human Rights: Prospects for the 1980s and Beyond." *Human Rights Quarterly,* vol. 8, no. 1 (February): 89–103.

O'Laughlin, Bridget. 1974. "Mediations of Culture: Why Mbum Women Do Not Eat Chicken," in Michelle Zimbalist Rosaldo and Louise Lamphere, eds. *Women, Culture and Society.* Stanford, Calif.: Stanford University Press.

Olenja, Joyce. 1988. "Gender and Agricultural Production in Samiya, Kenya." Oral Presentation to the Canadian Association of African Studies, Kingston, Ontario, May 12.

Ontario. 1989. *The Report of the Race Relations and Policing Task Force.* Toronto: Government of Ontario.

Onwu, Nienanya. 1990. "Theological Perspectives on Human Rights in the Context of the African Situation," in George W. Shepherd Jr. and Mark O. C. Anikpo, eds. *Emerging Human Rights: The African Political Economy Context.* New York: Greenwood, pp. 69–85.

Organization for Economic Co-operation and Development. 1988. *Future of Social Protection.* OECD Social Policy Studies no. 6.

Panikkar, R. 1984. "Is the Notion of Human Rights a Western Concept?" *Interculture,* vol. 17, nos. 1–2 (January–June): 28–47.

Park, Robert Ezra. 1950. *Race and Culture.* Glencoe, Ill.: The Free Press.

Partsch, Karl Josef. 1986. "Recent Developments in the Field of Peoples' Rights." *Human Rights Law Journal,* vol. 7, nos. 2–4: 177–182.

Patterson, Orlando. 1982. *Slavery and Social Death: A Comparative Study.* Cambridge, Mass.: Harvard University Press.

Perin, Constance. 1988. *Belonging in America: Reading Between the Lines.* Madison: University of Wisconsin Press.

Perlez, Jane. 1989. "Kenya's Plan for Tower Annoys Aid Donors." *New York Times* (International Edition), December 29, p. A5.

Petchesky, Rosalind Pollack. 1981. "Antiabortion, Antifeminism and the Rise of the New Right." *Feminist Studies,* vol.7, no. 2 (summer): 206–246.

Plant, Richard. 1986. *The Pink Triangle: The Nazi War Against Homosexuals.* New York: Henry Holt.

Poirier, Richard. 1988. "AIDS and Traditions of Homophobia." *Social Research,* vol. 5, no. 3 (autumn): 461–475.

Polivy, Janet, and C. Peter Herman. 1987. "Diagnosis and Treatment of Normal Eating." *Journal of Consulting and Clinical Psychology,* vol. 55, no. 5: 635–644.

Pollis, Adamantia. 1992. "Human Rights in Liberal, Socialist and Third World Perspective," in Richard Pierre Claude and Burns H. Weston, eds. *Human Rights in the World Community: Issues and Action.* Philadelphia: University of Pennsylvania Press, pp. 146–156.

Pollis, Adamantia, and Peter Schwab. 1980. "Human Rights: A Western Construct with Limited Applicability," in Pollis and Schwab, eds. *Human Rights: Cultural and Ideological Perspectives.* New York: Praeger, pp. 1–18.

"Prairie Backlash: Anti-Minority Campaigns Cause Heated Debate." 1990. *Maclean's* (March 19): 18–19.

Priest, Gordon E. 1988. "Living Arrangements of Canada's 'Older Elderly' Population." *Canadian Social Trends* [Statistics Canada], vol. 21 (autumn): 26–30.

"Racial Attacks Concern Toronto." 1977. *Canadian News Facts,* vol. 11, no. 1 (January 19): 1699.

Ranger, Terence. 1983. "The Invention of Tradition in Colonial Africa," in Eric Hobsbawm and Terence Ranger, eds. *The Invention of Tradition.* New York: Cambridge University Press, pp. 211–262.

Rawlings, Steven W. 1989. "Single Parents and Their Children," in U.S. Department of Commerce, Bureau of the Census, *Current Population Reports: Studies in Marriage and the Family,* Special Series P-23, no. 162. Washington, D.C.: U.S. Government Printing Office.

Reitz, Jeffrey G. 1993. "Statistics on Racial Discrimination in Canada." *Policy Options,* vol. 14, no. 2 (March): 32–36.

Renteln, Alison Dundes. 1990. *International Human Rights: Universalism Versus Relativism.* Newbury Park, Calif.: Sage.

Renteln, Alison Dundes. 1985. "The Unanswered Challenge of Relativism and the Consequences for Human Rights." *Human Rights Quarterly,* vol. 7, no. 4 (November): 514–540.

Rice, James J. 1990. "Volunteering to Build a Stronger Community." *Perception* [Canadian Council on Social Development], vol. 14, no. 4 (autumn): 9–14.

Robertson, Claire. 1987. "Developing Economic Awareness: Changing Perspectives in Studies of African Women, 1976–1985." *Feminist Studies,* vol. 13, no. 1: 97–135.

Robertson, Robert E. 1991. "The Right to Food—Canada's Broken Covenant." *Canadian Human Rights Yearbook, 1989–1990.* Ottawa: University of Ottawa Press, pp. 185–216.

Rushdie, Salman. 1989. *The Satanic Verses.* New York: Viking Penguin.

Rushdie, Salman. 1993. "Witch Hunt: Islam's War of Terror Against Secular Thought." *The Globe and Mail* (Toronto), July 17, 1993, p. D1.

Rybczynski, Witold. 1986. *Home: A Short History of an Idea.* New York: Viking.

Said, Edward W. 1978. *Orientalism.* New York: Vintage Books.

Samuelssohn, Kurt. 1957. *Religion and Economic Action: A Critique of Max Weber.* New York: Harper Torchbooks.

Sanday, Peggy Reeves. 1981. *Female Power and Male Dominance: On the Origins of Sexual Inequality.* New York: Cambridge University Press.

Sandel, Michael. 1984. "The Procedural Republic and the Unencumbered Self." *Political Theory,* vol. 12, no. 1 (February): 81–96.

Sartori, Giovanni. 1968. "Democracy," in David L. Sills, ed. *International Encyclopedia of the Social Sciences,* vol. 4. New York: Macmillan and The Free Press.

Schachter, Oscar. 1983. "Editorial Comment: Human Dignity as a Normative Concept." *American Journal of International Law,* vol. 77 (October): 848–854.

Schmid, Alex P. 1989. *Research on Gross Human Rights Violations.* Leiden: Center for the Study of Social Conflicts [C.O.M.T.].

Schur, Edwin. 1976. *The Awareness Trap: Self-Absorption Instead of Social Change.* New York: Quadrangle.

Schur, Edwin M. 1983. *Labeling Women Deviant: Gender, Stigma and Social Control.* Philadelphia: Temple University Press.

Second Canadian Conference on Aging, October 24–27, 1983. *Fact Book on Aging in Canada.* Ottawa: Minister of Supply and Services Canada.

Sen, Amartya. 1990. "More Than 100 Million Women Are Missing." *New York Review of Books*, vol. 37, no. 20 (December 20): 61–66.

Sennett, Richard. 1978. *The Fall of Public Man: On the Social Psychology of Capitalism.* New York: Vintage Books.

Seymour, James D. 1987. "China," in Jack Donnelly and Rhoda E. Howard, eds. *International Handbook of Human Rights.* New York: Greenwood Press, pp. 75–97.

Shils, Edward. 1981. *Tradition.* Chicago: University of Chicago Press.

Shivji, Issa G. 1989. *The Concept of Human Rights in Africa.* London: CODESRIA Book Series.

Shorter, Edward. 1977. *The Making of the Modern Family.* New York: Basic Books.

Shue, Henry. 1980. *Basic Rights: Subsistence, Affluence and U.S. Foreign Policy.* Princeton, N.J.: Princeton University Press.

Simmel, Georg. 1950. "The Metropolis and Mental Life," in Kurt H. Wolff, ed. *The Sociology of Georg Simmel.* New York: The Free Press, pp. 409–424.

Sinclair, Donna. 1992. "In Search of an Equal Voice: Native Women and the Constitution." *The Nation* [United Church Observer], vol. 56, no. 2 (August): 14–15.

Sommers, Christina Hoff. 1994. *Who Stole Feminism? How Women Have Betrayed Women.* New York: Simon and Schuster.

Stackhouse, Max L. 1984. *Creeds, Society and Human Rights: A Study in Three Cultures.* Grand Rapids, Mich.: William B. Eerdmans.

"Statement on Human Rights." 1947. Submitted to the United Nations Commission on Human Rights by the Executive Board, American Anthropological Association. *American Anthropologist* (new series), vol. 49, no. 4 (October–December): 539–543.

Staub, Ervin. 1989. *The Roots of Evil: The Origins of Genocide and Other Group Violence.* New York: Cambridge University Press.

Stohl, Michael, and George A. Lopez, eds. 1984. "Introduction," in their *The State as Terrorist: The Dynamics of Governmental Violence and Repression.* Westport, Conn.: Greenwood Press.

Strum, Philippa. 1989. "Women and the Politics of Religion in Israel." *Human Rights Quarterly*, vol. 11, no. 4 (November): 483–503.

Suro, Roberto. 1992. "Bush Gets Full Support at Religious Gathering." *New York Times*, August 23, p. A15.

Taeuber, Cynthia. 1991. *Statistical Handbook on Women in America.* Phoenix: Oryx Press.

Tawney, R. H. 1969 [1st ed. 1926]. *Religion and the Rise of Capitalism.* Harmondsworth, U.K.: Penguin.

Taylor, Charles. 1991. "Civil Society in the Western Tradition," in Ethel Groffier and Michel Paradis, eds. *The Notion of Tolerance and Human Rights.* Ottawa: Carleton University Press, pp. 117–136.

Taylor, Charles. 1985. "The Person," in Michael Carrithers, Steven Collins, and Steven Lukes, eds. *The Category of the Person: Anthropology, Philosophy, History.* Cambridge: Cambridge University Press, pp. 257–281.

Teson, Fernando R. 1985. "International Human Rights and Cultural Relativism." *Virginia Journal of International Law,* vol. 25, no. 4 (summer): 869–898.

Tigar, Michael E., and Madeleine R. Levy. 1977. *Law and the Rise of Capitalism.* New York: Monthly Review Press.

Tonnies, Ferdinand. 1957. *Community and Society.* Translated and edited by Charles P. Loomis. New York: Harper and Row.

Torgovnick, Marianna. 1990. *Gone Primitive: Savage Intellects, Modern Lives.* Chicago: University of Chicago Press.

Traer, Robert. 1991. *Faith in Human Rights: Support in Religious Traditions for a Global Struggle.* Washington, D.C.: Georgetown University Press.

Trevethan, Shelley, and Tajeshwer Samagh. 1992. "Gender Differences Among Violent Crime Victims." *Juristat Service Bulletin* [Statistics Canada], vol. 12, no. 21 (November).

Trevor-Roper, Hugh. 1983. "The Invention of Tradition: The Highland Tradition of Scotland," in Eric Hobsbawm and Terence Ranger, eds. *The Invention of Tradition.* London: Cambridge University Press.

"2 Million Users Expected by '93." *Vancouver Sun,* September 26, 1992, p. A7.

Turpel, Mary Ellen. 1991. "Aboriginal People and the Canadian Charter: Interpretive Monopolies, Cultural Differences." *Canadian Human Rights Yearbook 1989–1990.* Ottawa: University of Ottawa Press, pp. 3–45.

United Nations. 1966. Convention on Consent to Marriage, Minimum Age for Marriage and Registration of Marriages (1962). *Treaty Series,* vol. 521. New York: United Nations, pp. 232–239.

United Nations General Assembly. 1993. "Vienna Declaration and Program of Action [June 25, 1993]." A/Conf.157/23, July 12.

U.S. Department of Commerce, Bureau of the Census. 1989. *Current Population Reports,* Series P-60, no. 163. "Poverty in the United States, 1987." Washington, D.C.: U.S. Government Printing Office.

U.S. Department of Commerce, Bureau of the Census. n.d. (1991?) *Poverty in the United States: 1991.* Consumer Income Series, P-60, no. 181. Washington D.C.: U.S. Government Printing Office.

U.S. Department of Commerce, Bureau of the Census. n.d. (1991?) *Statistical Abstract of the United States, 1991.*11thed. Washington, D.C.: U.S. Government Printing Office.

U.S. Department of Health and Human Services. 1989. *National Nursing Home Survey: 1985 Summary for the United States,* Series 13, no. 97. Washington, D.C.: U.S. Government Printing Office.

U.S. Department of Labor, Bureau of Labor Statistics. 1992. "Union Membership 1991," in *Compensation and Working Conditions,* vol. 44, no. 2 (February).

U.S. House of Representatives. 1993. Committee on Ways and Means, *Health Care Resource Book.* Washington, D.C.: U.S. Government Printing Office, February 2.

Valentine, Charles A. 1968. *Culture and Poverty: Critiques and Counter-Proposals.* Chicago: University of Chicago Press.

Van Dyke, Vernon. 1974. "Human Rights and the Rights of Groups." *Midwest Journal of Political Science,* vol. 18: 725–741.

van Niekerk, Phillip. 1990. "New Victims of Ancient Fears." *The Globe and Mail* (Toronto), November 5, pp. A1 and A10.

Vincent, R. J. 1986. *Human Rights and International Relations.* Cambridge, England: Cambridge University Press.

"Violent Crime in Canada." 1990. In *Juristat Service Bulletin* [Statistics Canada], vol. 10, no. 15 (October).

Wai, Dunstan M. 1980. "Human Rights in Sub-Saharan Africa," in Adamantia Pollis and Peter Schwab, eds. *Human Rights: Cultural and Ideological Perspectives.* New York: Praeger, pp. 115–144.

Walker, Alan. 1990. "Poverty and the Welfare State: Can Poverty Be Abolished?" Public lecture at McMaster University, Hamilton, Ontario (March 6).

Walzer, Michael. 1983. *Spheres of Justice: A Defense of Pluralism and Equality.* New York: Basic Books.

Weber, Eugen. 1976. *Peasants into Frenchmen: The Modernization of Rural France, 1870–1914.* Stanford, Calif.: Stanford University Press.

Weber, Max. 1958. *The Protestant Ethic and the Spirit of Capitalism.* New York: Charles Scribner's Sons.

Weber, Max. 1964. *The Theory of Social and Economic Organization.* Ed. Talcott Parsons. New York: The Free Press.

West, Cornel. 1994. *Race Matters.* New York: Vintage Books.

Whitehead, Barbara Dafoe. 1993. "Dan Quayle Was Right." *The Atlantic Monthly,* vol. 271, no. 4 (April): 47–84.

Whitehorn, Alan. 1985. "New Democratic Party." *The Canadian Encyclopedia,* vol. II. Edmonton: Hurtig, p. 1238.

Wickberg, E. B. 1985. "Chinese," in *The Canadian Encyclopedia,* vol. I. Edmonton: Hurtig, pp. 336–337.

Wilson, Edward O. 1979. *On Human Nature.* New York: Bantam Books.

Wilson, William Julius. 1987. *The Truly Disadvantaged: The Inner City, the Underclass, and Public Policy.* Chicago: University of Chicago Press.

Winks, Robin W. 1971. *The Blacks in Canada: A History.* Montreal: McGill-Queen's University Press.

Winn, Conrad. 1988. "The Socio-Economic Attainment of Visible Minorities: Facts and Policy Implications," in James Curtis, Edward Grabb, Neil Guppy, and Sid Gilbert, eds. *Social Inequality in Canada: Patterns, Problems, Policies.* Scarborough: Prentice-Hall, pp. 195–213.

Wolf, Naomi. 1991. *The Beauty Myth: How Images of Beauty Are Used Against Women.* New York: Doubleday.

Woodard, Joe. 1992. "Gay 'Families' Await the Verdict: The Supreme Court Ponders Homosexual Marriage." *Alberta Report,* vol. 19, no. 37 (August 31): 23–24.

Woodward, C. Vann. 1989. "The Mississippi Horrors." *New York Review of Books,* vol. 36, no. 11: 15–17.

The World Bank. 1993. *World Development Report 1993: Investing in Health.* New York: Oxford University Press.

Wyatt-Brown, Bertram. 1982. *Southern Honor: Ethics and Behavior in the Old South.* New York: Oxford University Press.

York, Geoffrey. 1989. *The Dispossessed: Life and Death in Native Canada.* Toronto: Lester and Orpen Dennys.

Young, Iris Marion. 1990. "The Ideal of Community and the Politics of Difference," in Linda Nicholson, ed. *Feminism/Postmodernism.* New York: Routledge, pp. 300–323.

About the Book and Author

Some critics contend that the concept of universal human rights reflects the West's anticommunitarian, self-centered individualism, which disproportionately focuses on individual autonomy. In this book Rhoda Howard refutes this claim, arguing instead that communities can exist in modern Western societies if they protect the whole spectrum of individual human rights, not only civil and political but also economic rights.

Howard supports the case for the universality of human rights by showing community to be inherent in and essential to the realization of universal human rights. She makes an original contribution to the study of universal human rights through her review of those types of communitarian thought that underlie cultural relativist attacks on human rights. Howard defends individual rights against conservative and leftist communitarian challenges emanating from both the Western world and the Third World. Exploring conservative viewpoints, she examines traditionalists of the Third World—focusing on African and Muslim traditionalist schools—as well as reactionary conservatives of the Western world. Howard then looks at challenges from the left, including collectivists, who see universal human rights as the product of cultural imperialism or capitalist exploitation, and status radicals, such as feminists or black activists, who are critics of liberalism.

Howard also criticizes what she dubs "radical capitalism" or "social minimalism," the idea that there is a very narrow range of true human rights, including the right to property, and that citizens are responsible for no one but themselves. A community, in Howard's view, is a group of people who all feel a sense of obligation to all others in the group. For a community to exist in the modern world, everyone must be treated equally, enjoy societal respect, and be able to act autonomously in her or his everyday decisionmaking.

Rhoda E. Howard is professor of sociology at McMaster University in Canada and director of the university's Theme School on International Justice and Human Rights. She is the author of *Colonialism and Underdevelopment in Ghana* (1978) and *Human Rights in Commonwealth Africa* (1986), and is co-editor (with Jack Donnelly) of an *International Handbook of Human Rights* (1987).

Index